Like Bread on the Seder Plate

D1637384

BETWEEN MEN~BETWEEN WOMEN
Lesbian and Gay Studies

Lillian Faderman and Larry Gross,
Editors

Like Bread on the Seder Plate

*Jewish Lesbians and the
Transformation of Tradition*

Rebecca Alpert

Columbia University Press

NEW YORK

Columbia University Press
Publishers Since 1893
New York Chichester, West Sussex
Copyright © 1997 Columbia University Press
All rights reserved

Library of Congress Cataloging-in-Publication Data
Alpert, Rebecca T. (Rebecca Trachtenberg), 1950 –
  Like bread on the seder plate : Jewish lesbians and the transformation of tradi-
tion / Rebecca Alpert.
    p. cm. — (Between men—between women)
  Includes bibliographical references and index.
  ISBN 978-0-231-09660-7 ISBN 978-0-231-09661-4 (pbk.)
  1. Lesbianism—Religious aspects—Judaism. 2. Bible.—O.T.—
Feminist criticism. 3. Jewish lesbians. I. Title. II. Series.
BM729.H65A47 1997
296'.08'6643—dc20   96–43411
                                                                      CIP

Casebound editions of Columbia University Press books are printed on permanent
and durable acid-free paper.

Printed in the United States of America

Contents

Acknowledgments

In 1976 I was ordained as a rabbi. In 1986 I came out as a lesbian. My story is not unique; there are dozens of lesbian rabbis today. Each of us has found a way to make sense of these parts of our lives, and sometimes to fit them together. This book is my way. In it I seek to explore how lesbians have made our presence felt in the Jewish world. I also suggest some new directions for reinterpreting and transforming Jewish texts from a uniquely lesbian Jewish perspective, because for me our textual tradition forms the core of Jewish life.

These issues are of deep interest to me as one who has spent the past decade living both in Jewish and lesbian worlds. I do not claim a distant or objective perspective on this subject. As a feminist, I do not believe that such a perspective is either attainable or desirable. It is impossible to assume a detached position about events, because as human beings we are part of what happens in this world and our own perspective inevitably colors our ideas. I have no choice but to write out of my own experience. And while I know my experience is unique, I hope that it will be resonant for others.

I am not convinced that one must write from a personal and subjective stance in matters of identity; I believe that the voice of the outsider may also be an authentic voice and that sometimes writing from within one may lose perspective. But I am grateful for the opportunity to write about a subject so close to my heart.

I see this work as a continuation of the pioneering efforts by Evelyn Torton Beck, the editor of *Nice Jewish Girls*, and of Andy Rose and Christie Balka, the editors of *Twice Blessed: On Being Lesbian or Gay and Jewish*. *Nice Jewish Girls* broke the silence about Jewish lesbians. Its focus was on holding the feminist and Jewish communities accountable for the oppression of Jewish lesbians, both as Jews in the feminist world and as lesbian feminists in the Jewish world. The authors told incredible and passionate stories of coming out, revealing the pain they experienced around their identities. I must confess that I did not read the book when it was first published in 1982; it was too frightening for me to confront the possibility that I could put those worlds together, that I could be a lesbian and not have to surrender my Jewishness. But its existence influenced me nonetheless, making me aware of possibilities I had not yet dared to dream about.

Twice Blessed took the conversation about lesbians and Jews in some new directions. The book tackled religious issues. And it was coedited by a lesbian and a gay man, bringing gay men's issues into the conversation for the first time. Like *Nice Jewish Girls*, *Twice Blessed* continued to make an effort to reflect Jewish, gay, and lesbian cultural diversity, incorporating stories from working-class Jews, Mizrachi Jews, and Jews with disabilities. But its main focus was to demand recognition of gay and lesbian Jews by the organized Jewish community; it succeeded greatly in this goal.

I am also indebted to Judith Plaskow's *Standing Again at Sinai*. Though the focus of that book was on feminist and not lesbian issues, it provided me with a conceptual blueprint for the transformation of Judaism.

I have been profoundly influenced by these works and by the many novels, short stories, essays, and rituals that have explored Jewish lesbian identity over the past fifteen years. Two collections contain much of this material: the Lesbian Herstory Archives in Brooklyn, New York, and the Jewish Women's Resource Center in

New York City. Both places house extremely valuable resources for scholars, and I am grateful to the women who have donated their time and energy to make these collections available.

"In God's Image: Coming to Terms with Leviticus" is reprinted from *Twice Blessed: On Being Lesbian or Gay and Jewish*, edited by Christie Balka and Andy Rose, Beacon Press, 1989. "Celebrating Gay and Lesbian Awareness: Toward Open Jewish Communities" copyright © Rebecca Alpert. First published in *New Menorah*, the journal of ALEPH: Alliance for Jewish Renewal, 7318 Germantown Ave., Philadelphia, PA 19119. "Coming Out in the Jewish Community" is reprinted from *Lifecycles Vol. 1: Jewish Women on Life Passages and Personal Milestones*, edited by Debra Orenstein (Woodstock, Vt.: Jewish Lights Publishing, 1994). Copyright ©1994 by Debra Orenstein. "Finding Our Past: Lesbian Interpretation of the Book of Ruth" is reprinted from *Reading Ruth: Contemporary Women Reclaim a Sacred Story*, edited by Judith A. Kates and Gail T. Reimer (New York: Ballantine Books, 1994). Copyright © 1994 by Judith A. Kates and Gail T. Reimer.

I am deeply grateful to readers of earlier versions of this manuscript for their insightful and careful criticisms. It is stronger because of the efforts of Martha Ackelsberg, Christie Balka, Ellen Garvey, Robin Goldberg, Shirley Idelson, Alexis Jetter, Clare Kinberg, Michael Krausz, Lori Lefkovitz, Sarra Levine, Laura Levitt, Susan Lieberman, Denni Liebowitz, Rebecca Lillian, Eleanor Myers, Annelise Orleck, Judith Plaskow, Claudia Schippert, Sheila Weinberg, and Chava Weissler. Sarra Levine deserves to be mentioned twice since she actually read two complete earlier drafts and in the process more than illustrated the ancient Jewish teaching that we learn most from our students.

I could not have found the courage to write this book without the encouragement and example of so many people:

the Reconstructionist rabbis—Linda Holtzman, Deborah Brin, Jane Litman, Julie Greenberg, Leila Berner and Sharon Kleinbaum —who were both models and partners in this process with me;

the Jewish feminist community, B'not Esh, and, in particular, Faith Rogow, who gave me the courage to dare;

the editors at Columbia University Press—Larry Gross, who first believed in this project; Lillian Faderman who, with her insight and support, made it possible for me to sustain this effort; Ann Miller who calmly saw it through some difficult passages; and Susan Heath, who did inspired editing;

my children, Lynn and Avi Alpert, who have made being a parent magical in ways that I could never have imagined it to be, and their father, Joel Alpert, for his compassion and understanding.

When my mother ate she would always scoop off the sweetest layer of melon, or set aside the tenderest piece of meat, and save them for last. My ultimate words of gratitude go to my lover, Christie Balka, whose daily presence has kept me alive, whose belief in the possibility of a world of justice and peace has sustained my writing, and who, by her simple loving acts, has enabled me to reach this day.

Rebecca Alpert

Like Bread on the Seder Plate

One

Lesbian and Jewish: What's the Problem?

Lesbian Visibility

The twin social revolutions of the 1960s and 1970s—the feminist and gay and lesbian movements—have made it possible for women who define our primary commitments in life to other women to make these commitments public, to "come out," to name ourselves as lesbians. Although not every lesbian feels comfortable taking on this public role, and while many societal rights and privileges are still denied us, the social acceptance of lesbianism far surpasses the expectations of past generations of women who never dared to dream that this openness about sexual identity would come to pass.

As part of this change, we began to think about ways in which lesbianism affected other aspects of our lives. Reexamining Jewish identity was an important part of this process. In the winter of 1979 the Jewish Women's Group at the University of California Berkeley Hillel invited the rebbitzin from the campus Ḥabad House, Hinda Langer, to speak on the subject of "Women and Halakhah." Out of simple curiosity, one of the organizers asked Langer for her opinion about the place of lesbians in Judaism.

Or religious tchr wife of Rabbis

Langer treated the issue as a minor matter. She suggested that it was a small transgression, like eating bread during Passover. Something one shouldn't do, but for which there were few consequences.

Some time later that spring when some members of the Berkeley group were planning a Passover seder, Langer's comment surfaced. But for them, Langer's explanation did not mesh with their reality. In their experience, lesbianism was much more problematic and transgressive in a Jewish context than Langer's comment suggested. So they chose that year not simply to eat bread during Passover but to place a crust of bread on their seder plate in solidarity with lesbians who were trying to find a place in Jewish life.[1]

The idea of putting bread on the seder plate caught the imagination of various groups of Jewish lesbians, and the "Crust of Bread at the Seder Table" became a midrash that was incorporated into Jewish lesbian haggadot around the United States during the early 1980s. As the story was retold, it was a male rabbi, "the Febrente Rebbe," who declared that "there is as much place for lesbians in Judaism as for leavened bread at the Seder table." And the women responded:

> Why is this night different from all other nights and this Passover from all other Passovers? For until this Passover there was no place for ḥamez on the the Seder table, but this night, this Passover, there will be room for ḥamez, for a crust of bread. This Passover, there will be a place for lesbians in Judaism—for it is said: There are pharaohs in every generation and in every generation, a woman must leave her own Mitzrayim.[2]

While not all groups felt comfortable placing bread on the seder plate (a transgression of much greater magnitude than merely eating bread during the later days of the Passover holiday), the story itself served to make the point. At the Oberlin seder, they decided to leave an open space on the seder plate that was marked makom. This term literally means space, but it is also a word used in Jewish tradition as a name for God that is without gender. This "space" would leave room for Jewish lesbians, and others who have felt alienated, to enter.[3]

But the story does not end there. Moved by the ritual, but too uncomfortable with the symbolism of bread on the seder plate,

Jewish feminists substituted an orange for the bread and began placing it on the plate instead. Initially, this orange was placed there to symbolize the role of lesbians and, later, gay men in Judaism; bringing in these groups was strange but nonetheless something new to be explored and added.[4] The transgressive nature, both of the symbol and of the act, was again removed.

But over the years the legend changed. The story began to be told about a Jewish feminist who, speaking in Florida, was upbraided by a man who said to her that women rabbis had as much of a role in Judaism as oranges did on a seder plate, or alternatively that women had as much place on the bimah as oranges on the seder plate.[5] Putting an orange on the seder plate to represent women's roles in Judaism seemed to appeal to many people, and the practice has been incorporated into seders. Artists included oranges in their designs for seder plates and maẓẓah covers.[6]

And so a contemporary legend was born. Like any evocative story, it was not often told the same way twice. The complex variations of this story resonate with the complicated ways in which Jewish lesbians have been dealt with by the Jewish community. This process of transmission also made it clear that Jewish lesbians saw our treatment in the Jewish community quite differently from the way others, from the Ḥabad rebbitzin to the Jewish feminist, saw it.

When Jewish lesbians began to make ourselves visible,[7] in most respects the American Jewish community responded like any group facing a challenge from some of its members who have been excluded or ignored and are seeking a change in their status. The community reacted with ignorance, silence, homogenization, and exoticization as we see from the above tale. Group members do their best to protect the status quo, to incorporate change in the way that will least radically alter the nature of the group as it exists. They look to minimize and standardize difference. But the Jewish reaction was also informed by a unique set of attitudes that stem not from the surrounding American culture but from Jewish tradition.

Jewish Responses

Initially, many Jews responded with disbelief. When I first spoke to a congregation in New York City on the subject of Homosexuality and Judaism in the late 1970s, a venerable older member pronounced my talk irrelevant and absurd. "There are no Jewish lesbians," she proclaimed. It took the eloquent response of another member who knew many gay people to disabuse her of this idea. It is the notion that there are no Jewish lesbians that allowed the Habad rebbitzin in 1979 to consider lesbianism a minor problem. Like eating bread on Passover, it is something that can be ignored.

The 1982 publication of the watershed book, *Nice Jewish Girls: A Lesbian Anthology*, told the stories of women who defined themselves as lesbian and Jewish for the first time, helping to dispel the myth that Jews never, or even rarely, had same-sex erotic relationships. Even if the incredulous are now beyond doubting that lesbian Jews exist in great numbers, they often refuse to do anything to acknowledge our existence. Despite the availability of information, many Jews have avoided learning more about lesbian life. If members of the community do not inform themselves about the questions lesbian Jews are raising, then the community cannot begin to address the problems of integrating lesbian perspectives into Jewish life. Nor can they benefit from Jewish lesbian creativity.

Some who did not ignore us responded by asking us to keep our sexual identities hidden. Surely if there were women who saw themselves as lesbian, and those women were also Jewish, what difference did it make? Judaism welcomes everyone who is born a Jew or who has gone through a ceremony of conversion (although our definitions of who is a Jew certainly differ among religious denominations). What difference would it make if someone had a "sexual preference" that was out of the ordinary? How could it possibly affect their religious lives or Jewish identity? Why would it matter? The development of gay and lesbian synagogues and other groups beginning in the late 1970s challenged this reaction.

Gay and lesbian Jews made it clear that our needs, visions, and dreams are not entirely the same as those of other Jews and that there are special considerations that require our making our sexual identities visible. When I attend a synagogue where my partner and I are the only lesbians present, it is very difficult for us, for example, to feel comfortable expressing our affection for one another by holding hands or even kissing at the end of services, an opportunity that is taken for granted by heterosexuals who are in long-term relationships. And without supportive communities, special events in our lives such as coming out to parents or celebrating anniversaries often cannot be appropriately acknowledged.

Others who were more comfortable began to exoticize our differences, to be fascinated by us, turning us, as it were, into "oranges." They wanted us to explain everything about being lesbian to them.[8] Why are you gay? How do you have sex? How do you have children? What's it like to raise a baby with two mothers? How can you distinguish your friendships from your romantic involvements if both are with women? Don't you like men? Why are you wearing that funny symbol, the pink triangle in the Jewish star? What do you do at gay synagogues?

Others, embarrassed by their ignorance and discomfort about our lives, responded by keeping silent and ignoring us, substituting "women on the bimah" for "lesbians." Worried about saying the wrong thing and offending us, they would often say nothing at all, thus failing to acknowledge our existence or incorporate us into their visions of Jewish life. For many years our ideas and thoughts were completely excluded. We were never asked to write or teach about lesbian subjects anywhere in Jewish publications, schools, or conferences.

Recently, we have begun to be included, but mostly as tokens. More people who are writing on Jewish subjects will now include a line or a paragraph or even an article about gay issues in an anthology, or a special issue about gay Jews in a magazine. On several occasions I have been asked to contribute the "lesbian piece" to an anthology or to be the speaker at the one session of a conference devoted to lesbian themes. To tokenize means to give voice to only one lesbian Jewish perspective.[9] After all, we are a small minority, probably less numerous than the often quoted 10 percent figure that is based on very old studies of sexual behavior by Kinsey. How complicated could our small community be? Why should significant attention be devoted to our lives or our perspectives on Jewish issues?

Others saw us not only monolithically but as very much like themselves. They responded by focusing on the similarities between heterosexual and lesbian Jews. As Jewish lesbians began to demand ceremonies to recognize our relationships and to have children, some of the discomfort with us began to fall away. Really, they claimed, you are just like us. You are committed to the survival of the Jewish people and you share our traditional family values. You fall in love, make long-term committed relationships, have children, live "stable" lives: What's the need to focus on your differences? They are interested in welcoming us in, but at a price— the same price Jews paid when the nation-states of Europe proclaimed us emancipated two centuries ago.[10] As individuals, we are granted all rights and privileges. As a group, we are expected to shed public manifestations of our distinctive behaviors and practices, to conform. And those of us who do not conform, who do not want to raise children or live in committed relationships, are not welcome.

But there are also positive signs. Many individuals in the Jewish community have begun to understand the need of lesbians in the Jewish community to be affirmed as both similar to and different from other Jews in our spiritual, cultural, and social expressions and to recognize us as a complex group in our own right. Often positive connections begin with personal relationships as friend or family member. Our supporters have begun to appreciate that we do not feel welcome as equals in the Jewish community because we face much prejudice and hatred that we must deal with, and that for the most part we and our issues are still invisible in Jewish institutions. Our allies do not hesitate to challenge rules that exclude us, jokes and comments that diminish our humanity, or the assumptions about the norm of heterosexuality that make our lives invisible.

Problems with Jewish Tradition

However, even if all heterosexual Jews overcame their prejudice and supported us, that would not solve the problem of integrating lesbians into Jewish life. For the problem is not only with the reaction of Jewish individuals and institutions but with the ancient sacred texts that form the core of Jewish belief and practice. Whether or not we read these texts, share these beliefs, or observe these practices, they continue to have a profound effect on our lives as Jews. For example, on December 12, 1995, it was reported from Israel that

> An Israeli Rabbi and member of parliament quoted the Bible, sentencing homosexuals to death. Immediately after, homosexual activists received threat letters and a couple's apartment was vandalized. The letters keep coming in while their messages are getting more and more extreme—from "strange death" threats to expressions of admiration of Yigal Amir and promises to follow his way.[11]

These words, beliefs, and practices determine how others behave toward us. They also affect our self-perceptions and our feelings about being Jewish. We claim a connection to a culture whose sacred texts incorporate ideas that exclude and hurt us. It is no wonder that we identify with bread on the seder plate.

Traditional Jews excommunicated some of us, merely for being lesbian.[12] They banned us from marching in Israel Independence Day parades,[13] from publicly honoring gay victims of the Holocaust,[14] from planting trees in Israel in memory of our dead,[15] from making aliyah under the law of return. They expanded halakhic rulings against same-sex relationships by men to apply to women too.[16]

Liberal Jewish institutions, while more sympathetic, have not given us full access to religious life. At different times they have refused to ordain us, to allow us to teach in Hebrew schools, to serve on college campuses, or to have the opportunity to honor our relationships either through ceremonies or through a dues structure that includes us.[17] Religious feminist Jews have been frightened or alienated by our differences. I have had conversations with some women rabbis who have refused to speak publicly on our behalf, threatened by the possibility that people would think that they are lesbians too.

To deal with this dilemma, we must determine strategies for ourselves to react to them. That is the goal of this book. As the Jewish community grows more open to exploring the place of lesbians, we can now begin to look deeper into this dynamic: to discover what would make it possible for lesbians to participate fully, as lesbians, in Jewish life. For this to happen, not only Jews but Judaism and its sacred texts must be transformed from a lesbian perspective. This transformation must include new readings of ancient texts, an effort to find or rediscover Jewish texts from other eras that incorporate a lesbian sensibility and the creation of new sacred texts that are affirmatively Jewish and lesbian.

As a result of these efforts, not only will Jewish lesbians become more full participants but Judaism itself will be enriched with new interpretive strategies and stories. Like the tale of bread on the seder plate, there may be many versions and interpretations. And some of them may make us so uncomfortable that we will continue to try to exoticize them or make them disappear. But it is my hope that we are ready to face the questions that lesbians pose for Judaism with a new openness.

Defining Lesbian Perspectives

To understand what would be required to transform Judaism from a lesbian perspective, we must first understand what we mean by lesbian in contemporary society. While there is no simple agreed-upon definition, we can identify several phenomena that are associated with lesbianism: same-sex sexual desire and attraction; woman-identified romantic friendship and feminism; and gender nonconformity. This definition is important because the three dimensions of lesbian existence are in fact the key impediments that stand in the way of a lesbian transformation of Judaism. As sexual beings, we share the stigma that is attached to male homosexuality in Judaism, based on biblical prohibitions. As feminists, we are part of the invisibility of women in Jewish tradition. As gender nonconformists, we defy the rigid approach to gender roles in traditional texts. These three impediments are actually interrelated. That is, it has been argued that the lack of a strong prohibition against lesbian sexuality in traditional Jewish texts makes it possible to view lesbianism as permitted within Judaism. But it can also be argued that the reason that lesbian behavior was not stigmatized was precisely that what women do does not matter in the context of Jewish life. The absence of any severe prohibition against female homosexuality does not therefore make it permissible, it merely renders it invisible. And the extent to which we refuse to conform to gender roles makes us vulnerable to prohibitions against cross-dressing and stepping out of traditional women's roles.

Sexual Desire

In contemporary Western society, lesbians are characterized by same-gendered sexual desire. From this perspective, lesbianism questions the normative nature of heterosexuality by providing an alternative model for sexual relationships. In this way lesbians most closely resemble gay men, who also do not fit into normatively defined heterosexual roles. Beginning in the 1970s this affinity resulted in alliances with the gay liberation movement. Lesbian and gay groups have worked on issues that affect both groups, including sexual liberation and civil rights such as protection from hate crimes and freedom from workplace and housing discrimination. Some lesbian and gay groups are also concerned with gaining recognition for lesbian and gay relationships and the benefits that accrue to heterosexuals through marriage including tax support, inheritance rights, custody of children, and other intangible societal privileges. And we have also built organizations together, such as gay and lesbian synagogues.

Lesbians as Women

In other perceptions of lesbianism the central focus is not on sexuality but on the affinities between lesbians as women. Prior to the second wave of feminism, women whose worlds revolved around relationships with other women came to be known as "romantic friends."[18] Throughout the first wave of feminism, women's strong romantic attachments to one another were not considered a matter of public concern. But in the late nineteenth century, lesbian was the label given by male physicians and sexologists to women who loved other women, labeling them "sexual inverts," that is, women who hated being in a female body. In that era, women who had affectionate, lifelong, and often primary relationships with one another did not name themselves lesbian. But their relationships as lifelong companions were models for contemporary lesbian feminists.[19]

At the beginning of the second wave of feminism lesbians were often characterized as "women-identified women." Lesbian feminist theory posited a deeply rooted connection among all women. Lesbian feminists were among the leading proponents of feminist theory and saw lesbianism as an extension of their feminism. Their analysis emphasized the elements of patriarchy that needed to be changed. Lesbians were highly visible in the feminist movement and active in battles against violence against women, for reproductive freedom, and for workplace equality. In this context, Jewish lesbian and feminist study and prayer groups proliferated.

Gender Nonconformists

Early in the twentieth century lesbians were most often viewed as a "third sex," women who were "mannish," and who audaciously usurped male privilege. Women's sexual attraction for other women became a medical issue in the pioneering work of the sexologists. These "experts" saw lesbianism as inextricably linked with gender identity. Lesbian sexual desire was thought to be related to disdain for traditional women's roles and behavior. If a woman wanted to have sexual relations with another woman, it was assumed that she also desired other masculine privileges. The partners of these women who themselves maintained traditional women's roles were not defined as lesbian nor was attention paid to their desires.[20]

During the second wave of feminism some strands of feminist theory argued against connecting gender roles and sexual desire. This separation provided theoretical support for women to take on the roles and behaviors of men without the concomitant assumption that they were therefore not heterosexual. These feminists were uncomfortable with "butch-femme" roles in the lesbian culture of earlier eras that revolved around connections between sexual desire and unorthodox gender roles. Gender transgression still plays a significant role in lesbian communities today, and a complex gender identification is an important characteristic of lesbianism. The link between gender and sexual transgression opens up many possibilities for the expression of lesbian sexuality.[21]

More recently, lesbians have worked in coalitions with those who call themselves queer. Queer alliances are more broadly inclusive of all those who see themselves as outside of the heterosexual norm of monogamous marriage: bisexuals and others whose sexual practices are viewed by society as "deviant," including cross-dressers, sex workers, and transsexuals. Queer theory questions social constructions of dichotomies such as homo and heterosexual. Its goal is to eradicate fundamental social distinctions based on sex, gender, and sexual orientation and also to do away with the power relations that accrue according to these categories.[22]

Lesbians in Coalition

Each alliance that lesbians have made has been problematic in one way or another. Often in these alliances, lesbian interests go unvoiced and unaddressed. In feminism, lesbians have focused their energies on a critique of male dominance rather than on challenging the system of heterosexuality that benefits all heterosexuals, women and men alike.[23] And heterosexual feminists have often been reluctant to acknowledge lesbian contributions to feminist work such issues as reproductive health and sexual violence.[24] In the gay liberation movement, the dominant concerns reflected are often male, silencing lesbian feminist critiques on such matters as sexual violence. Queer and transgendered communities also define their issues in ways that subsume lesbianism under sexual preference, viewing it as one of many possible choices about sexual behavior without taking into account gender-determined power differences between gay men and lesbians.

This slippage often mutes lesbian voices. African-American feminists find themselves in a similar predicament, forced to choose between racial and gender identifications and rendered invisible in both contexts. Lesbians are similarly forced to choose between identification based on gender and sexuality. When multiple identities come into conflict, groups sometimes set out to define their own separate spaces. A lesbian separatist movement has been crucial for defining a unique lesbian voice.[25] Yet for many separatism is not the answer. As Bernice Johnson Reagon has suggested, creating a separate space can be helpful as a retreat but it can also become a barred room preventing lesbians from addressing the conditions that created the need for a separate space in the first place.[26] This perspective does not allow lesbians to work closely with others who are also questioning and struggling against the rigid sex/gender system that binds us all.

There are important connections for lesbians to feminist, gay, and queer perspectives, and my goal is to speak in a lesbian voice that takes all of those perspectives into account, recognizing both their contradictions and limitations. While it is important to differentiate among these various dimensions of lesbianism, it is also crucial to understand them as both partial and connected. A lesbian may identify with aspects of all of these perspectives either simultaneously or at different times in her life. It is because the term "lesbian" takes all these perspectives into account that I use it to name the subjects of this book.

Feminist Accomplishments

Over the past two decades enormous changes have taken place in putting both women's contributions and problems on the agenda in Jewish life. The inclusion of feminist perspectives has made it possible for Jewish lesbians to find a voice in the Jewish community. Recognizing that we share a silence with all other Jewish women has given us a context within which to understand and counteract our invisibility. Feminist Jews, heterosexual and lesbian, have already provided a paradigm with which to approach the process of transformation. A distinctly lesbian transformation of Judaism is informed by the vast outpouring of feminist Jewish writing and activism.[27]

Problems That Remain

But this is only part of the story. While enormous changes have taken place with respect to the feminist transformation of Judaism, negative attitudes about homosexuality remain entrenched in Jewish tradition. Lesbians bear the burden of biblical characterizations of male homosexuality as to'evah, "abomination."[28] We experience this prohibition as directed toward us not only because of our solidarity with gay men but because with our growing visibility leaders of traditional Judaism have made it clear that they believe the prohibitions to extend to us as well.

And while feminism has broken new boundaries with respect to the roles that men and women play in society, transgressing or defying gender roles and defining ourselves as queer is deeply problematic in traditional Jewish life. Lesbians who do not want to be mothers and prefer to devote themselves to work, or who present themselves in ways that are traditionally understood as male are not readily accepted. Judaism is still deeply influenced by the biblical commandments to be fruitful and multiply (Genesis 1:28) and the prohibitions against dressing in clothes of the opposite sex (Deuteronomy 22:5).

Our understanding of the role those prohibitions play in our lives as Jews is crucial to a lesbian transformation of Judaism. If we assume that those laws and practices are fixed for all time, then we may reject the religious perspective in its entirety. If however we assume that Judaism has undergone radical changes over time and that it is in fact the flexibility and dynamism of the tradition that has sustained it, then we may see an opportunity to reinterpret and transform these rules and prohibitions as well as to reject specific ones if necessary and build on a new foundation.

Defining Judaism

The possibility of a lesbian transformation of Judaism is predicated on an understanding that a new foundation can be built within the context of complex and changing definitions of Judaism. I agree with the many scholars who argue that there is no one monolithic Judaism nor was there ever such a phenomenon.[29] Individual Jewish communities have existed in all parts of the world. Each has adapted to and been influenced by the culture and attitudes of its host community. Judaism has flourished for many thousands of years in no small part because of Jewish communal adaptations to living among different nationalities, races, and religions. In all these circumstances, with the exception of the state of Israel, Jews have lived as outsiders within existing cultures.[30] This has of course had a significant impact on the way the Jewish community deals with the gay and lesbian people in its midst.

Moreover, within each national community of Jews, there exist separate communities. Each Jewish community is unique in terms of the language it speaks, its ethnic diversity, its degree of adherence to Jewish law, its expressions of Jewish culture, and its desire to identify with and support other Jews outside its frame of reference.

Differences in ethnicity, belief, practice, and focus have existed among Jews since biblical times. One need only remember that Christianity began as a Jewish sect, or look at the history of charismatic movements in Judaism, or examine the differences between Ashkenazic and Sephardic Jews today, to appreciate the breadth of Jewish cultures.

While many people today associate Judaism with its religious dimension, this association is an oversimplification. Since the emancipation of the Jews in Western countries in the eighteenth century, many Jews have retained a strong identification with the Jewish people without any involvement in religious observance. As Mordecai Kaplan, the founder of Reconstructionism, suggested, Judaism is a civilization that encompasses elements found in any culture: language, law, art, politics, folklore, and religion. Zionism and socialism are two powerful expressions of Jewish secular culture. Even Jews who affiliate primarily for religious reasons do not share a single set of practices and beliefs. As a Reconstructionist, I believe that the single unifying factor for Jews is our connection to the Jewish people and to Jewish civilization. From this perspective, Judaism includes all who claim identification with the narrative history of this particular people, its values and practices, however they define them.[31]

Complicating Factors

The complexity of Jewish life adds another interesting dimension to the lesbian transformation of Judaism. In the process of this transformative work, we must keep in mind that lesbianism is only one of many dimensions of Jewish identity. In some situations Jewish lesbians find that other aspects of Jewish experience are more salient. The lesbian rabbi at times finds that her sophisticated

Jewish knowledge and observance gives her greater status than those without advanced Jewish education. The white Jewish lesbian whose grandparents came from Russia feels more comfortable in most North American settings than will the Moroccan Jew. The Jewish lesbian by birth will be more at home at a family seder than will her partner who is a convert to Judaism. An older Jewish lesbian may find more compatible associations in many Jewish organizational settings than the younger lesbian who defines herself as queer. Able-bodied lesbians have more access to Jewish institutions than those with disabilities. And some of these factors may work in reverse in those parts of the Jewish community where different groups are in the majority. These factors of difference must be taken into account when speaking about a lesbian transformation of Judaism. They remind us that there is no universal Jewish lesbian perspective. Any view of Jewish life from a lesbian standpoint is always only partial.

Judaism and lesbianism are complex phenomena that do not allow for simple definition. However, there is a relationship between the experiences and ideas of lesbian Jews that forms what African-American feminist thinker Patricia Hill Collins has called "a unique angle of vision" from which to examine the values and ideas of Judaism in its various manifestations.[32] It is through a lesbian Jewish angle of vision that I will examine ancient, modern, and contemporary Jewish texts to begin the process of a lesbian transformation of Jewish textual tradition that will serve as a basis for a larger social transformation.

In this first chapter I have suggested that, despite advances in the Jewish community toward the acceptance of lesbians, no real change is possible without also confronting Jewish texts, reinterpreting them, and adding our own. I have argued that the ability to confront and challenge these texts is predicated on seeing lesbianism and Judaism as complex phenomena whose definitions change over time and space. In the chapter that follows, I continue this process by examining the troubling texts that have rendered us invisible and reviled. Looking at these texts is a necessary step that begins the process of transformation. Only by confronting the deep-rooted sources of our alienation can we truly begin the process of finding a place for ourselves as lesbians in Jewish life.

After looking at these troubling texts from Torah in chapter 2, in chapter 3 I suggest possibilities for understanding these texts in new ways, by reading them through a lesbian lens. Chapters 4 to 6 examine other biblical texts that provide an opening to a broader transformation of Jewish belief and practice from a lesbian perspective. In chapters 7 and 8 I call attention to modern texts that have gone unnoticed but are an important part of constructing a Jewish lesbian past. Chapter 9 suggests that contemporary Jewish lesbian fiction makes our lives part of this textual transformation as well. The concluding chapter dares to imagine what Jewish life would be like based on a lesbian transformation of textual traditions.

Two

Troubling Texts from Torah[1]

The Torah, the most sacred text of the Jewish people, contains passages that are highly problematic for Jewish lesbians. For example, the Torah includes a passage that calls male homosexual acts abhorrent: "Do not lie with a male as one lies with a woman; it is an abomination." (Leviticus 18:22); another passage that insists that humanity is defined through male-female partnership: "And God created humanity in God's own image, in the image of God He [sic] created it; male and female He created them." (Genesis 1:27); and another that has been interpreted to suggest that lesbian sexuality is alien to Jewish practice: "You shall not copy the practices of the land of Egypt where you dwelt . . . nor shall you follow their customs." (Leviticus 18:3). No doubt these passages cause consternation among those of us who are involved in religious life. We need new strategies to overcome their effects.

Even if we are not religious Jews, these ancient Jewish texts can affect us. Torah is used by others to support their belief that homosexuality is wrong. (This is true not only for Jews. Torah is quoted by right-wing Christian religious groups to the same end.) These uses to which Torah is put can undermine our pride in ourselves, feeding our own homophobia as well as that of others. Even if we don't attend synagogue or religious school where we read these words, we are not immune from them. Passages from Torah are taught in university classrooms as literature. Assumptions based on these words find their way into newspapers, movies, and television. We cannot ignore the fact that in the sacred literature of our people lesbians are either trivialized or reviled. This chapter examines these three troubling Torah texts and the ways in which they have been interpreted throughout Jewish history that have served to increase our sense of alienation.

The Significance of Torah

Before we look at these texts, it is important for us to understand the central role of Torah in Jewish religious life. The Torah consists of the first five books of the Hebrew Bible. Torah is also known as the Pentateuch, or the Five Books of Moses. These books contain stories of the origins of the world, the birth of our people, and the beginnings of the Jewish legal system. Traditionally, they are understood as revelation—God's words, written down by Moses, God's prophet, on Mt. Sinai. Thus, these words are considered not only a record of our past but God's explanation of God's will for the people of Israel. Studying and interpreting the words of Torah has been a central occupation of Jews for the past 2,500 years, since the time of Ezra.

Torah forms the basis for the entire corpus of Jewish law. Laws codified in these books are the ultimate source of authority and are the starting point for the later development of Jewish civilization. According to strict interpretation of Jewish law, no pronouncement in the Torah can ever be nullified or abrogated. And many laws that were written later were given authority by linking them in some way to a Torah passage, in the same way that the prohibition against "the practices of Egypt" was later identified as the source for prohibitions against lesbianism.

Beyond its implications for the Jewish legal system, Torah has deep symbolic power. It is preserved on a handwritten parchment scroll. It is kept in the ark, a sacred space at the front or center of every synagogue, under a flame that burns perpetually. It is adorned with a special cover and ornaments. It is removed from the ark with great pageantry to be chanted aloud three times weekly and on holy days. The public reading of Torah is the central event of the Sabbath morning service. To be called to the Torah to recite the blessing for reading from the scroll is a great honor. Blessing and reading from Torah forms the core experience of the bar/bat mitzvah ceremony.

Clearly, the words of Torah cannot be dismissed lightly, nor would we wish them to be. For although the Torah does contain troubling passages, it is also the source of concepts that are vital to us: that we should love our neighbors as ourselves and deal respectfully with the stranger, the poor, and the lonely in society. Torah instructs us to see ourselves as having been created in God's image and, therefore, as the bearers of holiness in the world. It also contains wonderful and challenging stories of the world's beginnings and our people's journey from slavery to freedom.

Those of us who choose to remain identified with the Jewish tradition do so in part because of the foundation laid by Torah. We cannot simply excise what we do not like; it is our heritage and the primary text of our people. Yet a piercing question arises and reverberates through our lives: How do we live as Jews when the same text that tells us to love our neighbors also tells us that male homosexual acts are punishable by death by decree of that same God? When the text that tells us that we are created in God's image is based on an assumption of male-female coupling? When our sexuality is associated with the "practices of Egypt"—the culture of people who enslaved us? We begin to answer these questions by taking a close look at the passages that are problematic for us and then deciding what resources we have to come to terms with them.

The Story of Creation

And God created humanity in God's own image, in the image of God He [sic] created it; male and female He created them.   —*Genesis 1:27*

We must address the question of how lesbians can live as Jews when the sacred text that tells us we were created in God's image also tells us that male homosexual acts are punishable by death and that lesbian acts are associated with "the practices of Egypt." These are contradictory notions; if God created all human beings in the divine image, then men who love men and women who love women must also be part of the divine plan. While it is necessary to come to terms with the legal prohibition against male homosexual acts in the Torah, it is also important to examine more closely the text that declares all human beings to be created in God's image. For this text which appears to support our dignity and humanity is not unproblematic. In fact, it raises even more troubling questions.

In this case, we are looking at myth rather than law. We should not underestimate the power of myth to define cultural norms, in ways more powerful even than legislation. One need only think of the way the story of Oedipus has affected our thinking about the relationships between parents and children, or the power of fairy tales to teach lessons about how to behave in the world, to understand the power myth has of determining our perceptions. Myths are often written descriptively, to explain how the world works, but they are used prescriptively, to explain how the world should work. In the case of the Hebrew myth of creation in which we find the idea that we are all created in God's image, both the prescriptive and descriptive assumptions present obstacles to the acceptance of lesbians in Jewish tradition.

Because this text is myth and not law, it is best to approach it "mythically," that is, through the language of midrash. The goal is not to uncover the "true" meaning of the text or even to understand what it meant in its own context. Why focus on this story and not other biblical tales? Precisely because this text makes a claim to define the nature of human beings in relationship to God, to our intimate relationships to other humans, and to our sexuality.

The Creation of Gender

The idea that human beings are created in God's image is found at the very beginning of the Torah text, in the first chapter of Genesis. The statement is embedded in the first of two creation stories in the Hebrew Bible. In this simple declaration, an entire world view is articulated.

The primary way that human beings are understood to exist in the world is through the definition of sexual identity: one is either anatomically male or female. For feminists, this statement can be read in a positive light. A feminist interpretation argues that men and women were created equal, simultaneously, and both in God's image. In this version of the creation story, men are not given dominance or primacy based on biological difference.

But making biological sex the primary defining characteristic of humanity is disturbing. This myth introduces a rigid binary identity system in which to be human one must be either biologically male or female. It leaves the status of intersexuals, those who are born with two biological sexes, subject to painful and prejudicial societal attitudes. Most frequently they are compelled to choose one sex rather than live in a more ambiguous state as male and female. In most cases parents decide on surgery to remove one set of sex organs before the child has a chance either to decide on one sexual identity or to retain both.[2] The myth that there are only two, mutually exclusive sexes is reinforced by the Hebrew creation narrative.

This description of human creation also implies a link between sexual identity and gender identity. Although most individuals who are anatomically male or female identify as such, there are many who understand themselves to be born in the wrong body, who feel that they belong in another gender. The need to define people as male or female as articulated in the text is reinforced throughout a person's lifetime, and those with alternative gender identities suffer profound discrimination because of their differences.[3]

The problem is further complicated by an oversimplistic understanding of the terms "male" and "female" from the perspective of culture as well as biology. As the text is most often read, "male" and "female" stand not only for anatomy, but also for role behavior, the positions that men and women are expected to occupy in society. Because the text implies a fixed understanding of "male" and "female," it leaves little room for exploring ambiguous gender identities, or for broadening the definition of what it means to be male and female.

The issues raised thus far about biological sex, gender identity, and gender roles are often understood as directly related to sexual orientation. Therefore if a woman decides that she wants to drive a truck for her profession, or if a man chooses to wear skirts rather than pants on occasion, they are assumed to be gay or lesbian. It is the threat of being labeled gay or lesbian that enforces rigid gender roles, keeping men and women from considering a wider variety of options for their behavior and also leading to confusion about lesbian identity.

No one understands how gender or sexual orientation is constructed; we therefore may not presume the nature of the relationship between these and biological sex. People who identify as lesbian may in fact be led because of our different sexual orientation to think in more complex ways about gender and sexuality; some of us may even choose to experiment with these identities more freely than heterosexuals. But many people with alternative gender and sexual identities do not necessarily consider themselves gay or lesbian.[4] Nonetheless, looking at the text through a lesbian lens heightens our concern about these issues, because we understand lesbian identity as part of a larger frame of reference that questions assumptions about gender and sexuality. We are therefore concerned about the oppression of others with different gender and sexual identities, and we must also look at the text from this perspective.

"And They Become One Flesh": Creation and Complementarity

The inextricable connection between the two genders is even more deeply disturbing. The creation of humans as male *and* female, not male *or* female, presents us with the paradigm of the complementary coupling of men and women as essential to human experience. This view of creation, alluded to in the first creation story, is made explicit in the second creation story about Adam and Eve. It is this creation story that supplies basic explanations about gender complementarity, sexuality, and compulsory heterosexuality.[5]

Through the centuries, biblical commentators and scholars have been puzzled by the fact that the story of creation is told twice in the text. In the first telling of the story, the creation of human beings is briefly described. The second creation story is more elaborate than the first, and is the one with which most people are familiar. It is commonly understood as an explanation of basic elements of human life—work, sexuality, procreation, clothing, shelter, and death. In this story, God creates Adam.

Adam's first task is to care for the garden. But Adam is alone, and God decides that this is not a good state. God creates animals, and Adam names them, but these animals do not offer fitting companionship. God solves the problem by anesthetizing Adam and creating two new beings, man and woman, to be companions for one another, as described by the Hebrew phrase, ezer c'negdo. The centrality of coupling in this story echoes and adumbrates the first. In the first chapter of Genesis, male and female are linked. In this second version, they bear a crucial relationship to one another as companion/counterpart.

Then the biblical author suggests that this companionship is the reason that marriage exists. Because they are ezer c'negdo, "a man leaves his father and mother and clings to his wife, so that they become one flesh" (Genesis 2:24). It is in this gloss that the connection between man and woman takes on a sexual connotation.

Thus according to this story of creation, the paradigm for human companionship is the male/female couple. It appears that at this point in the narrative, the lesson being taught is the primacy of companionship, defined through the union of male and female opposites. This part of the story thus understood raises some important questions. The first is about the necessity of defining relationships as dyadic pairs to overcome aloneness. We must question this basic assumption, given that many societies recognize the ability of individuals to function without heterosocial companionship and in predominantly homosocial groups. In fact, Jewish culture, like most premodern cultures, was, and remains in traditional circles predominantly homosocial, emphasizing the rigid separation of the sexes in every dimension of public life.[6] Yet the Jewish tradition has no place for people who do not crave the companionship of others of the opposite gender or who do not experience aloneness as an evil to be overcome but whose happy and productive lives belie the necessity of heterosocial coupling.

The second concerns the assumption that a union of opposites, defined as male/female, is the primary paradigm for couples. This presents the most significant challenge to lesbians who choose to live with partners. Even if we accept the notion that it is preferable to share companionship with one other individual, it is not at all clear to us that the relationship we choose needs to be with a man.

This focus on the complementary relationship between men and women is the basis for much antilesbian and gay sentiment outside the Jewish community and particularly among the religious right. "God made Adam and Eve, not Adam and Steve" has become an important slogan of the antigay movement. We see it on signs and placards as we march in gay rights parades from Washington to San Francisco. We read it on car bumper stickers in towns and cities. And it issues forth as truth from the mouths of fundamentalist preachers, TV talk show hosts, and students in college classes. The story of creation, for many in contemporary society, proclaims truth about what is right and natural for everyone.

A 1994 article by Reuven Kimelman expresses this idea from a Jewish perspective. Kimelman argues that the essential and immutable basis of Jewish family life is male/female complementarity. Given this reasoning, it is impossible for gay men and lesbians to be "good" Jews.[7]

"Your Desire Shall Be for Your Husband": Defining The Heterosexual Norm

Up until this point in the Genesis narrative the issue of sexuality has not been the focus. Now, as the story unfolds, the woman becomes curious about a tree that was forbidden to her and the man by God. Taking her cue from the snake and asserting her independent will, the woman decides to eat from the fruit of the tree and offers some to the man who is with her. From that point on they realize that they are unclothed and create clothing for themselves. This reference is generally understood as an awareness of their sexuality. God, noting that they had not obeyed the command not to eat of the fruit of this tree, makes many changes in the nature of their existence. The man will be alienated from his labor. The woman will have the same fate and, additionally, will suffer pain in childbirth. The issue of sexuality is raised when God tells the woman: "your desire shall be for your husband, and he shall rule over you." Furthermore, Adam is now given the power to name his wife. He calls her Eve, which means mother of all living. The myth assumes connections between sexuality, procreation, male dominance, and heterosexual desire.

For feminists the story now becomes problematic, because the relationship of equality between man and woman is replaced by a relationship of dominance: "and he shall rule over you." In addition, the story asserts woman's primary identity as childbearer.

For lesbians a different problem arises. The issue of male dominance as defined by the phrase "and he shall rule over you" is of less concern if we do not define ourselves among the group to whom "your desire shall be for your husband" applies. As women who do not desire men as sexual partners, lesbians do not fit under the "curse of Eve." Perhaps this is the most threatening aspect of lesbian existence, as it recognizes that there are women whose desires defy the assumption of the "naturalness" of heterosexuality. Lesbian desire complicates the assumption of the universality of this myth.

It may also lead us to question the nature of the myth and whether it prescribes or describes. If the myth is descriptive, then it is an effort to explain why men dominate women; why childbirth is both painful and dangerous, yet women endure it anyway; and why heterosexuality is the norm. But if the myth is prescriptive, then the author must have assumed that women's desire for their husbands must be made compulsory because women's desire is in fact diffuse and may be channeled in other directions.

The story is also complicated for lesbians because there is no necessary connection for us between sexuality and procreation. Although some lesbians do on occasion have sex with men, lesbian procreation is usually unrelated to heterosexual intercourse. For these reasons, the story excludes lesbian existence altogether.

The Prohibition Against Male Homosexual Behavior

Do not lie with a male as one lies with a woman; it is an abomination.

—*Leviticus 18:22*

Three times a year, on Yom Kippur afternoon and then twice during the annual cycle of Torah readings, every year for the past 2,500 years, Jews around the world have listened to the public reading of Leviticus declaring a sexual act between two men "an abomination." When the prohibition is read from Leviticus 20 during the reading from the annual Torah cycle in the spring, male homosexuality is declared not only an abomination but also a capital crime.

What could be more profoundly alienating than to know that the most sacred text of your people, read aloud on the holiest day of the year, calls that which is central to your life an abomination? What could be more terrifying than to know that what for you is a sacred loving act was considered by your ancestors to be punishable by death?

Coming to terms with this passage in Leviticus may be the greatest single struggle facing lesbians seeking to find a home within the Jewish community, despite the fact that lesbians are not specifically mentioned in this passage. There has been much speculation about this omission. Some have assumed on this basis that the Hebrew people never observed lesbian behavior. Surely, if they knew about female homoeroticism it would have been prohibited along with male homoeroticism. But this argument from silence does not take into account the differing attitudes about male and female sexuality in the Hebrew worldview. The main sexual concern of the Hebrew Bible is the emission of semen. What women did with one another was of no concern to the authors and redactors of the Bible. So it may be more likely to assume that female homoeroticism was not outlawed because that society paid no attention to the private sexual activities of women.

In either case, most Jewish lesbians today do not view the absence of the prohibition as giving them any particular privileged position in Judaism as compared with gay men. But it does provide an advantage for us. Because of this biblical prohibition, the most vituperative antigay sentiments are often directed at gay men, and lesbians are spared some of the hostility.

Even if we are not the objects of as much hostility, the silence is a problem. The fact that lesbian behavior is not considered in the biblical text marks the invisibility of lesbian concerns in our tradition. This invisibility is the source of the pain Jewish lesbians often feel when we confront the tradition. It doubles our burden when we face this text. We identify with the stated antipathy to gay male sexuality, and respond to that. Then in addition, we have to deal with the fact that we are not mentioned in the text—even though we feel a kinship with gay men, and even though we are often included anyway when people use the biblical prohibition to denounce homosexuality. Lesbians must still come to terms with Leviticus. The silence that surrounds us complicates this process.

With this understanding as our background, let us look at how Leviticus 18:22 and 20:13 have been interpreted by traditional Jewish commentators. We find that this prohibition is mentioned less often than others in Torah. Some have assumed that this lack of discussion is due to the fact that homosexuality was not common among Jews. We can only speculate about the extent of homosexual practice, but we can say with certainty that the subject was not considered problematic enough to require extensive public discussion. For whatever reason, to be sure, homosexuality was not a central issue in the Jewish world until contemporary times.

Most of the interpretations of Leviticus 18:22 hinge on an unclear word—to'evah—which is generally translated as "abomination." In fact, the meaning of this word is obscure. Therefore, interpreters have taken the opportunity to translate it in ways that explain the prohibition. After all, the text never tells us why lying with a man is to'evah, only that it is.

What might to'evah mean? According to second-century commentator Bar Kapparah, it means "to'eh ata ba—you go astray because of it" (*Babylonian Talmud, Nedarim* 51b). This play on words has been taken to mean that it is not intrinsically evil to engage in homosexual acts but, rather, that these acts have negative consequences. Bar Kapparah did not spell out those negative consequences. He left it to later commentators to interpret his interpretation.

Pesikta (Zutarta) and *Sefer Ha-Ḥinnukh* (209) suggest that homosexual acts lead a man astray from the main function of sexual behavior, procreation. *Tosafot* and R. Asher ben Jeḥiel assume that to go astray means to abandon your wife and to disrupt family life. This interpretation is reinforced by medieval commentator Saadiah Gaon's general pronouncement that the Bible's moral legislation is directed at preserving the structure of the family (*Emunot ve-Deot* 3:1). Finally, modern commentator R. Barukh haLevi Epstein, author of the commentary *Torah Temimah*, suggests that going astray means not following the anatomically appropriate manner of sexual union.

The most well-known biblical commentator, Rashi, who lived in eleventh-century France, had but one comment on Leviticus 20:13. Wanting to make the text clearer to his readers, he explained rather graphically the meaning of the phrase, "as with a woman": "he enters like a painting stick into a tube."

In the latter part of the twentieth century traditional Jews have had to come to terms with the fact that gay men and lesbians have made themselves a presence in the Jewish community. A widely disseminated article on homosexuality and Judaism was written for the *Encyclopedia Judaica Yearbook* in 1974 by Orthodox rabbi Norman Lamm, and has been reprinted in several volumes on Jewish ethics.[8] Lamm defines homosexuality as a sin and a sickness. He concludes that because it is a sin, the prohibition cannot be rescinded, but because it is also a sickness, the biblical punishment of death should not be carried out. Lamm's response affirms the text as it is simply understood—a strong prohibition against homosexuality. While he claims interpretation to be unnecessary to explain the text, in fact, he makes an interpretation of his own of the meaning of to'evah:

> The very variety of interpretations of to'evah points to a far more fundamental meaning, namely, that an act characterized as an abomination is prima facie disgusting and cannot be further defined or explained.[9]

Lamm's understanding of the term "to'evah" as "prima facie disgusting" clarifies the problem gay men and lesbians face when confronting Jewish tradition and leaves little room for conversation.

It is not only Orthodox Jews who employ interpretations to take a moral position against homosexuality. Note the following responsum by Reform rabbi, Solomon Freehof:

> In Scripture (Leviticus 18:22) homosexuality is considered to be an "abomination." So too in Leviticus 20:13. If Scripture calls it an abomination, it means that it is more than a violation of a mere legal enactment; it reveals a deep-rooted ethical attitude.[10]

Freehof goes on to indicate that this is an attitude that he shares.

As these traditional interpretations make clear, Jewish textual scholars understand the legislation in Leviticus to prohibit male homosexual behavior in no uncertain terms. These interpretations discern the plain meaning of the text by explaining difficult or unclear words in the verse. Their goal is to underscore the antipathy between their understanding of Judaism and the practice of homosexual behavior.

The Prohibition Against Lesbianism

You shall not copy the practices of the land of Egypt where you dwelt . . .
nor shall you follow their customs   —*Leviticus 18:3*

This biblical passage also says nothing about lesbianism. Yet it was used by later Jewish legal sources to prohibit lesbian behavior: "What did they do? A man would marry a man, or a woman a woman, a man would marry a woman and her daughter, or a woman would marry two men." This textual reference is from *Sifra* (*Aḥare Mot*), a compilation of commentaries on Leviticus from the Roman era, second century C.E.[11] It links the biblical prohibition against "the practices of Egypt" with, among other things, lesbian marriage. The biblical text itself does not suggest that the prohibition of behaviors that are "like those of the Egyptians" have anything to do with same-sex marriage, and we have no evidence to assume that there were same-sex marriages in Egypt during the time when Leviticus was being written.[12] But it is very likely that the author of *Sifra* knew of same-sex marriages from the Roman culture in which he lived and interchanged the identities of Rome and Egypt without regard to historical accuracy.

Female homoeroticism was considered the ultimate depravity in Roman society. Women who loved other women were seen as seeking male privilege and attempting to usurp the authority of men.[13] But lesbian marriage was known in Roman society, and we do have other examples of references to women-women marriages in the second-century Roman empire. A novel by Iamblichus, a contemporary of Lucian, tells the story of a marriage of a queen of Egypt, Berenice, who is said to have loved and married a woman named

Mesopotamia.[14] And Church Father Clement of Alexandria condemns female-female marriage as an unacceptable practice, contrary to nature.[15]

More evidence of the awareness of female homoeroticism from Jewish sources of the early Roman period (probably from the beginning of the common era) is found in the fragmentary extracanonical work, *The Sentences of Pseudo-Phocylides*. It was probably written by a Jew living in the diaspora. In this text, women are forbidden to imitate the sexual roles of men.[16] We do not know if this text refers to positions during heterosexual intercourse, to same-sex lovemaking, or to marriage.[17] But like the *Sifra* text, it reflects the era's awareness that such activities existed.

While there are other discussions of lesbianism in ancient Jewish texts, this connection to the biblical text is not mentioned again until the twelfth century. Other ancient texts took lesbianism less seriously. In the Talmud (c. 500 C.E.), female homoeroticism is referred to as engaging in mesolelot. Modern English translations define mesolelot as "practicing lewdness."[18] But there is no indication from the context that such a pejorative definition is warranted by the term. Apparently, this term was used for sexual behavior that did not involve penetration.[19] It is probably the Hebrew equivalent of "tribade," the ancient term used in Greek and Roman cultures for women who engage in sexual activity by rubbing their genitals against one another.[20]

The rabbis of the Talmud were concerned about mesolelot only insofar as this behavior might change a woman's status from that of virgin (betulah). Nonvirgins lose their eligibility for marriage to men of priestly descent (who were restricted to marrying virgins). The Talmud records two opinions. Rav Huna argues that women who practice mesolelot should not be eligible for priestly marriage; Eleazar says they should, and the law follows Eleazar. The text suggests that such behavior does not warrant punishment because it is prizut. This is generally translated as "mere obscenity" but might better be understood as "minor infraction."

The Babylonian Talmud refers to mesolelot in one other case. In *Shabbat* 65a, it is reported that R. Samuel prohibited his daughters from sleeping together. The question is raised in the text as to why he would enforce such a prohibition. The commentators suggested that he was following Rav Huna's interpretation and assuming that his daughters would be prohibited from marrying priests if they were engaging in mesolelot (in this case, incestuous mesolelot). But the conclusion of the text indicates that Samuel did not agree with Rav Huna. It suggests that he prohibited his daughters from sleeping together so that they would not grow accustomed to "a foreign body."

While I am tempted to argue that Samuel feared that his daughters might enjoy female homoeroticism so much that they would refuse marriage to a priest (or anyone else), it is more likely that these two texts illustrate a different point. The rabbis who wrote and edited these passages clearly knew of female homoerotic behavior but assumed that the women involved would certainly marry men. Thus their concern is probably with stopping this behavior, so that the women in question would be prepared for marriage. Samuel's daughters should not get used to sexual pleasure either because they were not yet ready for marriage or because when they did marry they would have to sleep separately from their husbands. Husband and wife were not allowed to share one bed because of the laws of niddah, which prohibited touching between husband and wife while the woman was menstruating and for seven clean days after. So sexual pleasure, while encouraged, was limited to approximately half of the month because of the demands of niddah. That is not to say that the daughters in question might not have preferred each other's company to a husband; of this we cannot be certain.

In the Middle Ages the Jewish laws found in the Talmud and other texts were codified by subject so that it would be easier for people to understand and gain access to Jewish legal precepts. One such codification, aptly titled *Mishneh Torah* (a second Torah) was compiled and edited by Moses Maimonides (1130–1205). Maimonides' compilation did not only reiterate the legal precedents. His text also reflects his analysis and gives us some information about mesolelot in his era that sheds light on the question of lesbianism in later Jewish societies:

> Women are forbidden to engage in mesolelot with one another, these being "the doings of Egypt" against which we have been warned, as it is said: "You shall not copy the prac-

tices of the land of Egypt . . ." (Leviticus 18:3). Our Sages have said: "What did they do? A man would marry a man, or a woman a woman, or a woman would marry two men." Although such an act is forbidden, the perpetrators are not liable for a flogging, since there is no specific negative commandment prohibiting it, nor is actual intercourse of any kind involved. Consequently, such women are not disqualified from the priesthood on account of prostitution, nor is a woman prohibited to her husband because of it. It behooves the court, however, to administer the flogging prescribed for rebelliousness since they performed a forbidden act. A man should be particularly strict with his wife in this matter and should prevent women known to indulge in such practices from visiting her and her from visiting them.[21]

From the text it appears that Maimonides' main interest is not with a hypothetical situation about marriages to priests, which he deals with perfunctorily, but with the problems of men who are married to women who keep company with women known to engage in mesolelot. Maimonides makes a connection not mentioned in the Talmud text between mesolelot and "women who marry [nosin, the technical legal term for Jewish marriage] one another."

While lesbian behavior was only a minor sexual infraction, lesbian marriage as a subversion of heterosexual norms would have been a serious threat to the legal system and would receive more attention, as Maimonides' comments suggest. The focus on the biblical source rather than the comments from the Talmud allowed Maimonides to view this behavior as serious and gave more license to punish it. Yet Maimonides still chose to define lesbian behavior as a minor crime of rebelliousness. This leniency is remarkable given his awareness of lesbian behavior in women married to men and his association of these practices with lesbian marriage, which he categorized among the biblically prohibited "doings of Egypt." Maimonides saw lesbianism as the problem of a husband who could not control his wife's behavior. But that behavior was not despised nor considered sinful. Lesbian behavior was not a serious crime, especially in comparison to male homosexuality, which was subject to capital punishment. It was taken lightly but not overlooked entirely. Punishment was to be meted out by the authorities of the community, the court, not simply by the man who was wronged by his wife.

In contrast to modern European practice, Jewish law punishes the wife and not the partner, the presumed lesbian, who entices her. The person presumed to initiate sexual contact is not the one who is blamed or punished. Lesbian behavior itself is not considered problematic unless it threatens the institution of heterosexual marriage.

Ancient Jewish sources were aware of, but not threatened by, female homoerotic behavior. This stance created a silence around the subject, for there was little to discuss. Now that lesbianism has become a more open topic in recent times, the neutrality of earlier sources tempers to some degree negative contemporary attitudes toward lesbianism.

In contemporary times there has been a limited response to lesbianism in Orthodox circles where the Jewish legal tradition has ultimate authority. In Norman Lamm's definitive 1974 article on homosexuality, he did not examine lesbianism in early Judaism in any substantial way. He devoted one paragraph to rabbinic sources on women, in which he denied that such behavior had any significant impact on Jewish life.[22] In Lamm's opinion, lesbianism is a lesser offense but is also not tolerated.

More recent awareness of the prevalence of lesbianism has led to stricter interpretations in traditionalist writings. In a 1994 book about women from an Orthodox perspective, Michael Kaufman briefly discusses lesbianism in a section on married women. Kaufman does not qualify lesbianism as a lesser offense but states boldly that it is prohibited by Jewish law, deriving the prohibition from the biblical injunction against Egyptian practices. According to Kaufman, lesbianism is not only legally prohibited but is "a perversion of nature and the divine order" and "intrinsically repulsive."[23]

Reading traditional Jewish legal texts on lesbianism leads to the conclusion that the private sexual behavior of women was viewed as trivial. As feminists, we reject the rabbinic sensibility that claims our sexual activities don't count and don't matter. However, now that lesbianism has become public and challenges heterosexuality, the response from traditional circles is anger and revulsion.

Taken together, these biblical texts are deeply troubling for Jewish lesbians. They make our existence invisible, pejoratize and trivialize our sexuality, and proclaim norms for human existence that leave out our way of life. These factors are enough to make some lesbians decide to leave Judaism entirely. Others choose to ignore the texts while maintaining their connections. But as I suggested at the beginning of this chapter, many Jewish lesbians feel a deep commitment to struggle with these texts and to find ways to counteract them.

The Halakhic Response

Since Torah is the foundation of Jewish legal writings (halakhah), it is logical to assume that we could use halakhic method for dealing with these texts. If we don't like the way laws about lesbian behavior have been interpreted, why not write new laws?

This process would only be possible if certain changes were to take place in the halakhic process. Transforming Judaism from a lesbian perspective begins from the assumption that lesbian identity and behavior is no more or less valued or holy than is heterosexual behavior. The question is not whether one is lesbian or heterosexual but rather how one creates values in a Jewish world in which lesbian is as normal as heterosexual. Transforming Judaism through a lesbian lens can only happen in a world where we would no more consider the question of the ethics of homosexuality than we would consider whether it is more ethical to be Jewish, Buddhist, or Christian.

Because of this assumption, it is difficult to work within the framework of halakhah. Of course, it could be argued that halakhah never interdicts lesbian behavior. Since there is no biblical injunction against lesbianism, it must be acceptable in Jewish law. But this would be an erroneous argument. As we have seen, later Jewish law does punish lesbian behavior, and efforts have been made by Maimonides and others to find biblical roots for the prohibition. While most of the legal discussions about lesbianism are not ethical in tone, it is considered rebellious behavior and a minor sin. And, more significantly, halakhah is predicated on the normative nature of heterosexuality. Jewish law commands heterosexual marriage and requires that procreation take place within marriage. Halakhic precepts circumscribe the role of women and define women as possessions of their husbands.[24]

Another problem with using halakhah in the formulation of Jewish lesbian transformation of tradition is that halakhah is generally understood to emanate from the authority of revelation. For many Jewish lesbians this perspective is problematic because it requires a belief in a God who reveals truth, who watches and judges, who rewards and punishes individual behavior.

The last difficulty with the halakhic system is that it can only be interpreted by certain rabbis who are considered to be halakhic experts, and it is most unlikely that Jewish lesbians will have the opportunity to serve in this capacity. It makes no sense to transform Judaism from a lesbian perspective to create a situation in which Jewish lesbians still have no voice in the decision-making process.

Jewish lesbian transformation must look beyond halakhah for resources to reinterpret and challenge these texts. We will discover these resources through our own efforts to define a body of Jewish texts that includes us. Some of these texts will be found in the Torah itself, some in other sacred Jewish literature, and some in works that we redefine as sacred for ourselves. The rest of this book is dedicated to that task.

Three

Jewish Lesbian Interpretation of Torah

The Torah is the formative document of Jewish life. It has been the common text of the Jewish people throughout time and in different cultural circumstances. While most contemporary Jews do not interpret it literally, it remains the source of our ideas and ideals. The Torah contains law, history, and myth that define basic Jewish values and from which we draw inspiration.

One approach to addressing troubling passages is to realize that the Torah is only a partial record of our people's early history. It contains that part of our story that men in positions of authority chose to record. We come to this 3,000 year old text with an understanding that human needs and sensibilities change over time, and that we must revisit the text in each generation to see what insights we can glean from it from our own perspective.

Female homoeroticism is not mentioned in the Torah. It is not directly interdicted in legal pronouncements. And the few stories that include relationships between women in the Bible are mostly about sisters, cowives, mothers, and daughters. But the absence of these laws and stories does not mean that lesbian concerns are absent from ancient Jewish civilization.

Making lesbian concerns visible in these texts is the first step toward a lesbian transformation of Jewish tradition. Let me suggest, then, three methods of reading Torah through a lesbian lens, using both the passage from Leviticus that calls male homosexual behavior an abomination and the story of creation in order to illustrate my approaches. We can, as did our ancestors, interpret the text to enable us to function with it on its own terms. We can, like biblical scholars, treat the text as historical record and draw conclusions based on the way the text functions in a given context. Or we can encounter the text directly with our emotions and our self-knowledge, allowing it to move us to anger and then beyond anger to action.

Each method comes to terms with the text's authority in a different way. Through interpreting the text we use the text's own language to give it new meanings. Through historical reasoning we place limits on the text's authority by examining it with the lens of another system. Through encountering the text emotionally we confront it and therefore use it as an instrument of social transformation.

The Interpretive Method

Midrash—the process of making commentary to interpret the text—is a vital aspect of attempts throughout Jewish history to make the Bible come alive. Throughout the generations, interpreters have sought to make the text accessible to their contemporaries, who may not understand its original meaning. The text may be ambiguous, unclear, or redundant. A word or custom may be unfamiliar and need explanation, as we saw in the case of the word "to'evah." One part of the text may contradict another part, like the two creation stories, and a resolution of the conflict is necessary. The same word or phrase may be repeated, seemingly without purpose, and commentators have sought to explain these repetitions by assigning different meanings to them. For example, the commandment to observe Shabbat is described first with the word "shamor" (keep) and then with the word "zakhor" (remember). For this reason, we light two candles on Friday evenings, to observe both commandments. Finally, there are cases in which the grammar or syntax is unusual and lends itself to a new interpretation. While interpretive methods are legitimate and widely practiced, it should be noted that many Jews would claim that the text is not really in need of interpretation. It stands on its own as God's word.

Yet the interpretive method is also used to alter the meaning of biblical verses, sometimes even contravening the original meaning. For example, the ancient rabbis interpreted the mandate of an eye for an eye as meaning monetary compensation as the punishment for a crime. This perspective creates an opportunity for commentators to change or expand the meaning of a verse.

Contemporary commentators see a contradiction between Leviticus 18:22 and the idea as stated in Genesis that we were all created in God's image. This contradiction must be resolved. We must assume that those of us who were created lesbian and gay are also in God's image, and that acts central to our identity cannot therefore be an abomination.[1]

Another interpretation has pointed out that the text refers only to certain sexual *acts*, not to same-sex love *relationships*.[2] Therefore the text is not relevant to a style of life and love and family of which it was ignorant. Or perhaps the text is suggesting that any heterosexual man who wants to experiment sexually with "lying with a man" should consider that such a "fling" might be hurtful to his current partner and should therefore refrain from this action.

Another contemporary commentator, Yehuda ben Ari, focuses his comments on the phrase "as with a woman," suggesting that the text is only trying to tell us not to make love to a male *as if* he were a female—that is to say, gay love and straight love are indeed different. One should not be confused with the other, because the acts do not evoke the same feelings or fulfill the same commandments.[3]

Gay Orthodox Jews have also begun to confront Leviticus 18:22. Yaakov Levado, a gay Orthodox rabbi writing under a pseudonym that means "alone," suggests that since the phrase "as one lies with a woman" only refers to anal intercourse, only this behavior should be halakhically prohibited for gay men. He recommends that gay men agree to this prohibition and that halakhic experts consider accepting gay men who are willing to live with it.[4]

A similar method can be employed to think about issues raised by the creation story. Feminist Bible scholar Phyllis Trible translates Adam as "earth creature," for "Adam" is formed from "adamah," the earth.[5] In this interpretation Adam at the moment of creation is neither male and female, nor male or female, nor he or she.

Trible's interpretation opens up important possibilities. In the second story, at least initially, the human race begins life as a primordial being who has neither gender nor sex. Positing that life begins with an earth creature that has neither sex nor gender raises doubts about how essential these characteristics are to human beings. Looking at the first human as "earth creature" enables us to imagine a world in which gender and sexuality are irrelevant—one in which people would not automatically be judged and labeled based on these two societal constructions.

Following this interpretation, the creation of man and woman from the earth creature brings about two entirely new beings, male and female, to be companions for one another, as described by the Hebrew phrase, ezer c'negdo.[6] In this regard, the Hebrew term "ezer c'negdo" is helpful. It can be understood to mean one who is equal but not like oneself. We may therefore argue that the goal of choosing a companion is related to finding someone who is equal to but not totally like oneself. Difference is an important factor in establishing significant relationships. The issue raised by lesbian relationships is whether anatomical or gender difference is the most salient characteristic in defining an appropriate ezer c'negdo.

Eve and Lilith

Another way to respond to problematic texts is to weave new elements into the stories that expand or explain them. For example, in the first story of creation the man and woman are never given names. All we learn about them is that they are created equal, in the image of God. Ancient midrashic writers were puzzled by this first story and sought to illuminate it. According to these legends, Adam was the same individual in both stories but there were two women involved. The woman created in the first story was Lilith. Why was

Lilith not in the second telling of the creation story? Midrash relates that Lilith refused to submit to Adam's will and so was banished from the garden by God. In Jewish legend she is a demonic figure who murders children.[7] Contemporary Jewish feminists, however, have redeemed Lilith as a woman who sought equality and refused to submit to male domination.

Following this tradition, Judith Plaskow wrote a midrash entitled "Applesource" that suggests further possibilities and new directions. In her retelling of the legend, Plaskow creates the opportunity for Lilith and Eve to meet and develop deep affection for one another:

> They talked for many hours, not once but many times. They taught each other many things, and told each other stories and laughed together and cried, over and over, till the bond of sisterhood grew between them.[8]

Their connection is charged with erotic energy. Although not explicit, Plaskow sows the seeds of possibility for a lesbian relationship between the two. Eve and Lilith are adventurous, playful, and delighted by one another's company. They have clearly entered into the world of romantic friendship. Perhaps "Applesource" could continue to describe their loving relationship in erotic terms. Adam meanwhile might be contented with his special relationship with God. This connection between Adam and God is in fact prototypical of the passionate relationship between Jewish men and God throughout Jewish history.[9] As Jewish women begin to explore female images of God, these relationships will be complicated even further. Lesbians may begin to eroticize our relationship with God as men have done for centuries.

To some readers, this whole process of textual interpretation may seem irrational and unnecessary, even amusing. Why go to the trouble to validate this text? Why play by these rules? But there are many gay and lesbian Jews who feel compelled by the absolute authority and immutability of the Torah text. This is the only solution that enables them to affirm both their gay and Jewish selves and helps them to feel whole. And all of us, as I have already noted, are affected by the traditional interpretations in subtle and destructive ways. It is for these reasons that more creative work needs to take place in the area of interpreting the text of the Torah.

The Historical Approach

A little more than one hundred years ago Jewish and Christian thinkers began to study the Bible as a document created by human hands. The early biblical critics' questioning of divine authorship is viewed as commonplace today, but in their times these views were heretical.

Biblical scholars sought to place the Bible in its context in the Ancient Near East. They explained much of what was unclear in the biblical text by reference to practices in other cultures and explained redundancies as the result of the compilation of documents of multiple authorship. They introduced the concept of evolution and attempted to date biblical materials. Biblical critics developed sensitivity to the nuances of the text, developing concerns about linguistic and literary patterns.

Biblical criticism enables us to look at a passage from Torah in an historical, linguistic, and cultural context and understand it in a new, more objective light. Of course, we must bear in mind that complete objectivity is unattainable. Looking at the text from outside we are bound by our own cultural norms and expectations. In truth, we are looking at a text through another kind of lens. While biblical criticism is a valid way to approach the text, this method is not a way of obtaining "the truth."

This method begins by locating the simple meaning of the verse in Leviticus—that in biblical times, certain homosexual acts were forbidden.[10] Yet this method does not require that we affirm the truth of that reality for today. We can, as biblical critics, acknowledge the need for a reexamination of biblical norms. (After all, the Bible also countenanced other things we no longer accept as moral—stoning a rebellious son or giving second-class status to women and the disabled, for example.)

Furthermore, biblical criticism can explain why homosexual acts were considered to'evah from a different perspective, by examining parallel linguistic uses of the word. "To'evah" may be a technical term used to refer to a forbidden idolatrous act. From this linguistic understanding it is possible to conclude that the references in Leviticus are specific to cultic practices of homosexuality and not to sexual relationships as we know them today. This explanation is supported by reference to the other uses of the term "to'evah," which often refers to ritual violations.[11]

Second, many laws in Torah have as their goal making separations between acts considered pure and those considered impure, to define the boundaries of the community. Accordingly, the sexual prohibitions described fit into the larger category of laws about mixing things: defining food as kosher and treif (forbidden), separating the sexes and their clothing, concern over pollution from bodily fluids, and the prohibitions against plowing with two types of animals and of mixing certain types of fabric in a garment.[12] Today, we can reexamine which of these separations are still meaningful.

Biblical criticism also sheds light on the issue of repetitions in the text. A biblical critic would argue that the injunction against homosexual acts was repeated because the text incorporates two different sources, written at different times. This explains why one injunction demands the death penalty and the other does not. The death penalty may have been applied at one period in biblical history but not at another time.[13]

Through this approach we are able to step back from the text and ask questions about how the text functioned. We can see from some of the suggestions above that the text functioned to define purity and to make boundaries between the Israelite people and the practices of their neighbors. This approach disengages the values expressed in the text from the specific laws in which they appear, allowing for the possibility that there may be other means, outside the law, of perpetuating values—if we indeed still share those values today. Further, if we are not bound by the assumptions of divine authorship, we can conclude that while the prohibition against homosexual acts functioned in its time, it is no longer appropriate to our ethical sensibilities today.

Encountering the Text

There is one last approach for facing the challenge of troubling texts. In this method, we confront the text directly. We do not look to the midrashist or the scholar to interpret the text for us. Rather we face the text in its immediacy—seeking its meaning in our lives, coming to terms with all that implies, and then going beyond it.

To face the simple meaning of Leviticus 18:22 is to acknowledge the source of much of lesbian and gay oppression. The Bible does tell us that sexual acts between men of the same sex are to'evah—an abomination—and that they are punishable by death. And we know very well that this text has given generations the permission to find those of us who are lesbian or gay, in Norman Lamm's word, disgusting; to hate us; and even to do violence against us.

In our encounter with Leviticus, we experience the pain and terror and anger that this statement arouses in us. We imagine the untold damage done to generations of men, women, and children who experienced same-sex feelings and were forced to cloak or repress them. We reflect on those who acted on those feelings and were forced to feel shame and guilt and to fear for their lives. We remember how we felt when we first heard those words and knew their holy source. And we get angry—at the power these words have had over our lives, at the pain we have experienced in no small part because of these words.

In our encounter with the creation story, we face its simple meaning and are furious about being denied the privileges of heterosexual coupling—from the right to the legal protections of marriage to the simple courtesies accorded to heterosexual couples in restaurants, hotels, and all public spaces.

In our encounter with the text that associates lesbianism with the "doings of Egypt" we feel our anger about the way we are associated with evil in our tradition; we are reminded of the story of the rabbi who compares us to bread on the seder plate and we know in our hearts the pain of always feeling as though we don't belong.

And then, if we can, we grow beyond the rage. We begin to see these words as tools with which to educate people about the deep-rooted history of lesbian and gay oppression. We begin to use these very words to begin to break down the silence that surrounds us.

In this way, we can transform Torah from a stumbling block to an entry path. We become more honest with ourselves and with our community about the barriers to our involvement, about our need for separate places to worship, and about our demand to be accepted as an integral part of Jewish life.

Whether we try interpreting, criticizing, or confronting, there are no easy answers for coming to terms with these troubling texts from Torah. We marvel at the fact that words written over 3,000 years ago still have so much power to affect our lives. Words are powerful. Now it is up to us to make the words that will transform our lives and give new meaning to our existence as lesbian Jews, and to challenge other Jews to work with us toward this goal.

We cannot desist from the challenge of finding creative solutions to deal with text. To be whole as Jewish lesbians we must acknowledge with what great difficulty those pieces of our lives fit together. But we must also demand—of ourselves and of our community—that those pieces be made to fit. Reinterpreting these difficult texts is an important place to start this process.

Redefining Sacred Texts

Reinterpreting troubling texts is only one part of a lesbian response to Jewish textual tradition. Another approach seeks out other Jewish texts as potential sacred texts for us. A text is sacred if it tells a story about how to construct our lives and how to think about the world we live in. It is sacred if it challenges perspectives that deny the humanity of lesbians. In other words, a lesbian transformation of Judaism requires that we expand the concept of Torah, of sacred text. There is ample precedent in Jewish life for this expansion of the concept of Torah. Reading the biblical text to understand contemporary situations has been an important part of Jewish tradition since biblical times, as suggested in the Mishnah: "turn it and turn it, for everything is in it," (*Avot* 5:25). The Hebrew word "Torah" does not only refer to the Five Books of Moses; the word itself means "teaching" and frequently refers to all Jewish texts that express sacred values.

The goal for Jewish lesbians is to enlarge and complicate the idea of what is sacred text, not to define a new canon. What is sacred to some Jews may not be sacred to others. As lesbians, we define new dimensions of Torah for ourselves, but that does not mean creating a Jewish lesbian canon. Rather, we need recognition that for Jewish lesbians, reinterpreting painful texts is not enough. We also seek out texts that more fully celebrate our lives.

Textual reinterpretation and exploration of new sacred texts is a form of cultural resistance. It is an opportunity for Jewish lesbians to define our relationship to Jewish texts in new ways that allow us to remain connected to ancient Jewish traditions but also to alter them to meet our own needs. This process enables Jewish lesbians to find our place within the Jewish community.

We can find lesbian themes in Jewish texts once we are willing to ask the right questions. In order to read a lesbian perspective into ancient texts, we must search beyond the obvious to explore what the texts could possibly mean to lesbians claiming a place in contemporary Jewish society. A similar effort to reclaim the biblical text for women has been made by Jewish and Christian feminists.[14]

"Whither Thou Goest": Lesbian Interpretations of the Book of Ruth

A good place to start this process of defining new sacred texts is the biblical story of Ruth and Naomi. This story is generally understood as a tale of the loyalty of a young woman who, after the death of her husband, continues to support and care for her mother-in-law. But for lesbians it is the story of the relationship between two women, and lesbians have begun to use this story in our search for biblical texts that include us in some way. Consider the following scenarios:

A lesbian is ready to convert to Judaism. She has lived a Jewish life for several years, and wants to make her status official. She requests that the ceremony take place around the time of Shavuot, when Ruth is read in synagogue, for she feels deeply connected to Ruth, a convert whom she understands to be like herself, a lover of women.

Two Jewish lesbians plan a ceremony of commitment. They know they cannot say the traditional wedding vows, which speak of being joined according to Jewish law. They choose instead to say Ruth's words to Naomi to one another, "Wherever you go, I shall go. And wherever you find rest, so shall I."

Another Jewish lesbian couple plans to celebrate the tenth anniversary of their relationship. To honor them in the ceremony, a friend writes and sings a musical setting for Ruth 1:16.

A book about lesbian ceremonies of commitment is published, called *Ceremonies of the Heart: Celebrating Lesbian Unions*. In it, Ruth 1:16 is mistakenly assumed to be the traditional Jewish wedding vow.[15]

A major motion picture, *Fried Green Tomatoes*, uses Ruth 1:16 as the secret message sent by a woman to let her "friend" know that she wishes to leave an abusive marriage and come live with her.[16]

A gay and lesbian synagogue sponsors a conference on the theme "Ruth and the Meaning of Female Friendship in the Jewish Tradition." As the keynote speaker, lesbian rabbi Linda Holtzman interprets the story of Ruth and Naomi as a model for the powerful love that is possible between women.

A book on gay and lesbian Jews includes an article by a gay Jewish scholar entitled "In Search of Role Models." He, too, refers to the story of Ruth and Naomi as a positive example of a primary relationship between women in the Bible. He suggests that the story hinges not on Ruth's devotion to the Jewish God but rather on her devotion to Naomi. He suggests that Ruth marries Boaz to ensure the two women will have a source of financial support and be able to remain together.[17]

A closeted lesbian minister tells me she has been preaching about Ruth for years. "The people who are really listening," she tells me, "know what I mean."

Given the difficulties with the other biblical texts we have looked at, the search for a Jewish past that includes us requires an effort to locate ourselves somewhere in the biblical tradition. We look carefully for women in the Jewish past who might have been, like ourselves, lovers of women. The search is a difficult one. For centuries in Western cultures, lesbian love has not been spoken of in public. Recovering lesbian origins has been hampered by the lack of written records. As I have already noted, lesbianism is mentioned in Jewish legal texts only as a sexual behavior that husbands should vigilantly prohibit their wives from engaging in. If there are to be lesbian role models, they must be found between the lines through imaginative reconstruction of the text. Because the story of Ruth describes a loving relationship between women, it is a logical place to begin.

Rarely do relationships between women receive prominence in Jewish texts. There are some stories about sisters or cowives and a few about mothers and daughters. When women do appear in relation to one another, they are most often competitors and antagonists, as in the case of Sarah and Hagar or Rachel and Leah. The story of Ruth and Naomi is an exception. Ruth clearly loves Naomi, and pledges a lifelong commitment to her when she says:

> Do not press me to abandon you,
> To turn back from following you.
> Wherever you go, I shall go.
> And wherever you find rest, so shall I.
> Your people shall be my people,
> And your God shall be my God.
> Where you die, I shall die,
> And there I shall be buried.
> Thus may YHWH do to me,
> And thus may YHWH add
> If even death will separate me from you.
>
> *(Ruth 1:16–17)*

When these words are read through the lens of lesbian experience, they point toward something greater than a relationship of loyalty and obligation between these two women. This story of female friendship resonates powerfully with Jewish lesbians in search of role models. Ruth and Naomi have a committed relationship that crosses the boundaries of age, nationality, and religion.

Ruth makes a commitment to Naomi to stay with her, even to their death. Lesbians hear in Ruth's vow a foreshadowing of the commitment they may now, in contemporary Western societies, make to one another to be life partners. Today many Jewish lesbians live in committed relationships that are marked by public ceremonies. It is not surprising that the vow Ruth makes to Naomi has been incorporated into lesbian rituals as the vow that a couple makes to one another. The frequency with which this vow is used in lesbian circles makes quite understandable the mistake made by the non-Jewish editor of *Ceremonies of the Heart* when she assumed that the line from Ruth actually was a part of the standard Jewish wedding vow.

Taken out of context, Ruth's declaration indeed sounds like a statement of primary commitment. Had the speakers been of opposite sexes, Ruth 1:16–17 would certainly have been read as a poetic statement of love. In *Eros and the Jews*, David Biale underscores the connection when he notes that the phrase used to describe Ruth's remaining with Naomi, that she "clung to her" (davkah bah) is the same "clinging" described in the creation story when it is explained that a man leaves his mother and father to "cling to" his wife.[18]

In addition, Ruth and Naomi are making a commitment to maintain familial connections. More and more Jewish lesbians today are forming alternative family arrangements, relying on friendship networks to replace families who may have rejected them. They are also raising children together as couples, not unlike heterosexuals.

Ruth and Naomi's relationship has meaning for Jewish lesbians in another dimension as well. Differences other than gender are crucial to lesbian relationships. Many Jewish lesbians find themselves in relationships with women that cross the boundaries of age, race, nationality, and religion. Ruth and Naomi model a relationship across differences. Jew and Moabite, they come from different cultures and worship different deities. Given the fact that Naomi is the mother of Ruth's deceased husband, they are clearly from different generations. Yet they overcome their differences and make a permanent connection. Ruth's vow to share Naomi's faith in YHWH is one possible model for lesbian couples to deal with difference.

Finally, Ruth and Naomi are friends. They exemplify a caring relationship between women. Lesbian relationships incorporate the connections of female friendship and affection celebrated by lesbian and heterosexual women alike. That Ruth is willing to leave her homeland, marry a man of Naomi's choosing, and cast her fate entirely with Naomi speaks worlds about how deep the connection was between these two women. This bond is celebrated when lesbians examine the story of Ruth.

The connection between these two women is a fertile field for midrash. The Hebrew Bible tends not to focus on the motivation of its human characters, and it is up to later commentators to add explanations. Why is Samson persuaded to cut off his hair? Why doesn't Abraham protest the command to sacrifice his son? What convinces Moses to listen to the voice in the bush? Why does Joseph trick his brothers? What made Ruth want to follow Naomi? Lesbian midrash can answer this last question in ways that may fill in the blanks about Ruth and Naomi's relationship. Did they bond in common love for Ruth's dead husband? Was Ruth really persuaded to follow Naomi because of her love for YHWH? Or did Ruth and Naomi become special friends, companions, or even lovers when they lived together in Moab?

Only through this sort of midrashic suggestion do Naomi and Ruth become true models for contemporary Jewish lesbians. While public vows of commitment, familial connections, female friendship, and cross-cultural and intergenerational relationships are important aspects of lesbian culture, sexuality is central to lesbian identity. Many heterosexuals mistakenly assume that all that is different about lesbians is that they are women who have sex with other women. Jewish lesbians have sought to establish that lesbian culture includes other elements, including those I have already described. Yet without romantic love and sexuality, the story of Ruth and Naomi loses much of its power as a model for Jewish lesbian relationships.

A Jewish lesbian midrash on Ruth requires that we read between the lines of the text and imagine Ruth's words as a manifestation of her sexual desire for Naomi. To lesbians, this is not implausible. Throughout the centuries, sexual love between women was hidden from public view. As I have argued, the absence of an interdiction of lesbian behavior in the Bible may not necessarily imply that this behavior was unknown in that culture. The fact that Ruth was married does not detract from the plausibility of this suggestion. The only references to lesbianism in Jewish legal texts are those prohibiting married women from engaging in this practice, so one would assume that it was married women who engaged in it. It is possible to argue that Ruth had to marry Boaz to protect herself and Naomi, since it was not possible for women to survive in biblical times without the protection and financial support of men.[19] The suggestion that the story of Ruth comes from an oral tradition of women storytellers[20] further supports the plausibility of this interpretation.

When nonlesbian scholars and commentators look at the Book of Ruth, they fail to see what we see. They are sure that Ruth means only to dedicate herself to Naomi's God. They are convinced that the important love relationship is the one between Ruth and Boaz. With the exception of feminist critic Ilana Pardes, most can't imagine that there is a theme of love between women written between the lines.[21]

Establishing literary, historical, and logical possibilities that the story of Ruth and Naomi could be read as a lesbian love story will certainly distress some readers. Yet less plausible midrashim have been accepted throughout the ages. The explanation that Isaac did not return from Mount Moriah after the Binding because he was sent to yeshivah is one such example. It is not the goal of midrash to prove that the story actually happened this way but to make room for change within tradition while providing historical antecedent for the change. Making room for lesbian interpretations of the Book of Ruth is a way of welcoming lesbians into the contemporary Jewish community.

To find what is written between the lines has been the essence of midrashic interpretation throughout the ages. What makes biblical narrative so powerful is that it can be reinterpreted in every generation. A midrash works when it enables people to see the story in a new light or with an added dimension. Midrash gives us an opportunity to embellish the stories of the Bible and Jewish history and to look at our heroes from new angles. It is not surprising that— now that women have taken a more active role in Jewish life— midrashim are being written about Sarah, Miriam, and Deborah. When martyrdom was an important theme in the Middle Ages, many midrashim were written to reinterpret the binding of Isaac. And when the Zionists were interested in proclaiming Jewish military abilities, new emphasis was placed on the heroism of the Maccabees.

Lesbian midrash plays the same role. It inspires us to ask new questions of the text: Why when Shifrah and Puah are mentioned do they always appear together? How did Miriam and Pharoah's daughter know one another?[22] What did Jephthah's daughter do when she went away with the women? Where did Dina go when she left the house of Sheḥem?

Lesbians have had to read between the lines for centuries in Western cultures, looking for role models where all traces were hidden. For those of us women whose love of women has had no public acknowledgment, writing midrash has given us an opportunity to make our presence known and to lend validity to our relationships. We must insist on our right to find hints of the existence of women like ourselves in the past where we can find them. Reading the stories of Ruth and Naomi, Eve and Lilith, and other texts in this way should be considered an obligation to our nameless ancestors, to give them, too, an opportunity to speak. It is our hope that our midrash will find an honored place in Jewish tradition.

Textual interpretation has other facets. We can also use biblical texts as a starting point for the expression of Jewish lesbian perspectives. In the following chapters, I examine the ways in which a prophetic text can function as a framework for examining the concerns of contemporary lesbian Jews.

Four

Haẓnea Lekhet Im Elohekha:
Jewish Lesbian Visibility

Thus far the lesbian transformation of Judaism that I am propos-
ing has concentrated on challenging and reinterpreting biblical
texts from a lesbian perspective. In addition to this process, we can
look to other parts of the Bible that lend themselves to conceptual-
izing a broader transformation of Jewish belief and practice from a
lesbian perspective. As I suggested when discussing the troubling
texts in Genesis and Leviticus, we cannot simply excise the biblical
text or ignore it, because it contains precepts that define the very
reasons that we remain connected to Judaism and the Jewish people in the first place. To put in place a lesbian transformation of
Judaism we must not only respond to difficult texts, we must also
use the texts that speak to us as the source of our work.

It is common practice among Jewish commentators to use a biblical passage as a starting point or proof text for contemporary
ideas. The passage I have chosen as a framework for examining
Jewish lesbian concerns is found in the book of Micah, the writings
of a minor prophet thought to have lived in the sixth or seventh
century before the common era. Micah summarizes his understanding of "what is good" as follows: "do justice (asot mishpat),

love well (ahavat ḥesed),[1] and walk modestly with God (haznea lekhet im elohekha)" (Micah 6:8). The next three chapters comprise a Jewish lesbian reading of this prophetic saying, which focuses on some of the problems facing Jewish lesbians today. In addition, they offer some resolutions to those dilemmas: questions about public disclosure of our identities, our relationships to our families, and how to contribute to a more just and peaceful world from our unique (and currently problematic) position. Although this reading is specific to Jewish lesbians, it is my hope that the model created here for dealing with these dilemmas may be applied to questions faced by nonlesbian Jews as well.

Micah's threefold precept suggests three areas of particular concern: how to live with and present oneself in the world (how to walk modestly with God), how to establish social relationships (how to love well), and how to make the world a better place (how to do justice). My interpretation inverts the order of Micah's precept. As he states it, the precept culminates with the individual's relationship with God, which is in keeping with the biblical authors' theocentric worldview. From my human-centered perspective, it makes sense to begin with the individual's relationship with God, expressed through her relationship with herself. It is this relationship that enables her to love others and then to translate that love into acts of justice for all humanity—which is for me the ultimate goal.

The Process of Coming Out

The process begins where Micah ends, with the enigmatic phrase "haznea lekhet im elohekha." Traditionally, this has been translated "walk humbly with your God," but more recent translations have suggested it to mean to walk modestly or with decency. I interpret this statement to be about the way an individual understands her own place in the world. I assume that the way in which a person approaches her own life will determine her ability to behave ethically toward others. A central Jewish precept demands that we love our neighbors as ourselves. Commentators have understood this to mean that we can only learn to love our neighbors if we learn to love ourselves.

Walking with God is a metaphor for the way each person approaches her own life. It is a way to conceptualize one's innermost feelings and thoughts. It is not necessary to hold a traditional concept of God, or to imagine God in human form, to appreciate this metaphor. To see oneself walking with God requires a vision of God as the most important value in life, that which is with the individual always and everywhere. God may be in the image of a human being, but God could also be a power, force, feeling, idea, or anything that helps one perceive holiness in the world.

As Jewish lesbians, we begin with the assumption that we can only walk with God if we know and accept ourselves for who we are. Walking with God begins with self-acceptance and requires that we tell ourselves the truth about ourselves. This stance describes coming out, declaring oneself to be lesbian, as a necessary prerequisite to walking with God. Walking with God requires self-knowledge. Those who walk with God know their way and consciously claim a path in the world. They are guided by the understanding that all human beings are holy, having been created in God's image. They respect the mysterious process, whether it derives from nature or society,[2] that makes them women who are erotically attracted to other women and who prefer to build their lives with them. This is not an easy task to accomplish. I share my own coming out story as an example:

> There was no one else about when Joseph made himself known to his brothers. His sobs were so loud that the Egyptians could hear. (Genesis 45:1–2)

As a child reading the Bible, I was always deeply touched by the story of Joseph and his brothers. I was moved to tears when Joseph, forced to hide his true identity, was finally able to tell his brothers who he really was and to be reconciled with them after years of estrangement.

It was not until I was much older that I identified Joseph's story as similar to my own. Like Joseph, I hid part of my identity for many years. And also like Joseph, the experience of revealing that hidden dimension of myself made me feel whole. Joseph hid his identity as a Hebrew. I hid my identity as a lesbian.

I grew up knowing that I was strongly attracted to members of my own sex. But everything I saw in society—movies, popular songs, my parents' relationship, Bible stories—pointed to heterosexuality as the norm. I often had crushes on girls and women teachers and had sexual relationships with girlfriends in high school. Yet as an adolescent I would never have called myself a lesbian; I assumed I was going through a stage. When I was growing up, lesbians were found in bars, underground magazines, and pulp novels. They were assumed to be poorly adjusted women who wanted to be men, not courageous women who dared to be different. I did not want to be one of them.

My experience in Hebrew school reinforced my own discomfort with my sexual feelings and fostered the development of my heterosexual identity. Lessons about the importance of marrying a Jewish man and raising Jewish children were well taught, and I wanted desperately to belong. There was nothing in Judaism as I was growing up that would indicate any possible acceptance of lesbians.

For me, focusing on my Jewish identity provided a perfect alternative to exploring my sexual identity. I married, became a rabbi, and had two children. Despite my wishes to the contrary, the strong erotic attraction I felt toward women never left me. After a while I began to think of myself as bisexual. But at some point it became clear to me that I needed to make a choice. It was then that I left my marriage and developed a primary relationship with a woman.

Coming out to myself, calling myself a lesbian, was not an easy thing to do. I had achieved status and visibility in the Jewish world as a rabbi, and I was afraid that if I came out I would be forced to give that up. I was concerned that people I had worked with would be uncomfortable around me or that they would no longer respect my ideas and judgments.

But at a certain point I developed a strong conviction that it would be better if people knew and that I couldn't worry if they did or not, at least most of the time. I came out because I got tired of hiding and lying; it had a corrosive effect on my soul. In coming out I experienced a sense of pride in being a lesbian. I gained peace of mind and a sense of freedom unattainable in the closet. That year, Pesaḥ took on new meaning, for I had truly experienced the journey through the narrow straits of miẓrayim to freedom. And I finally knew what Joseph felt like when he revealed his identity to his brothers.

The Ethics of Coming Out and Outing

Accepting and acting on this erotic attraction is an example of ha*z*nea lekhet because it indicates self-acceptance. Jewish lesbians claim our sexual attractions as a holy pursuit. What makes our sexuality holy is not intrinsic to it. It is the acceptance in ourselves of our sexual joys and pleasures, of not seeing our erotic lives as cut off from the rest of ourselves, but integral to making our lives rich and meaningful.[3] Too often lesbians, especially when our homosexuality is first awakened, feel shame about our feelings and desires. Ha*z*nea lekhet means accepting desire and finding creative ways of expressing it. Of course, those expressions must conform to other ethical standards of behavior toward ourselves and others. But those desires and behaviors will also unleash our creative powers and enable us to be in the world in a holy and positive way. When the connection between the sexual self and the rest of the self is cut off, we cannot walk with God. It is important for Jewish lesbians to affirm the link between our sexuality and the rest of our lives as Jews.

From this perspective, there is no holy way for a lesbian to be closeted to herself. In the closet, we relinquish the opportunity to express our own inner needs and desires. The lesbian who hides her sexual desires from herself stays still and cannot walk in the direction of self-acceptance. This is true for anyone who makes a choice that does not lead to her own self-fulfillment and growth. Coming out reminds us that God is with us; that when lesbians come out we have the support of the power in the universe that gives us strength to do courageous things.

Walking with God is not limited to self-acceptance as a lesbian in the privacy of one's own inner world. The next stages of self-acceptance suggest being out with family and friends and in the lesbian and gay or Jewish lesbian worlds. But I want to suggest that truly walking with God moves beyond this stage. The ultimate way to walk with God with self-acceptance also requires coming out publicly. The reluctance to do so may be caused by real discrimination and bigotry or the threat of losing one's job or custody of one's child. But it may also be the result of feelings of shame about one's sexuality and fear of loss of status. It is clear that the visibility of lesbians and gay men in our society has made possible civil rights and societal respect for gay people unknown in prior human history. Lesbians must be willing to write about our lives, talk about ourselves in newspaper and television stories, testify and work for laws that will increase our civil rights, be involved in test cases for the courts to expand our rights, and especially speak out in synagogues and Jewish communal organizations who want to learn about us. The more of us who speak out publicly about our commitment as lesbians and Jews the less likely that anyone will be able to deny our humanity based on the claim that they don't know anyone who is lesbian or gay.

There is another dimension to the ethics of coming out. Hazṇea lekhet also requires us to be honest people: honest with ourselves about our sexuality and honest with others in our lives. Coming out publicly keeps us from having to lie—to doctors whom we sometimes don't visit because we don't want to talk about our sex lives; to coworkers with whom we omit pronouns when referring to our partners; to acquaintances who want to introduce us to men. The lies we tell may be small, but they inhibit our ability to live openly and lead us into patterns of lying incompatible with walking with God. And they draw nonlesbians into our lie as well, requiring them often to deny what they see.

Not lying has another consequence. If every lesbian came out, then we would not have to lie for each other, to pretend that the rabbi, cantor, person applying to teach in the Hebrew school or editor of the Jewish newspaper is not the same person we saw with her lover at the women's music concert the other night. The gay and lesbian community has for a long time agreed to a conspiracy of silence, never to expose a closeted gay man or lesbian outside of the gay community (although gossip of this sort within the lesbian community is commonplace). This conspiracy of silence is a burden placed upon open lesbians by our closeted friends, to the detriment of lesbian life. To walk with God requires that we stop demanding of one another that we keep secrets; it also requires that we persuade the closeted to come out.

But the quotation from Micah suggests not only that we find a way to walk with God but that that way be modest, decent, and humble. Ḥaznea lekhet does not carry with it the assumption that we are not proud to be lesbians. The fact that being open and comfortable with being a lesbian is understood as a way to walk with God should illustrate this clearly.

It does imply, however, that we are not so arrogant as to assume that we can determine the right way for everyone. Walking humbly with God means self-acceptance, not requiring that others follow your example. This is not a mandate for outing others. Our humility must keep us from arrogant assumptions about who must declare their lesbian identity. This humility outweighs the burden placed on us by closeted lesbians to keep their secrets. We must be mindful of the idea that we cannot judge others until we have stood in their place (*Mishnah, Avot* 2:5). Once a person has come out, it is difficult for her to comprehend what compels another person to remain closeted or to be unable to accept their sexuality. While it is important to promote the value of coming out as exemplary of self-acceptance and an appropriate way to walk with God, not everyone will be comfortable enough with their sexuality or with their family to feel safe coming out. While those who are out may wish to persuade other Jewish lesbians to come out in public ways, we must respect each person's process and decision.

Those in the gay community who have popularized outing argue that there are two reasons to out people—as role models and as hypocrites. First they argue that the dead should be outed as role models and that outing them does no harm. Given the importance of role models, especially in Jewish circles, I also see no harm in bringing to light the same-sex erotic inclinations of Jewish women in the past who lived when being public about one's lesbianism was the equivalent of confessing to mental illness and moral turpitude. They clearly were denied the choice to be open about their sexual orientation. One may argue that the Jewish value of honoring the dead would lead us not to name lesbians in prior generations. But that perspective is predicated on the assumption that lesbianism is a source of shame. As lesbians are visible and accept ourselves as walking with God, so we name lesbians in past generations to honor their memories, not to bring shame on them.

Advocates of outing also argue that celebrities should be outed as role models. Celebrities may reach many people but they are not necessarily role models. As feminists, fame should mean something quite different to us. Lesbians want to write history in a different way, to celebrate the acts of courage and decency of all people. Criteria for celebrity should have more to do with walking with God than achieving fame as a movie star or politician. While there is no doubt about the value of visible lesbians, it is better if they come out because they want to identify and to contribute to the development of community than if they are outed against their own inclination.

What about outing hypocrites? Hypocrites are defined as those who themselves work against the rights of the gay and lesbian community while at the same time using the privileges of communal spaces (gay synagogues, book stores, bars, and community centers) that we have worked hard to attain. Sometimes included in this category are those who may personally support the work for lesbian and gay rights but who work for and represent institutions that repress us, such as seminaries, the legislature, or the military.[4]

These hypocrites are negative role models. Why should the lesbian community want to claim them? Of course, they should not be denied a place if they wish to claim it. Outing hypocrites may give the lesbian community political advantage, but it is not a helpful way to further the cause because it makes us behave like those who wish to deny our rights. It is not that different from the blackmail that our enemies perpetrated in the 1950s that forced many lesbians out of the closet. Many of these hypocrites may not in fact see themselves as part of a lesbian community. They may take a minimalist approach that argues that sexuality is a private matter and that their sexual attraction to someone of the same sex is the only thing that distinguishes them from other people. Out lesbians would disagree and would want to argue that there is a great difference between enjoying lesbian sexuality in private and living openly as a lesbian. Our goal may be to persuade the hypocrites that their approach is not in keeping with the Jewish ideal of walking with God—but all we can do is persuade them. Coercion and embarrassment are not acceptable methods of achieving that goal.

It is not surprising that outing has been rejected by gay and lesbian Jews, and by lesbians in general, as a tactic.[5] No matter how much we want the world to change, decisions must be based on our values about acceptable ways of doing this. However, the opposite of outing—the intentional omission of someone's status as a Jewish lesbian—must also be strenuously opposed. Role models are important. Visibility makes a statement. Journalists from the Jewish press and elsewhere should not keep us in the closet. They must be reminded whenever possible to include sexual orientation, even if lesbianism may not be particularly relevant to the story.

I am suggesting that we encourage coming out as a value. Only by accepting who we are as Jewish lesbians can we enable others to understand and accept us. While we cannot coerce others into being public lesbians and Jews, we can use our powers to persuade those who can to speak out. The more Jewish lesbians who publicly acknowledge their sexuality, the easier it will be for all of us to gain the acceptance in the Jewish community that is a prerequisite to transforming the community. Nonlesbians will then have the opportunity to see that we are a varied group, who look and behave in a multiplicity of ways. And they will begin to understand that we are Jewish in a variety of ways as well. There is no one specific way to follow the precept of haznea lekhet.

The Role of the Jewish Community

Lesbians will only come out in the Jewish community when Jewish environments are safe places for them to do so. For this to happen, Jewish lesbians will have to promulgate the idea of coming out as self-acceptance and a valid way to walk with God. The Jewish community will have to make coming out a value, so that those who are closeted and those who keep them in their closets through insensitive speech or actions are understood as acting in unholy ways.

To walk with God in humility, modesty, and decency is a daunting task. It is not easy to eschew arrogance; it is not easy to be modest about our accomplishment of self-acceptance in the Jewish world that tells us daily that we do not fit, do not belong. Haznea lekhet im elohekha requires a delicate balancing act between feeling pride and joy at being able to be at peace with ourselves but not expecting others to travel the same path. Our goal is to create a world where coming out is not an issue because sexual orientation is not stigmatized. We still live in a society where falsely calling someone gay or lesbian is susceptible to charges of libel, as it was to call someone a Jew prior to 1950.[6] It is this reality that we are working to change.

The Jewish community will play an important role in this process by viewing coming out as a holy act. And nonlesbian Jews can also apply this model of walking decently with God to themselves. That may mean being more accepting of themselves and honest about the way in which they, too, hide parts of themselves in closets.

One important way in which coming out can be sanctified in the Jewish community is through the creation of ceremonies that celebrate the individual's coming out. With the creation of coming out rituals, lesbians have a unique life cycle event to bring to the Jewish community.

Rituals for Coming Out

Coming out is the central rite of passage for lesbians and gay men. It marks a change of identity and also a change of status in the world. Like other life passages, it is both exciting and dangerous. A coming out ritual provides the opportunity to make this important life change in the context of a community and with its blessing.

Coming out is about establishing a new identity and sense of self in the world. For many women, being a lesbian means participation in a new culture. It may involve a new aesthetic or contact with new institutions. It can involve reading lesbian and gay newspapers, magazines, and books or listening to programs with gay and lesbian themes on radio or television. It will probably involve attending communal gatherings—gay pride parades, concerts of lesbian comics or musicians, or political rallies. It may even involve travel to places such as Provincetown, San Francisco, or the Michigan Womyn's Music Festival, where lesbians can walk around comfortably holding hands in public.

Since there is no definitive moment of coming out (although for many lesbians, the first sexual experience and telling their parents may be the most crucial points in the process), it is difficult to pin-point a precise moment for a coming out ritual. I would therefore like to offer three different possibilities.

Even when we have been public about our identities for years, we are time and again faced with decisions about whether or not to make ourselves known in certain circumstances, and we will continue to experience the fears that arise when we need to make that decision. Although I have written and spoken publicly as a Jewish lesbian for many years, and for the most part feel great comfort in doing so, I also occasionally experience discomfort. For example, when I spoke on a panel on being lesbian and Jewish at a conference sponsored by the National Jewish Women's Resource Center several years ago, I never expected to run into Doris, an older woman who had been an informant for my dissertation research fifteen years earlier. I must admit that I did not tell her what I was speaking about and honestly hoped that she hadn't read the program. I did not want her image of me as a proper Jewish woman to change. No matter how comfortable I have become, the fear that someone I respect might not approve of me still surfaces on occasion.

Since coming out is a continual process, it is fitting to say a blessing or a prayer each time the process is furthered. Whether we are telling someone we haven't seen in a while about our identity or marching in a gay pride parade, we can acknowledge our courage by saying a blessing:

Nevarekh et Eyn HaHayyim asher natna lee haozmah lazet min hamezarim.

Let us bless the source of life for giving me the courage to come out.[7]

Beyond using this blessing in private, individual circumstances, many gay and lesbian Jews may feel a need to have a public ritual among friends or in the synagogue. The ritual may be very simple, consisting of the recitation of the blessing, followed by an additional blessing that a friend, the service leader, or the rabbi may say on the occasion:

May the One who blessed our ancestors, Abraham, Isaac, and Jacob, Moses, Aaron, and David; Sarah, Rebecca, Leah and

Rachel, Miriam, and Ruth, bless — bat —, who has come forward bravely to proclaim her lesbian identity to this congregation. May she grow in self-understanding and rejoice in her
newly claimed identity. May her courage be a model for others who yearn to reveal hidden parts of themselves. May she
receive love, warmth, and support from her community, family, and friends. May her public act inspire us to deepen our
commitment to work for a time when gay men and lesbians
will no longer suffer from hatred and prejudice and when all
will live in harmony and peace. Amen.

This ceremony could take place at any home gathering or synagogue service, but might be most appropriate when the Torah is
read, accompanied by an aliyah to the Torah. In this way it would
take on the resonance of the bat mitzvah. To become a bat mitzvah
means to make the transition to being a responsible Jew; to take on
a new identity as a Jewish woman. Similarly, coming out is a life
cycle event that demands the proclamation of a new identity; the
link is therefore most appropriate.

Another option is to link the coming out ritual to an aspect of
Jewish history as it is marked on the Jewish calendar. The experience of yeẓiat miẓrayim, going out of Egypt, resonates powerfully
with a public coming out for a Jewish lesbian. Jewish tradition
demands that each individual Jew must experience herself as going
out from Egypt. The historical event is a celebration of freedom, of
coming out of a restricted life as a slave into life as a free person.
For the Jew, this freedom is not merely individual liberation; it is
also the acceptance of responsibility for claiming a Jewish identity
and living as a Jew in the world. When a lesbian comes out, she too
leaves the restrictions of the closet behind to experience haẓnea
lekhet: the joy and freedom of a new identity and the weight of
responsibility that this new identity entails.

These themes of going out of Egypt are evoked during Shabbat
Shirah when we read the Torah portion about crossing the sea. It is
that moment of transition that best exemplifies the experience of
coming out, both because of the courage necessary to cross the sea
into a new life of freedom and the exultation experienced when the
crossing has been completed. The Torah service during Shabbat
Shirah is therefore an appropriate time for a coming out ceremony.

And the haftarah (prophetic portion) for this week is about Deborah, the only woman in the Bible who is herself not connected to a man.[8]

The story of Joseph revealing himself to his brothers, the reading of which occurs in the annual cycle around the time of Ḥanukah, could also be a powerful backdrop for the ceremony of coming out.

Readings in the service could include stories of courage from Jewish or lesbian literature. The midrash about Naḥshon, the first Israelite to cross the sea (B. Talmud, *Sotah* 36b) is most fitting to include. When the other Israelites held back in fear at the raging sea, Naḥshon stepped into the water, an action based on faith and the courage to dare. Midrashim about Joseph's revelation could also be included.

The following passage from Adina Abramowitz's story, "Growing Up in Yeshiva," would also be appropriate:

In my second year after graduating from college, in December 1980, I attended the founding conference of New Jewish Agenda and signed up for the lesbian and gay affinity group. That may have been my first conscious act of self-acceptance and pride. I was twenty-two years old and had been carrying around the conflict between my Jewish and lesbian identity for five years. Just being in a room with over thirty people who put the words "gay" and "lesbian" together with "Jewish" was immensely healing . . . After all of the years of debate, I decided on New Year's Eve, 1980, to try calling myself a lesbian for one month. Almost immediately I felt enormous relief. Although my struggles with my sexual orientation were by no means over, I have not questioned my lesbian identity since that moment.[9]

The person who is coming out should define her own role in the service. She could give a d'var Torah on the meaning of this change in her life. She could read from the Torah, or perhaps write new words for Miriam's rejoicing as she crossed the sea. She could lead a song or dance to celebrate her new status. Minimally, she may recite the blessing for coming out—"Nevarekh et Eyn HaḤayyim asher natna lee haoẓmah laẓet min hameẓarim (Let us bless the source of life for giving me the courage to come out)"—and be called to the Torah for an aliyah. The blessing will have special resonance on Shabbat Shirah, as the Hebrew for coming out, "lazet min hamezarim," echoes the idea of coming out from Egypt, Mizrayim. The ritual could conclude with some joyous song to reflect the mood of celebration. As the Israelites sang at the crossing of the sea, so should the Jewish community when anyone of us chooses to liberate ourselves from old enslavements to follow the precept of haznea lekhet.

When someone celebrates coming out in so public a way, it is crucial that the community clearly and unequivocally manifests its support. The risk involved in coming out in public is still great today, and the person who celebrates this ritual will probably feel a mixture of pride and vulnerability. Members of the community may wish to say mazzal tov, to write a note, or to make a contribution of zedakah in the person's honor, preferably to an organization that works for gay and lesbian rights. Because these ceremonies highlight gay and lesbian visibility within the Jewish community, they provide inspiration to the Jewish community to work for gay and lesbian liberation and civil rights.

Jewish lesbians will only be comfortable celebrating coming out with a communal ritual when the Jewish community becomes more supportive of people making choices to live as lesbians, when coming out is recognized as haznea lekhet. Until this occurs, many lesbians and gay men will remain in the closet. Some will also choose to come out selectively to individuals but will ask those individuals to keep the information confidential.[10] It is important for the community to understand that deciding to come out is difficult for most of us who come to identify as gay or lesbian and that the process is different for each of us.

The fact that increased visibility ultimately leads to increased acceptance has been a major factor in helping lesbians to take the risk of coming out. In many ways it is easier to remain closeted. As long as lesbians remain in the closet, they need not fear other people's negative assessments, nor must they worry that they will lose their job or promotion, the warm love of parents or other family members, or the custody of their children. It is hard work to deal with friends who have problems with issues of sexuality; it is not comfortable to disagree with a colleague's judgmental comments. And it is so comfortable to blend in, to be just like everybody else, as Jews are also often tempted to do.

Coming out is not easy, but it is vital for the health of individuals, for lesbians, and for the Jewish community. It is imperative that today young lesbians have models for their process of self-discovery and have public spaces, Jewish spaces, in which they can feel at home in a world that is still hostile to people who define themselves as different.

Visibility as a Group

Coming out and being visible as individuals in the Jewish community is not the only dimension of Micah's injunction to walk humbly with God. The self-acceptance that is implied here also relates to Jewish lesbian visibility in groups as well. Haznea lekhet means in this context the opportunity to have Jewish lesbian visibility on our own terms in the form of gay and lesbian synagogues, organizations, and community centers.

Making Jewish lesbians visible in the community requires that our groups be validated and recognized. Often we are asked why we need separate spaces. Aren't we separating ourselves from the community by creating Jewish gay and lesbian spaces? On the contrary, these communal spaces are opportunities for us to make contributions to the community. To bring our unique perspective into the Jewish conversation we need our voices to be distinct. Our institutions and publications provide vehicles for lesbians who have been alienated from the Jewish community to find a way back.

Gay and Lesbian Synagogues

The gay and lesbian synagogue movement has proven to be a key factor in making gay and lesbian concerns visible in the Jewish community. Because of sexism, however, both in the gay Jewish movement and the Jewish community at large, gay men's issues have been at the heart of the gay synagogue movement and lesbians, ironically, have had to fight to become visible in the gay Jewish world. Nonetheless, from its beginnings in the early 1970s the gay and lesbian synagogue movement has focused on becoming visible and playing a role in the Jewish world.

Gay synagogues began in the United States in the early 1970s. The Los Angeles group, Beth Chaim Chadashim (BCC), was begun in 1972 by Jewish members of the Metropolitan Community Church. These Jews began to feel like outsiders in a Christian environment and realized that they wanted a Jewish religious experience.[11] The beginnings of Congregation Beth Simchat Torah (CBST) in New York City were similar.[12] By 1975 there were congregations in Philadelphia, Boston, Washington, and San Francisco, and in 1976 the International Conference of Gay Jews met for the first time. Their first meeting outside the United States took place in Israel in 1979 and included delegates from Bermuda, West Germany, Mexico, and South Africa. In 1978 the name was changed to the World Congress of Gay and Lesbian Jews.

The role of lesbians in these groups has from the beginning been problematic. In 1978 "Lesbian" was added to the title of the international organization.[13] Lesbians within the World Congress have always faced sexism. Many male members of gay congregations thought they could recreate the synagogues of their childhoods, where women were invisible. They were often oblivious to issues of sexism in the traditional prayers and texts, and liturgical compromises were often hotly debated.[14] Aliza Maggid, a movement leader, has written about conflicts that arose when men dressed in drag at Purim. Feminists in the late 1970s viewed this behavior as mocking and satirizing women.[15]

In the early years men vastly outnumbered women in the gay synagogue movement. As the movement has grown, however, the presence of greater numbers of lesbians has helped to shift the balance of power in many cases. Separate women's groups arose in some synagogues, feminist liturgical changes were incorporated, and women's leadership (lay and rabbinic) became more common. In 1981 the World Congress had its first keynote speech by a woman rabbi, Linda Holtzman, who soon came out as lesbian. Lesbian rabbis have served gay congregations in Los Angeles, New York, Atlanta, and Philadelphia. Beth Chaim Chadashim in Los Angeles hired a heterosexual woman, Janet Marder, as its first rabbi. Marder became a great advocate for lesbian and gay rights in the Reform movement and helped the congregation deal with issues of sexism as well.[16] The work of lesbian rabbis Linda Holtzman, who serves as rabbi of Beth Ahava in Philadelphia, Denise Eger and Lisa Edwards who followed Janet Marder at Beth Chaim Chadashim, and Sharon Kleinbaum at Congregation Beth Simchat Torah in New York City, has also been of considerable importance in changing the climate for lesbians in the Jewish community.

Most of the gay and lesbian synagogues have joined the Reform movement, and one the Reconstructionist. Most congregations have chosen to affiliate with the Reform movement because of the strong example that movement set in the early 1970s by doing outreach to the first gay and lesbian congregations, helping them to organize, and providing them with meeting spaces, prayerbooks, and Torah scrolls.[17]

Gay synagogues have created a "safe space" for lesbian Jews, if not always a comfortable one. In gay synagogues lesbians often confront their differences with gay men on feminist issues and specifically lesbian issues often take second place to gay issues. In addition, much of the Jewish community's response to these congregations has focused on gay men, based on an assumption that lesbians are simply a female equivalent and do not have special issues and needs of our own. Nonetheless, the gay and lesbian synagogue movement has provided a place for lesbians to be visible as lesbians in the Jewish community and to be open about who we are in a Jewish context.

Visibility in the Jewish Mainstream

Walking humbly with God can also take place in other Jewish settings. Jewish lesbians must be visible as a group in mainstream contexts as well. The experience of CBST and the Israel Independence Day Parade of 1993 in New York City is an example of a time when gay and lesbian Jews were prohibited from being able to walk humbly with God.

The predominantly Orthodox organizers of the Israel Day Parade in New York refused to let CBST participate. This incident received a great deal of publicity, particularly in light of the very public struggle that gay groups had for several years been engaged in to be included in New York's St. Patrick's Day parade. The CBST members were divided about how to respond. The synagogue leadership attempted to effect a compromise that would have allowed them to march with the Reform movement, including the name of the congregation on the banner but omitting the words gay and lesbian. This compromise was first accepted and then rejected by the parade organizers. Ultimately, the congregation did not march but held its own gathering at a Reform synagogue on the day of the parade. Other liberal groups also boycotted the march in solidarity with the gay congregation.

But this affair raised conflicts over loyalty. CBST members wanted to be part of the larger Jewish community and express their support for Israel. For some members, their investment in being part of the Jewish community made them more susceptible to compromise. Others remained angry. This event also brought a great deal of attention to the existence of a gay and lesbian Jewish community because it was covered extensively in the mainstream press.[18]

But for lesbian Jews to walk humbly with God, it is important that the community supports every opportunity for us to be visible, to proclaim our identity by saying the word "lesbian" in public. It is imperative that the Jewish community take up this responsibility, since the United States Supreme Court has denied gay and lesbian people the right to march in parades organized by other communities. Unless the Jewish community stands up for our right to be a visible part of the community, all Jews are in effect denied the opportunity to fulfill our obligation to walk humbly with God in the Jewish community.

Walking humbly with God, individually and collectively, is a prerequisite to following the other virtues that Micah suggests: a commitment to love and justice. It is only those who come to self-acceptance, including a sense that they are loved by God and by the Jewish community, who can begin to work toward creating a world of love and justice.

Five

Ahavat Ḥesed:
Transforming Relationships

The second part of Micah's precept is about loving well. Loving is the connection we make to others, whether in intimate or social relationships. Loving in social relationships means respect for the other person; loving those with whom we are intimate involves passionate feelings and intense closeness in addition to respect. Ahavat ḥesed forms the link between individual self-acceptance, haẓnea lekhet im elohekha, and universal justice, asot mishpat. We cannot love others unless we accept ourselves. And we cannot bring justice to a world where people do not know how to treat others with whom they are in relationships.

While ahavat ḥesed is applicable to heterosexuals and lesbians alike, the concept raises several issues that are particular to lesbian lives. There are differences in the ways that lesbians create loving networks with people around us. Lesbians also have a different perspective on coupled relationships and on the bearing and raising of children. Looking at the subject of loving through a lesbian lens contributes a new perspective to the ongoing Jewish conversation about human relationships.

A New Concept of Family

Jewish families are typically created through biological ties, institutionally sanctioned marriage, adoption, and conversion. Jews inherit or claim a place in the Jewish community. We may choose to belong to a different religious or secular community from our family of origin, but for most of us, our primary connections to Judaism are set in our early lives.

Lesbian connections are not based on biological ties. Like converts to Judaism, most lesbians are not raised by parents who share our orientation. Unlike converts, the children we raise are mostly not like us either. While lesbian social groups and events in public spaces make it possible for us to find others like ourselves, there are no official ways to define oneself as lesbian or to join a lesbian community through marriage or conversion. Our lesbian family is a loosely defined network that incorporates our parents, children, and other family members who are willing to support us along with friends, former lovers, and members of their families.

It is imperative that the Jewish community comprehend and support the new concept of family that is derived from the context of Jewish lesbian existence. Changing the concept of family itself implies transformation. But it also demonstrates the need for new forms and rituals to celebrate this concept of family and deal with the problems that arise within our families of origin.

Lesbians and Our Families of Origin

Ahavat ḥesed is often difficult for lesbians to find in our families of origin. These spaces are often a source of tension and pain for us. Coming out to our families is perhaps the most difficult dimension of lesbian existence. Jewish families often have strong expectations that children should make their parents proud by living a typical American life: settling down with a partner of the opposite sex, raising children, and living comfortably in the confines of a nuclear family. Of course, many parents get used to the idea that their child is a lesbian, especially if we have children and live in what at least resembles a long-term nuclear family arrangement, but others do not.

Unique issues about achieving ahavat ḥesed arise in family settings for lesbians who may have complex relationships with their families of origin. Tensions may exist with family members who do not know about a lesbian's sexual orientation. How do you introduce a new partner to a cousin you haven't seen in many years, at the funeral of her mother who disapproved of your life choices? Tensions also arise about public acknowledgement of your relationship. Can your partner come to your mother's funeral if your mother disapproved of your relationship? Is it all right for you and your partner to dance together at your sister's wedding when you know it will embarrass her new husband? Should you and your lover demand to have an aliyah together at the bat mitzvah of her daughter from a previous heterosexual marriage? What if you receive an invitation to a cousin's wedding and your partner is not invited?

Jewish Communal Support for Lesbians and Our Families of Origin

These are difficult questions. Because they arise in a Jewish setting, the Jewish community must begin to address new ways to support ahavat ḥesed for lesbians and their families of origin. The community cannot allow homophobia to be the focus for the strife and contention that exist in families.

Other situations arise that also demand new patterns of behavior when lesbians and their families are involved. The customs and ceremonies associated with death and grief are a good example. When a lesbian dies, even if she has prepared all the necessary legal documents that will enable her partner to enter her hospital room, make decisions for her if she is not able to do so, inherit her property, and make her funeral arrangements, there is no mechanism for her partner to be recognized as a mourner within Jewish law. Only at the discretion of the rabbi who is presiding will she be allowed to stand as a mourner, to rend her clothes, to have her relationship to the deceased mentioned in the eulogy, or to sit shiva with the family—whether it be parents or children. While we hope that in most situations today the family of origin is comfortable with the relationship and the mourners can grieve their loss together, it is possible that the lesbian partner's grief will not be appropriately acknowledged. While there is no remedy to this situation, ahavat ḥesed suggests that lesbians and their families discuss these issues in advance with one another and with a rabbi and funeral director with whom the family has a relationship.

Around the time of death it is most important that the families that lesbians create among their friends take up the role that the biological family of the deceased would have played. If Jewish lesbians are in communities with lesbians who are not Jewish, it is important that they teach their friends about Jewish funeral and mourning customs. *Cancer in Two Voices*, by Barbara Rosenblum and Sandra Butler, describes the rituals surrounding the death of a partner in the context of a Jewish lesbian community. It is a very useful text with which to begin this discussion.

Issues Raised by Holiday Observances

Holidays are a focal point for tension between lesbians and our families and ahavat ḥesed becomes especially important to strive toward at such times. Passover is one point on the Jewish calendar when these issues come up most poignantly. After all, Passover tells the story of the liberation of the Jewish people from slavery. The struggle of our people for freedom resonates for lesbians with our own liberation from the oppression of hiding and points towards a time when all gay and lesbian people will be free to speak out about who we are. As a symbol of liberation from bondage, it is the Jewish holiday to which many lesbian Jews are deeply attached. It is not surprising that *Nice Jewish Girls* begins by asking the question: Why is this book different from other books?[1] It is also not surprising that the bread on the seder plate story is connected to Passover. This holiday is a time for reflection on belonging to the Jewish people.

The Passover seder is a time when the family gathers, and it is of extreme importance for lesbian Jews to feel liberated enough to bring their partners home for seder or to invite family members to seders in lesbian communities. Passover is also a time when lesbians feel most acutely estranged from their families. This is poignantly illustrated in the Passover scene in Judith Katz's novel, *Running*

Fiercely toward a High Thin Sound, which describes the missed opportunity for reconciliation and new beginnings for the lesbian protagonist and her family.[2]

For some lesbians Passover is a time to celebrate as a Jewish lesbian community, and hagaddot have been written for that purpose. By incorporating readings from these hagaddot, Jews who do not have lesbians in their families can include the lesbian experience of liberation in their seder ceremonies. This would constitute an act of ahavat ḥesed for people in the Jewish community who otherwise don't think about Jewish lesbian issues. A seder without a lesbian present might be enhanced by including one of the following parts of Jewish lesbian seder rituals.

Judith Stein's lesbian *New Hagaddah* includes four children that are very different from the four sons in the standard haggadah. She describes the "four sons" as different ways of being lesbian and Jewish. For example, the wise Jew knows the customs and rituals but accepts only those that are meaningful to her as a Jewish lesbian. The wicked Jew excludes herself from Jewish tradition because of self-hate. The Jew who is unable to ask must be brought into the ritual. Stein's reading is very useful for raising discussions of the lesbian's role in Judaism, and the different approaches we have taken to integrate ourselves.

It is also common practice to read from the Song of Songs at the seder. While the Song of Songs is a decidedly heterosexual love poem, it can be read in a lesbian voice by two women. In the context of the seder this way of reading honors the idea that sexual love exists between two women and is a profound gesture toward ahavat ḥesed.

The cycle of holidays around the new year lends itself to the reconciliation between lesbians and our families of origin. Rosh Hashanah is the holiday of individual new beginnings and ushers in a period of taking stock of our lives and asking forgiveness of those we have wronged. It is customary for Jews to reconcile with those from whom we are estranged during the ten days of repentance between Rosh Hashanah and Yom Kippur. This is the perfect time for family members to make peace with one another around the issue of lesbianism, to antidote the Yom Kippur afternoon reading of the Leviticus text that condemns male homosexuality and has been used to define lesbianism as "the doings of Egypt." A reconciliation of family conflicts around the High Holy Days is a powerful act of ahavat hesed.

Of course reconciliation is not always possible. Sometimes our families of origin reject us and are not prepared to reconcile. Sometimes people are not ready for reconciliation until it is too late, and one or the other person involved has died. These difficult situations remind us that sometimes ahavat hesed requires us to love those who do not or can no longer love us in return. While it is surely painful to love someone who does not return your love, ahavat hesed suggests that we make the effort to forgive.

New Jewish Lesbian Families

Whether our Jewish families accept or reject us, we often feel a need to create Jewish lesbian families for ourselves. Ahavat hesed is often based on familial attachment; for lesbians to experience such love we sometimes have to create those bonds among those usually defined as friends.

It is through the bonds of friendship that lesbian families are created and ahavat hesed is developed. Throughout the last two decades groups of Jewish lesbians have formed and provided the kind of love and support for one another that biological families are traditionally expected to provide.[3] Friendship networks among Jewish lesbians are powerful connections.

Some Jewish lesbians are blessed both with lesbian and Jewish families and can bring them together or divide their time between them. In these cases, family and friends become indistinguishable. What matters is not the biological definition of relationship upon which the bond between the people involved is based but the quality of ahavat hesed that exists among people.

Like biological families, chosen families should be expected to love loyally but not unconditionally. Families must maintain the ability to disagree and to challenge rather than to accept without question. An important part of ahavat hesed is to ask ourselves and those whom we love about what we value in life and if we are in fact living according to our values.

Ahavat Ḥesed Among Jewish Lesbians

Too often we begin to confuse our expectations of family and community, because the lines of chosen familial connections are not fixed. Individuals should expect intimate love from their biological families and the families they have made up out of their friends rather than expecting it from the Jewish or lesbian community.

A different kind of ahavat ḥesed needs to exist among networks of Jewish lesbians. The fact that two people both identify as Jewish and lesbian does not automatically make intimate love between them possible. Often Jewish lesbians express the expectations that we should love one another. Lesbian Jews can understand and be accepting of differences, without the expectation that our similarities will give us an automatic and lasting connection to one another. But we also must make room for one another's strengths. Jewish lesbians will not always agree. We will not always appreciate each other's ways of expressing ourselves. Each of us can make an effort to watch the way we behave with one another and make a commitment to treat each other with respect, the dimension of ahavat ḥesed that can be expected amongst members of a community. Respect does not only mean acceptance. It means challenging difficult group behaviors in as gentle a way as possible. It means not walking away from problems but discussing them until they are resolved. It means accepting differences and not expecting people to conform to one's own sense of what is right for Jewish lesbians. It means remembering that this is a complex group with different religious, spiritual, and personal needs and preferences. It means struggling when any of those elements seem to be in conflict with one's conception of ethical behavior. It means a willingness to leave things unresolved sometimes. These are the basic obligations of ahavat ḥesed within a community.

Sexual Relationships

Ahavat ḥesed is also important in defining lesbian sexual relationships. Jewish tradition emphasizes the importance of coupled relationships and hallows the institution of marriage as the only acceptable way in which two adults, one male and one female, should connect. The acceptance of lesbian couples has been accomplished in some Jewish circles; love between two women is deemed acceptable provided that they are in a monogamous long-term relationship. But such relationships are not the only way that lesbian Jews connect with one another sexually.

While there must be respect for couples as well as total acceptance of lesbian couples, coupled relationships are not necessarily the ideal. Ahavat ḥesed cannot mean that Jewish lesbians merely accept the traditional valorization of coupled relationships and therefore reject other possibilities for people to express love in their lives—from being single to having significant relationships with more than one individual, of either or both genders. The shame attached to being single or bisexual is greater today in some liberal Jewish contexts than is the shame of being part of a lesbian couple. Neither of these ways of being in the world should be stigmatized. Rather, we emphasize the importance of loving well, of taking human relationships seriously and treating those with whom we have established loving relationships with respect and caring. Rather than examining the form the significant relationships in our lives may take, we should examine the quality of ahavat ḥesed in our relationships and be held accountable for it.

There will inevitably be differences in intensity in the nature of the bonds of friendship people create. In some relationships these bonds are stronger and deeper. But the persons with whom we are sexual may not necessarily be the persons with whom we are closest at every stage of our lives. The separation between sexuality and procreation suggests the possibility of the same separation between sexuality and intimacy. While for many those are linked, it is not necessary that they should be. We demean nonsexual relationships when we define sexuality as the factor that determines intimacy.

Love in Coupled Relationships

Because lesbian couples comprise two women, they may have different expectations of friendship between them. Unlike heterosexual couples, lesbians often start as friends. Courting and romance for heterosexuals is inculcated through the culture; this is not the case for lesbian couples. Part of the meaning of ahavat ḥesed for

Jewish lesbians is thinking about ways to negotiate beginning these relationships.

Given the difficulties of creating lasting coupled relationships, there needs to be a focus on developing ahavat hesed in coupled relationships. How can couples succeed in loving one another in respectful ways? Some of these issues can be addressed through the vehicle of ritual. The process of creating commitment ceremonies helps couples figure out what ahavat hesed means in their lives. The Jewish community can help by making lesbian and gay commitment ceremonies part of Jewish ritual life. Rabbis are often uncomfortable with the idea of performing lesbian commitment ceremonies because they understand marriage to be a state that only applies to the union of male and female. They see the purpose of marriage as enabling the couple to have children who are recognized by society. By taking this position, they are making a statement about the way they view the legitimacy of the children of lesbian unions—and of nonprocreative heterosexual marriages as well.

For some Jewish lesbians commitment ceremonies are a diversion from the ultimate goal of the acceptance of all relationships. They see marriage as an institution in which women are the property of fathers who "give them away" in exchange for other commodities and services to husbands. Because traditional marriage oppresses women, some lesbians do not see the value of making a life commitment in a public and religious way. They think that the appropriate approach is to work toward the abolition of all marriage because that would keep people from treating married people as more valued members of society than the unmarried.[4]

Despite the opposition to lesbian commitment ceremonies from both traditionalists and feminists, more and more of these ceremonies are taking place. This is happening for a variety of reasons. Lesbians understand our relationships to be as valid as those of heterosexuals and wish to express that point by having these relationships validated publicly through ceremonies. Many see commitment ceremonies as a way of reconnecting to religious traditions, to have a spiritual way of confirming love relationships. Others want affirmation of their relationships by a religious tradition.[5]

Given the absence of protection of lesbian relationships in this society, a religious ceremony provides a means of public validation that will support the effort to legalize gay and lesbian marriage. In no state in the United States, with the pending exception of Hawaii, and in no country in the world except for Denmark, Norway, Iceland, and Sweden are same-sex couples afforded the privilege of marriage or the rights related to this privilege, which include the ability to inherit or transfer property, automatic citizenship for an immigrant spouse, immunity from testifying against one's partner in a court of law, tax benefits, and the right to custody or adoption of children raised by the couple. Domestic partnership benefits, which are available in over fifty municipalities around the United States, are largely symbolic ways of gaining official recognition of same-sex relationships. Some have consequences in terms of employee benefits but even those benefits are hard to obtain. Domestic partnership is not recognized for health benefits by much of the nation's health insurance industry, and it is unlikely that same-sex partnerships will receive benefits under any proposed national health insurance policies in the United States.

In the absence of these benefits, the public and religious validation given to same-sex couples by virtue of participation in a commitment ceremony is of tremendous symbolic importance. Because religious institutions are at the forefront of opposition to gay and lesbian rights, it is crucial that those who support these rights in the context of the religious community make their voices heard. One way of doing this is actively to support lesbian commitment ceremonies and to get involved in the fight for gay and lesbian marriage.[6] There is no doubt that if rabbis perform these ceremonies, and Jewish communities affirm them, they will have an impact on changing societal views that oppose same-sex marriage.

The Jewish Wedding: Spiritual and Legal Aspects

The traditional Jewish wedding is an opportunity for heterosexual couples to make a public statement of ahavat hesed. Lesbian couples must decide about the extent to which they desire their commitment ceremonies to resemble this ceremony, which is based on halakhah, Jewish legal precedent. There are three factors that make the Jewish wedding ceremony binding from the perspective of halakhah. First is the giving of a ring from the man to the woman as a token of their commitment; this act is accompanied by a vow that asserts that the woman is being made holy or reserved to the man "according to the laws of Moses and Israel." Second is the signing of a marriage contract, or ketubbah, which in its traditional form outlines the requirements that the man and woman must meet in order to be married (including financial arrangements and issues surrounding the bride's virginity) and must be witnessed by two men who are Jewish, ritually observant, and unrelated to the bride or groom. The last requirement is that sexual intercourse take place after the ceremony. In ancient times this act was actually part of the wedding event, and the bloody sheets that proved that the woman was a virgin were displayed for the witnesses. In contemporary ceremonies, sexual union is symbolized by the huppah and by the performance of yihud, a private time a couple spends after the ceremony.

To truly perform a Jewish wedding for same-sex couples that is meaningful within a Jewish context, these legal elements must be incorporated in some way. There is no reason why the elements of sexual relations, the exchange of a token and vow, and the writing of a marriage contract cannot be meaningfully transformed in a ceremony for lesbian couples. For most nontraditional Jews, halakhah is a symbolic matter, better understood as having the power of custom and tradition rather than of the law. Heterosexual ceremonies performed in a nontraditional framework have already changed and challenged the necessity of conformity to ancient law. For example, feminist innovations have made common the double ring ceremony; giving the ring no longer symbolizes the possession of the woman by the man but rather indicates their mutual connection and their agreement to have a primary relationship with one another.

The vows lesbian couples say to one another need not necessarily be "according to the laws of Moses and Israel" but might be more focused on the connections between the women involved. The lines from the prophet Hosea (2:21), "I will betroth myself to you forever"; the words of Ruth to Naomi (see chapter 3); or even the words used by a woman in the traditional ceremony when she is permitted to give her husband a ring "I am my beloved's and my beloved is mine" from the Song of Songs (2:16) are all acceptable alternatives to the traditional vow. Or women might decide to write their own vows.

A ketubbah can also be created for same-sex couples.[7] Many lesbian couples favor writing their own contracts, as have heterosexual couples. Models of alternative ketubbot are readily available, although I have yet to see any that incorporate language for same-sex couples. It would be an important sign to have such documents available from Jewish denominations, although lesbian couples can adapt contemporary documents fairly easily by using the forms that are available and changing the gender designations on them. Using the word "bride" raises the issue of terminology. We have yet to find appropriate terms for lesbian partners that convey both the romantic and sexual nature of the relationship.

The issue of sexuality and its relationship to the marriage ceremony has been avoided for many centuries. We no longer require women to produce bloody sheets, and the topic of virginity is rarely mentioned outside Orthodox circles. Of course, defining virginity takes on a wholly different connotation for lesbian relationships. Nonetheless, it is important at a lesbian commitment ceremony to affirm the sexual relationship between the couple and to hallow it in some way. Standing under the huppah is a symbol of the home and bed that the lovers share. Creating a huppah—with colors that have been symbolic of lesbian lives (lavender, pink, rainbow)—might be a good way of making the connection. Reciting romantic poetry is another possibility for those who are comfortable doing so.

There is a spiritual dimension in addition to the legal one—the goal of these ceremonies is to unite two people in a loving union. The spiritual dimension of the ceremony is most often the focus of the couple. They want the opportunity to have communal support and public celebration of their sacred relationship. The Jewish wedding ceremony acknowledges this ideal through the Sheva Berakhot, the seven wedding blessings, which are expressions of gratitude for the opportunity to love and rejoice. These blessings also reflect a focus on procreation. While sexuality and procreation may not be linked for lesbian couples, some do have commitment ceremonies to make a public statement about their interests in raising children together. Variations on the wedding blessings can be created to incorporate these differences.

It is also customary to stop for a moment in the context of the ceremony and to remember deceased parents. It may be that in a lesbian ceremony some of the parents (or children) of the couple are not comfortable enough to be present. It may be helpful to pause and think about them, perhaps offering a prayer for the healing of that relationship.

The final element in the traditional Jewish wedding ceremony is the breaking of the glass. The explanations have varied over time and usage, but its original stated purpose was to remind those celebrating that they should temper their joy with feelings of sorrow about the destruction of the Temple. Other explanations have ranged from taking up the broken pieces of the world to a symbolic deflowering of the bride. More than any other element of the wedding, breaking the glass is the symbol that gives the ceremony a uniquely Jewish flavor. Lesbians often struggle with this part of the ceremony. Certainly, it is not difficult to reinterpret the symbolism to relate to the brokenness of the world, the need to remember sorrow even at the most joyous times, the smashing of hatred and evil, or shattering the silence about women loving women in the Jewish community.[8] Yet for some this is a violent act and must therefore be omitted. Others have trouble deciding which of them will break the glass, for it may be seen symbolically as the kind of stereotypical role-playing they wish to avoid. Others see parody in the experience, and have the more male-oriented partner (when they can decide who that is, of course) do it. Occasionally, they agree to both do it together, although it is a daunting task if they are both dressed as brides and wearing high-heeled shoes!

For some lesbian couples, the idea of trying to fit their commitments into the form of a Jewish ceremony designed for heterosexual unions is untenable. They see the ceremony as antifeminist and are not comfortable making minor changes. They plan commitment ceremonies that exclude or radically alter the traditional elements. Despite these differences, they want this experience to feel Jewish. For some it is enough to go to synagogue for an aufruf (special aliyah) before the wedding.

They may also choose some form of mikveh to celebrate together their changed status. In traditional Judaism, mikveh is a very private ceremony for converts and for married women to mark the end of their menstrual cycle during which they must refrain from sex. A woman goes to mikveh for the first time before her wedding. This tradition of mikveh before the wedding can be adapted for a lesbian commitment ceremony. For many lesbians, going to mikveh has erotic overtones. Instead of going to mikveh at a ritual bath run by a traditional Jewish community, the ceremony can take place in any natural body of water. And the two women need not go separately. They can perform this ritual together and, if they choose, in the company of friends. In this context, it can be an experience that underscores ahavat ḥesed.

Others choose to focus on one element of the traditional ceremony to the exclusion of the others. They may exchange rings and vows, accompanied by other forms of celebration such as singing and eating. They may decide to write a contract and have that contract witnessed. Or they may incorporate some ceremony into their first experience of love-making.

It is also common for lesbians not to have ceremonies until many years after they have been together, since no official wedding is expected and their families may initially have difficulty getting used to the idea of them as a couple. Couples may have commitment ceremonies on anniversaries of important events in their lives: the first conversation, the first kiss, the first sexual encounter, or the time they moved in together.

Whatever they do, these are complicated decisions for lesbian couples. There is usually no simple answer about how to blend being lesbian and being Jewish. Jewish lesbians want both to claim the ways in which we are different and at the same time to remain within the context of Jewish life. And experimentation is not easy. Many couples, after deciding to make a public commitment, find the work involved in creating a ceremony that is uniquely theirs an overwhelming task and choose a traditional ceremony. Their focus is on making a statement about the ways in which they are connected to their Jewish roots and are similar to other Jewish couples who wish to make a public statement about their love and commitment and even about their desire to raise children together.

Lesbian wedding ceremonies that are based completely on traditional heterosexual ones risk losing the opportunity to give unique definition to who we are and what our relationships mean as les-

bians, so it is urgent that those couples who are interested in exper-
imenting with different forms feel comfortable doing so. We need
continued creativity about these new forms and a willingness to
take risks with alternative ceremonies.

Difficult questions also arise around dress. In Ashkenazi tradition, the bride is expected to wear a white gown with a train and
veil, the groom a tuxedo. Many feminists have opposed these customs as reinforcing rigid gender stereotypes. Yet some lesbians have
embraced them, often in gestures of irony.

The issue of interfaith relationships is a difficult one in the
Jewish lesbian community, as it is in the rest of the Jewish community. The Jewish community is for the most part unsympathetic to
interfaith wedding ceremonies, and most rabbis, including the most
liberal, will not perform these ceremonies. These rabbis see interfaith weddings as contributing to the demographic decline of the
Jewish community. Many synagogues make an effort to welcome
interfaith couples once they are married, but for many this is too
late. Jewish lesbians also have questions about whether to become
involved in interfaith relationships. Those who would refuse to
date non-Jewish men find themselves in conflict when they begin an
interfaith lesbian relationship. They may question whether they are
taking the relationship seriously if they're willing to interdate.

In this respect, Jewish lesbian couples should be treated differently from their heterosexual counterparts. Lesbian couples do not
have places in the Jewish community to meet one another, and so
relationships are more likely to develop in lesbian settings. While
openness in the Jewish community may change that reality, we
must also recognize a crucial difference about lesbian relationships
that makes taking a more positive view of interfaith and interracial
relationships important.

In all relationships, it is important that partners have both commonalities and differences. For heterosexual couples, the difference
of gender is salient. Lesbian couples need to make up for this particular absence of difference in another way in order to maintain
their individuality within the couple. Age, religion, and class make
for important differences for some lesbian couples. But these differences often make communication difficult between partners, as
do gender differences in heterosexual couples. Lesbian couples

need to work hard on understanding the differences between them. This is especially important in cases of differences that reflect power imbalances in society such as religious identification, race, and class.

Over the years it has been common for lesbians to convert to Judaism because of their love relationships with Jewish women. In other cases, couples blend their religious and ethnic identities, as is the case in the "Gospel under the ḥuppah" ceremony between an African American and a Jewish woman described in *Ceremonies of the Heart*. Yael and Luana were married by a rabbi under a ḥuppah. Wine was drunk from a kikombe cup from the celebration of Kwanzaa, and the seven blessings became eight principles, also derived from Kwanzaa.[9] Such creative solutions are helpful for Jewish lesbians who find themselves in interfaith relationships. Perhaps the Jewish community can learn from the challenges lesbians face as they find ways to handle religious and ethnic differences. Interfaith relationships between lesbians create important opportunities to mark differences for two people who share their gender in common. We need to be careful in our efforts to make lesbians equal to allow room for differences. Respect for lesbian relationships does not necessarily require applying all standards set for heterosexuals to these relationships.

Lesbians must have the room to decide if they want to have ceremonies that are similar to the traditional or that are radically different; both options must be celebrated as public declarations of ahavat ḥesed. It is the combination of these forms that sends a message to the Jewish community that we are both different and at the same time like everyone else. Honoring lesbian lives means insuring that a variety of opportunities exists for the expression of lesbian desire in the Jewish community.[10]

Lesbians and Heterosexual Weddings

It is also important to recognize how the Jewish community contributes to the difficulties that lesbians experience around issues of coupling. Heterosexual weddings pose a great challenge to lesbians. We attend as friends and family members to witness this important event in the lives of people we love. We want to be included among the well-wishers, yet we often feel like outsiders. Part of the obligation of ahavat ḥesed for heterosexual Jews is to find ways to acknowledge and include lesbians, even in a ceremony in which we cannot participate.

Weddings are often preceded by ceremonies known as aufrufen, a time before the wedding when the couple is called to the Torah for an aliyah, receives special blessings, and is showered with candy for good luck and fertility. Of course, lesbian and gay couples may also have an aufruf prior to a commitment ceremony. But the aufruf often celebrates not only the individual man and woman but their heterosexuality as well. This can be avoided if service leaders are careful to include a reading or blessing about the privilege of marriage mentioning those people who are unable because of law and custom to state their love and receive communal approval in such a public way. Congregations may also consider eliminating the custom of the aufruf entirely as a way of making a statement that the group does not single out heterosexual coupling for communal approval.

At heterosexual wedding ceremonies it is important for the couple to express gratitude for the privilege to marry and to include a statement in the liturgy that indicates the couple is aware that having this ceremony is part of heterosexual privilege. This imbalance can be remedied by adding an element into the ceremony that acknowledges that the commitments made by lesbians and gay men are not sanctioned by the state nor acknowledged by much of the Jewish community. This may mean spilling some wine from the cup that the couple drinks to indicate that their joy is diminished because lesbian unions are not recognized. It may mean rewriting parts of the seven wedding blessings.[11] In their traditional form these blessings are a pronouncement of communal joy surrounding heterosexual weddings that refers to the importance of procreation and compares the wedding couple to Adam and Eve. Another alternative is to add some words at the breaking of the glass that ends the ceremony. The breaking of the glass is commonly explained as a way of remembering that the world itself is broken and in need of repair. At this point in the ceremony, the officiant may indicate that the lack of civil rights for lesbians and gay men is one important aspect of this brokenness. Heterosexual couples and their wedding guests can donate money to organizations that are fighting for gay marriage or domestic partnership or become involved in working toward those benefits for gay and lesbian people at their workplace or in their hometown.

Ending Coupled Relationships

Like their beginnings, the endings of lesbian relationships often differ from the heterosexual model. Unlike when heterosexual couples divorce, there are expectations within the lesbian community that lesbian couples will remain friends when they end their relationships as lovers. Most likely, and especially if they are both involved in the Jewish community, they will remain in contact and continue to see each other at public events. More thought has to be given to the ways in which lesbians who were partners behave toward one another. It is true that many lesbian ex-lovers maintain ahavat hesed with one another, doing the emotional work it takes to establish loving friendships, and becoming a significant part of one another's support network. This is a wonderful model that heterosexual couples might learn from. But in other cases, the idea of remaining friends may be unrealistic, and this needs to be accepted.

Even if it is impossible to remain friends, lesbian couples have a responsibility to end their relationships through amicable mediation. Ahavat hesed also involves maintaining a respectful relationship with those whom we no longer love intimately. Although it may be necessary to be angry to separate from a partner, it is not necessary to carry that anger to the point where it is disruptive to others or to the fabric of a local community's sense of ahavat hesed. We should consider the wisdom of setting up a new system of batei din, religious courts, training lesbian Jews in mediation so that couples can address problems in a forum that does not require the use of a state judicial system that does not recognize lesbian relationships as legally binding.

Future Generations

As Jewish lesbians, another part of understanding ahavat hesed is finding ways to provide love for future generations. While we may not be obligated by the commandment to be fruitful and multiply, we heed its implications: to bring forth another generation who will continue the story of the Jewish people. While some of us are involved in the biological process of reproducing Jewish children, we cannot create another generation of lesbians by reproduction. This fact makes us aware that the obligation of ahavat ḥesed to the future generation is met in many ways, not only through bearing and raising one's own children.

Jewish Lesbians and Lesbian Youth

Jewish lesbians' obligation to ahavat ḥesed should extend to nurturing and supporting lesbian youth. As it becomes more acceptable to be lesbian or gay in our culture, youth are coming out at an earlier age. Gay and lesbian adolescents are at great risk of being targets of homophobia and are more at risk for suicide than other youth. Thus our obligation of ahavat ḥesed to the next generation is to provide gay and lesbian youth, and particularly Jewish gay and lesbian youth, with public places to gather and meet one another, homes to go to when their own homes don't feel safe, big sisters to go to lesbian communal events with, speakers for their high schools, day schools, and youth groups, and counselors for their camps. This population above all needs our help. They often find themselves in home situations where they do not receive the love and support they need. Parents of lesbian and gay youth often, even with the best intentions, do not know how to communicate with their children. Adult lesbian Jews can fill that gap. These youth, Jewish and non-Jewish alike, should be able to rely on lesbian Jews who can provide ahavat ḥesed for them.

Jewish Lesbians and Jewish Youth

Those of us who do not want to bear and raise our own children have an obligation not only to lesbian youth but to all Jewish youth. We can be visible in their lives to provide role models and to help them grow up accepting lesbians. When objections are raised to lesbian and gay leadership in the Jewish community, the greatest fear that is expressed is often about our contact with young people.

Along with keeping us from leadership roles in the Jewish community, such as rabbi and cantor, we are often told that we should not be teachers in religious schools or youth group leaders, as if our lesbianism could contaminate young people. Yet how will the next generation of Jews ever see us as human beings, understand the ways in which we are both different and like them, allow us to give to them our energy and knowledge if we cannot function in leadership roles and have contact with them?

Clearly, some Jewish communal leaders operate with the assumption that lesbianism can be taught and that seeing self-accepting lesbians will encourage students to choose this lifestyle. Of course, they would be comforted to know that lesbianism is genetic and not learned behavior. We cannot assure them of that, nor do I think it would be a good thing even if we could, for it would imply that we accept the notion that growing up lesbian or gay is inferior. Providing young people with healthy role models may mean that some of them may decide to experiment with a lesbian relationship as adolescents. It will definitely mean that they will feel more comfortable and supported in doing so, no matter at what age these feelings arise.

Ahavat ḥesed on the part of Jewish communal leaders means that they must fully accept lesbian behavior and relationships in the Jewish community and be able to say publicly that it is good to be lesbian or gay. They must be able to say that children may be lesbian, bisexual, or heterosexual and that these options are blessed by families and by the Jewish community. Tangibly, this acceptance will demand that rites that celebrate heterosexuality, as I suggested in the last chapter, also celebrate lesbian lives. When this comes to pass, Jewish lesbians will be able to fulfill our obligation to the community and to become an integral part of that community, helping to raise the next generation by serving simply as involved, caring adults.

Lesbians Having Children Of Our Own

Spending time with young people is not necessarily the only way to play an important role with future generations. Making sure that the world is a better place for them to live, creating works of art that will enhance their spirit, providing support to their parents are all included in our obligation to future generations.

Yet the urge to reproduce and raise our own children is strong among lesbians, and among Jewish lesbians in particular.[12] Our desire to raise children as part of the Jewish community, well aware that they are unlikely to be lesbian or gay, should be understood as a deep commitment of ahavat hesed that we express as Jews, and the Jewish community must do everything in its power to welcome our children. This includes education that reflects the reality of their lives: that is, which acknowledges the role of lesbians in Jewish history and in the Jewish community, which respects different family configurations, and that makes a positive effort to include rituals that celebrate lesbian relationships.

New rituals are also needed for new circumstances. For example, when a lesbian brings children from a previous heterosexual marriage into a new relationship with a woman there is a need for a different kind of ritual. Community recognition of the step-parenting role (and not only for lesbians but for heterosexuals as well) would go a long way to provide support and comfort for a new family. When my partner and I moved in together, our friends threw her a "shower" to mark her status as a new parent. The public recognition was important for a role that is fraught with difficulty. Rituals for new step-parents are important as a recognition of the changes in their lives.

Lesbian Jews also have to deal with unique questions about ways of bearing and raising children that have an ethical dimension and require a particular understanding of ahavat hesed. This is true not only of lesbians who decide together to start a family but also of lesbians who bring children with them (either from previous heterosexual or lesbian relationships) into a new relationship.

Most heterosexuals grow up assuming that they want to bear and raise children. Lesbians do not always make that assumption. In past generations, deciding to live as a lesbian was more likely to mean giving up the desire to raise children. While some lesbians have become stronger in asserting their rights to bear and raise children, others do not want their own children. This may be a very difficult issue to resolve in lesbian families, especially when a lesbian who never wanted children becomes involved with one who has children already. While heterosexuals also face this dilemma, it may be more difficult to resolve in lesbian relationships because of the already complex relationship between the lesbian step-parent and her partner's children.

Ahavat ḥesed requires that these women work hard to resolve differences in ways that do not have a negative impact on the children. This will require work on the part of all the adults involved to make it possible for them to give the children what they need.

In the case of two lesbians who disagree about raising a family together, loving well requires much discussion and compromise. Here we find the possibility that two dimensions of love are in conflict—the responsibility to a partner and the responsibility to future generations. When choices must be made, they must be made thoughtfully and lovingly, acknowledging how difficult such choices may be.

Lesbians who are clear about having children together also face questions about finding a method that is acceptable to both. First, the lesbian couple must decide which one will bear the children or, if both want to do so, in which order to do it. This will mean dealing with a variety of feelings about competition in motherhood. In a relationship of equals, it is sometimes difficult to figure out how to play these different roles, especially because the woman who is not bearing the child will often get cast by society in the role of father. While this is an interesting way to challenge the assumption that father must be a man, it may not always be comfortable for a woman to assume that role.

Second, their children will be conceived without a connection to their sexual relationship. This is also true for many heterosexual adoptive couples, and this separation of sexuality from procreation has an impact on the couple's relationship. Lesbians have yet to really talk about how this difference affects them.

Couples must also decide whether to work with a known donor, who will continue to play some role in the life of the family, or go to an anonymous donor through a sperm bank or hospital. Introducing a third parent may be very helpful, but it also may raise problems for the couple related to the connection between procreation and sexuality. The nonbiological parent may have a difficult time adjusting if there is another, biological parent in the picture.

She may have difficulty figuring out her role and problems dealing with the presence of another adult figure in the child's life. On the other hand there are also problems associated with using anonymous donors. Because the sperm usually comes from a hospital or infertility clinic, the primary experience of conception takes place in a medical setting that is often cold and sterile. Medical professionals who are strangers become involved in an intimate moment, and this may lead to discomfort. Anonymous donors also raise the difficult issues of explaining to a young child the circumstances of his or her birth, dealing with the absence of a biological father in the child's life, and informing the child about his or her genetic makeup.

Procreation in this environment requires a deep commitment and consciousness on the part of a lesbian couple. There are no accidents or hasty decisions. Each child of a lesbian couple is conceived in care and thought. This thinking and planning is even more significant in the cases of lesbian adoptions. These families are becoming more prevalent as adoption agencies have made it easier for single women to adopt and have begun to acknowledge lesbian partners in adoptions. Now that several states in the U.S. have accepted second parent adoptions, this route may be most helpful in allowing both parents an equal role in raising a child, if that is what they desire.

Adoption often raises questions of difference. Most North American Jewish lesbian adoptions involve children who are not Jewish and who come from different races and parts of the world. In these cases lesbian parents have much educational work to do with their children, initiating them into lesbian and Jewish culture in addition to the culture of their origin. While many heterosexual couples also adopt across nationalities and races, they face one less complicated "difference" with which to deal.

In each of these situations, ahavat ḥesed becomes a crucial element. There are no right ways to go about facing these challenges. But they must be faced and they can be if there is a strong enough commitment both to partners and to the future generation. Lesbians may also decide to raise children with only one adult in the household. All lesbian families need communal support to help them raise their children in ways that will provide love and nurture the relationships. Jewish lesbians must be committed to providing support for single-parent families with young children. These children need to be in contact with other lesbian families and to be welcomed in a Jewish context.

Rituals at the time of birth play an important role in helping the parents and child identify as part of a Jewish community. Lesbian couples should have the opportunity to celebrate their child's birth or adoption in traditional ways if they choose to do so. Stories of lesbians who have requested the service of a mohel (ritual circumciser) for a brit milah and been denied such service, or of lesbians who were unable to have public Jewish recognition of their child's birth for fear that they would not be accepted are commonplace. For the children of lesbian couples to achieve equal status in the Jewish community, those who perform ritual circumcision must be educated about the growing prevalence of lesbian parenting. Perhaps Jewish lesbian medical professionals should also begin to perform this ritual.

Like other feminist Jews, some lesbian parents may decide that ritual circumcision is not a good alternative and will refuse to circumcise their sons. Those who choose this option do not want to make such a strong differentiation between male and female children's opportunity to identify as Jews; they therefore choose ceremonies for their sons that would be the same as those for their daughters. Many Jewish lesbian feminists who might reject circumcision for political reasons circumcise their sons to avoid imposing yet another difference between their children and other Jews.

When lesbians have female children the problems are less complex. Ceremonies that welcome girls into the Jewish community have only appeared within the last few decades as a feminist innovation. Lacking ancient precedents, these ceremonies are more amenable to adaptation. It would also be helpful if "stage directions" were written into all of these ceremonies that did not assume the existence of a father and a mother as primary parents. Special prayers may be included in these ceremonies that focus on the experience of having two mothers raise a child, like the one that follows:

> Creator of all, may these mothers draw strength from You as together they raise this child. Grant them the ability to listen

to one another as they face the difficult task of nurturing and caring for this new life. May they never lose sight of the wonders of creation that live in this new person. And may they never lose sight of the love between them that made this life possible.

As is the case with heterosexual weddings, when babies are born to heterosexual couples in the Jewish community, certain assumptions are made that make lesbians invisible. It is automatically assumed for example that the child's behavior will conform to stereotypical gender roles and that the child will make a choice of heterosexual partners throughout his or her lifetime. There is no better time than at a brit or baby naming to interrupt those assumptions. The standard wish for a child is that he or she grow up to a life of Torah, ḥuppah (marriage), and good deeds. While we should not assume that two women will not choose "ḥuppah" as a life option, we must make the reference more general and accepting of a variety of choices. It is preferable to wish the child a life of Torah, reyut (passionate friendship), and good deeds, remembering that while intimacy is a value, the form that that intimacy takes will vary.

The children of lesbians also need communal support as they grow older. Adolescence is an especially difficult time for lesbian and gay youth, and it is also a difficult time for the children of lesbians and gay men. These children also must "come out" about their families being different and face the homophobia that is so prevalent in adolescent settings. Jewish settings can become a safe place for these children, so that they can have opportunities to talk openly about their families if they need to do so. This will only happen when gay and lesbian issues are publicly acknowledged in Jewish settings and Jewish educators include them in their curricular planning.

Very little attention is paid to the bat mitzvah who at age thirteen already knows she is different and is exploring same-sex feelings and fantasies. (Imagine, for example, what it might feel like for a thirteen-year-old girl who thinks she might be a lesbian to have to read the passage from Torah condemning male homosexuality at her bat mitzvah.) The community needs to find ways to express respect for the choices that this young woman might be making.

This means providing lesbian role models in religious schools and summer camps and discussing homosexuality openly and positively in the context of religious education. This will be valuable not only for the young woman who thinks she might be a lesbian but for all students as they develop sexual identities.

Questions about same-sex step-parents are also raised at the time of bar and bat mitzvah. The partner of the lesbian parent has a complicated role. No matter what kind of relationship the child who is celebrating bar or bat mitzvah has with the nonbiological partner, this is a time when difficult issues may surface. If the Jewish community provides support and respect for same-sex relationships, the problems of integrating same-sex step-parents can be dealt with the way any problems related to divorce are handled. But if the community fails to recognize lesbian relationships, even those children with good relationships with their step-parents may be unable to find an appropriate public role for them within the bar/bat mitzvah ceremony.

Lesbians who raise children make a special contribution to the Jewish community. We provide part of the next generation that the Jewish community needs to remain alive. We and our children deserve a warm welcome and a sense that we are an important part of the community that is so important to us.

While the struggles I have described in creating ahavat ḥesed specific to Jewish lesbians are many, the goal of creating strong loving networks that involve parents and children, friends and partners is one that we share with all Jews.

Ultimately, ahavat ḥesed requires much hard work. To love well we must take our responsibilities to others seriously and give careful consideration to the contribution we want to make that will enable the Jewish and lesbian communities to thrive. And ultimately to love well within the Jewish community, we lesbians must in turn receive ahavat ḥesed from that community.

Six

Asot Mishpat:
The Commitment to Justice

Having examined the commitments of haznea lekhet im elohekha, walking humbly with God, and commitments of ahavat ḥesed, to love the people in our lives well, I now end where Micah began, with asot mishpat, a commitment to justice. The commitment to do justice requires us to go beyond our own lives and to look at larger issues in the world around us. In the conception of Micah's precept that I describe here, these efforts are intrinsically interconnected. We cannot make a choice between accepting ourselves, caring for our circle of loved ones, and doing justice in the world. These efforts must be woven into one framework.

What, then, is the justice that we seek as human beings who are Jewish lesbians? Our goal is to live in a world where every person has what it takes to satisfy basic human needs: food, clothing, and shelter. Where every person has the opportunity for health care, safety, education, and work. Where all people have the opportunity to participate in decisions that affect their lives. Where nations do not make war against one another. And where the planet itself, and all that lives on it, is treated with dignity and respect. These are the goals of a just society.

We cannot begin to envision such a world unless we have created the possibilities within ourselves and our community of working toward this plan. As Jewish lesbians, we begin with the idea that to walk with decency with God is measured by our self-acceptance and willingness to be visible. This is the beginning of justice. For only if we speak out about who we are can we create the opportunity for justice for ourselves.

But this is insufficient: love is also a prerequisite to justice. In relation to justice ahavat hesed means respect not only for those whom we love particularly, but for all humanity. This means figuring out how to deal with hatred that is expressed in violent words and deeds. Many acts of violence in our society are perpetrated by those who hate others whom they judge to be inferior to themselves. While hate crimes and hate speech are often committed by individuals or groups who are not powerful in our society, they are often sanctioned by the powerful. And hate creates an environment inimical to a just society. We must remain vigilant in combating this type of violence and speak out publicly against the perpetration of such acts. As Jews we are mindful of the experience in Nazi Germany that began as the hate speech of a fringe group and turned into the rule of the state. Only if we remain vigilant against those who hate difference can we begin to speak about asot mishpat.

Some feminists have severed the connection between love and justice. In an effort to demonstrate the value of love, feminist philosophers such as Carol Gilligan have posited that a female way of being is to focus more on intimate caring, whereas the masculine approach is to demand abstract justice.[1] This dichotomized notion demeans both love and justice. It places them in opposition rather than as connected parts of a single obligation as Micah states.

On the other hand, Carter Heyward, a white Christian lesbian theologian, argues that justice is love. In doing justice, one is creating a loving world.[2] From the perspective of Micah's precept, however, these values are not one and the same. I interpret Micah's precept to make distinctions between loving well and doing justice—seeing them as separate but connected values—and pay attention to ahavat hesed among Jewish lesbians and between Jewish lesbians and the rest of the Jewish community. These actions are related to, but do not equal, the efforts all of us make to bring about a just society.

Asot Mishpat for Lesbian Issues: Gay and Lesbian Awareness Week[3]

Our first step in seeking justice is to demand that the Jewish community work toward justice for lesbians in the world: we seek an end to discrimination against us; we want legislative initiatives that would gain for us the right to housing, child custody and employment, and the opportunity to marry and serve in the military. The American Jewish community must also fight for our rights in Jewish life as well: to marry, to serve openly in leadership positions, and to be accepted fully for who we are.[4]

The Jewish community can begin to work on its responsibility to help us achieve justice for ourselves by initiating a new Jewish observance: Gay and Lesbian Awareness Week. To designate the first week in the spring when the weekly Torah portion Aḥare Mot (which includes both the prohibition against male homosexuality and the reference to "the doings of Egypt") is read to be devoted to issues related to gay and lesbian Jews will be enormously helpful in creating an opportunity to work toward asot mishpat. Gay and Lesbian Awareness Week can take a variety of forms and include many different activities. What follows are some suggestions for ways to observe this week.

The most obvious activity is a text discussion of the passages in Leviticus. Study sessions can be held about this portion or some other text under discussion in this book. Discussions could take place about issues of concern to gay and lesbian Jews such as the treatment of people with AIDS in the Jewish community, the relationship of homophobia to anti-Semitism, or the special contributions of gay people to Jewish life. Perhaps a rabbi will choose to make this a sermon topic or discuss his or her own process of coming to terms with feelings about homosexuality and Judaism. A Jewish community center could introduce the subject through a lesbian and gay film festival.[5]

If a Jewish group wants to begin a dialogue with lesbian Jews about issues we face, there are several options. If there is a gay and lesbian synagogue or group in the area, a representative will be happy to speak, perhaps to discuss the ways in which this passage in Leviticus has been problematic for lesbian Jews. A mainstream congregation can hold a joint service with the local gay congregation, like the one that took place in Cleveland several years ago. If there is no specifically Jewish gay and lesbian group, most cities also have a civil rights group, or bookstore, or community center. Often a Jewish member will be pleased to come to speak about issues of importance to the gay and lesbian community. Another good source for speakers is the organization known as P-FLAG—Parents, Families and Friends of Lesbians and Gays. P-FLAG's members have faced many of the issues that nongay people face in coming to terms with the homosexuality of someone close to them.

These activities are important first steps for Jewish groups to take when they begin to confront issues facing gay and lesbian Jews. If the group wants to go further, there are other things that can be done to foster work toward justice for gay and lesbian Jews. For example, if people begin to get in touch with their feelings about homosexuality, they may want to participate in a workshop designed to help people explore their feelings.

Groups can do outreach to openly gay and lesbian Jews, inviting them to become more actively involved in their activities. It is likely that there already are members of any Jewish group who are gay or lesbian. If they have chosen not to reveal this information, a process of reaching out to openly gay and lesbian Jews should not involve forcing them to give up their privacy. However, a process that opens up the issues and creates a welcoming environment for gay and lesbian Jews will allow them and their relatives and friends to begin to open up. Something as simple as saying "those of *us* who are gay, lesbian, transgendered, or bisexual"—instead of talking about *them*—is a good start.[6]

If there are openly gay or lesbian Jews in a synagogue, Gay and Lesbian Awareness Week will become an appropriate time for them to celebrate some life-cycle event with the congregation. An individual or a group of individuals might choose to participate in a "coming out" ceremony. A couple can renew their commitment to one another or celebrate an anniversary in the congregation. A special memorial service can be conducted for all those gay and lesbian Jews in history who left no children to say kaddish for them.

A Jewish school is also an appropriate place to begin to discuss issues related to being lesbian and Jewish. Some students will have a lesbian parent or will know someone with a lesbian parent; others will themselves be asking questions about their own sexuality. Speakers, books, and pamphlets are available to help teachers deal with these issues.

A Jewish library can prominently display books and periodicals that have gay or lesbian themes during Awareness Week. Often, reading is a good and private first step for people who are struggling with their own homoerotic feelings or with the homosexuality of someone close to them.

Finally, any group can become involved in the struggle for gay rights. There are a variety of issues to work on:

Plan to march in the annual Gay Pride parade.

Get involved in AIDS work. Investigate the practices of Jewish funeral homes and their treatment of people with AIDS. Find out if any of the Jewish social service agencies offer services for people with AIDS and their families.

Contact legislators about legal issues facing the gay community. These include fighting for domestic partnership legislation and gay marriage, the inclusion of sexual orientation in antidiscrimination laws, getting statistics reported on antigay crime, support for AIDS funding and anticensorship campaigns.

Establish ẓedakah projects for organizations that work for gay, lesbian, bisexual, and transgendered rights. One such project is to have heterosexual couples make a donation to support domestic partnership legislation or gay and lesbian marriage on the occasion of their wedding. This will increase their awareness of the fact that gay people are not able to get married legally and be afforded the rights, privileges, and protection of a marriage contract.

Work within the Jewish community for change. Meet with leaders of other local organizations to discuss their policies about outreach and openness to gay and lesbian Jews. For example, the Jewish Family and Children's Agency in Philadelphia has sponsored "coming out" groups, and the Jewish Federation has a task force on Gay and Lesbian issues. Groups could work to initiate programs like these in their own communities.

Foster change within synagogues. Is the rabbi open to doing gay and lesbian commitment ceremonies? Has there been an effort to hire openly gay or lesbian staff members? Synagogues can become arenas for change within the community.

These suggestions should indicate the enormous potential that Jewish organizations have for making justice for gay and lesbian Jews, enabling us to take our tradition seriously rather than ignoring it. Gay and Lesbian Awareness Week provides an opportunity to begin a process of making the Jewish community a place where lesbians feel at home.

Model Case: New Jewish Agenda

The group New Jewish Agenda provides an example of an organization that has applied its concept of justice to work for the rights and inclusion of gay and lesbian Jews. Agenda's case illustrates how a Jewish group that is not primarily focused on gay or lesbian issues can seek justice for gay and lesbian Jews.

New Jewish Agenda was founded in 1980. Its focus was on challenging the Jewish community to pay greater attention to issues of economic and social justice. Agenda's founders included gay men and lesbians, and the original platform of Agenda welcomed gay and lesbian members.[7] Lesbians and heterosexual feminists within Agenda were involved in a feminist task force that published an important pamphlet "Coming Out, Coming Home: Lesbian and Gay Jews and the Jewish Community." The text made suggestions for incorporating gay and lesbian concerns into the Jewish community. Agenda also sponsored a Havdallah ceremony and concert, which was attended by several hundred people, the night before the Gay and Lesbian March on Washington in 1987.[8] Agenda sponsored homophobia workshops in local chapters and incorporated many sessions on gay and lesbian Jewish issues in its national conferences.

Gay men and lesbians became significant leaders in the organization. Two of them, Andy Rose and Christie Balka, were inspired to edit the book *Twice Blessed: On Being Lesbian or Gay and Jewish*, which included essays from gay and lesbian perspectives on Jewish history, ritual, and community. The goal of the book was to demand full acceptance of gay and lesbian Jews into the broad spectrum of Jewish life. The editors of *Bridges*, a Jewish feminist journal that focuses on lesbian issues, also met one another in Agenda, and the organization helped facilitate the magazine's founding.[9]

Agenda continued to be a place where lesbian and gay Jews were at home in the Jewish community. The organization pursued issues that were crucial both to Jewish lesbian feminists and its own founding principle: the acceptance of the stranger. Under the leadership of lesbians, gay men, and their allies, and until its demise in 1993, Agenda continued to take strong stands on issues that were unpopular in the 1980s, such as a two-state solution to the Israeli-Palestinian conflict.

Appeals for Justice Based on Similarities

Lesbians have made gains in terms of recognition and acknowledgement in the Jewish community. There are now other organizations like Agenda where gay men and lesbians are included and appreciated. Lesbians have also been able to work on issues of inclusion of others and pursue careers as Jewish professionals—at least in some fields. We are beginning to experience justice within the Jewish community, but much work remains to be done.

For the most part, the acceptance of lesbians in the Jewish community has come about when we emphasize the ways in which we are like other Jews. Like all Jews, we are outsiders. We experience anti-Semitism because of our identification as Jews. We build Jewish institutions such as synagogues and communal organizations. We practice Judaism from a variety of perspectives, from traditional to nonobservant. Some of us commit ourselves to Jewish values such as long-term monogamous relationships that are sanctified through religious ritual and focused on raising another generation of Jewish children.

Our situation is not unlike that of the Jews in Western Europe at the beginning of the eighteenth century. In exchange for individual freedom, Jews were forced to give up our corporate identity. Some Jews gave up our differences entirely in order to gain acceptance in the Christian world. Most made Jewishness a private matter, as enlightenment leaders suggested: "Be a Jew at home and a man (sic) in the streets." It has taken almost two hundred years for Jews as a group to find acceptance by the outside world of our differences as well as our similarities.

For some lesbian Jews, particularly those who fit conventional gender roles and whose lifestyles are family oriented, fashioning our appeal for justice and inclusion on the basis of our similarities to other Jews has been rather successful. Jewish lesbians are very clearly part of some Jewish communities, and our presence cannot be ignored. Of course, our work for inclusion is not complete. We will not have succeeded until we are accepted by all segments of the Jewish community and not included only as tokens. But becoming part of the community is not enough. We have gained this inclusion by de-emphasizing those factors that make us outsiders in the first place. Now we must focus our energies on pursuing justice for lesbians who define ourselves as sexually different.

Justice for Jewish Lesbians as Sexual Beings

As David Biale has suggested, Jewish women are not perceived as being sexual.[10] It is not surprising that lesbians have underplayed our sexuality in a Jewish context. Our difference is based in no small part on our erotic attraction to other women. That fact cannot be hidden in our lives in the Jewish community. We must be able to express our sexuality, to flirt, to look for partners in the context of that community. Sex education in a Jewish context must include references to the ways in which lesbians are sexual with one another. Homophobia based on fear of lesbian sexuality must be confronted directly.

The sexual textures of our lesbian relationships are varied. In our dialogue with the Jewish community, we must be open about the fact that not all lesbians desire long-term, committed, monogamous relationships and not all lesbians want to be parents of children. Lesbian sexuality must be acceptable even if it takes less traditional forms.

Experimentation is part of a healthy approach to sexuality. Jewish lesbians may be involved in sex with multiple partners, the production of erotica, or sexual role-playing. Some are also involved in sadomasochism (s/m). S/m sexuality is broadly defined and may include fantasizing and role-playing. While part of s/m is the domination of one person over another, s/m activists claim that this domination is only a form of role-playing. In fact, the person who is being dominated takes control of the sexual encounter. Those who are engaged in s/m argue that it is parody that works to draw our attention to the inequitable power relationships in society. While we may argue that aspects of s/m like sexual violence and use of Nazi imagery are physically and psychically harmful, s/m sexuality requires a full discussion in the Jewish community. It cannot merely be ignored.

Often the acceptance of lesbians in the Jewish community has been predicated on the assumption that we have no choice about our sexuality, that being attracted to women is part of our genetic makeup. But if we are truly to be accepted in the Jewish community, it must be with the understanding that many of us do understand lesbianism as a choice for us.

Most lesbians have at some time in their lives engaged in heterosexual relationships. Many of us were married to men, often happily. Being open to lesbian relationships is a choice that we made based on a willingness to live a life without all the privileges of heterosexuality and on a desire to express our love of women in a sexual way. It means that we have opened ourselves to exploring erotic feelings toward other women that most women experience at some time in their lives.

For our acceptance in the Jewish community to be based on the assumption that lesbians are incapable of engaging in satisfying heterosexual relationships and therefore have no choice but to be in relationships with other women is not an acceptance based on justice. We cannot accept the assumption that heterosexuality is superior and that lesbianism is only for those who can't succeed in heterosexual relationships. Without true acceptance of the choices that make us different, we will never be partners in the Jewish world.

Jewish Lesbian Work Toward Justice for Others

Working toward achieving our goals for justice for Jewish lesbians is not sufficient. While it is important for us to be able to articulate what others must do for us, that cannot be our only concern. We must also talk about issues of justice that affect other Jews in our community and everyone in the world. There is no more important project for Jewish lesbians than to work on issues that will make justice possible not only for us but for others who are not like us.

Jewish lesbians have not taken up this responsibility sufficiently. Our inability to focus our efforts on an ethic of doing justice is related to the understanding of oppression from which our existence as Jewish lesbians originated. Many Jewish lesbians have focused on the ways in which we have been oppressed in society as Jews and as lesbians. While oppression theory argues that we must empower ourselves in the world, it is often the case that we retain and perpetuate our status as victims.

Doing justice must be based on a new understanding about the role of victims and oppressors. Micah's invocation is to do justice. That means that we must take an active role in creating opportunities for justice in this world. Asot Mishpat means that we cannot persist in perceiving ourselves as victims or in perceiving the world as split between the oppressed and the oppressor. This kind of dualistic thinking keeps us forever focused on the ways in which justice has not been done to us; it limits our ability to take power into our own hands and makes it impossible for us to engage in the task of doing justice.

From the position of victims we underestimate our own power to do justice. When we identify as victims we do not think about how to change power relations to bring about a more just world. All we see are the ways in which we are not being treated fairly ourselves.

Claiming the status of victim is seductive. It gives us credibility in a world where the victim is a hero. But victims are beloved only if they are willing to remain victims. When victims are no longer downtrodden, there is no role for them in our current system except as oppressors. Being a victim draws sympathy but does not give the victim the opportunity to change the dynamics of power.

Claiming the role of victim creates a situation that leads groups such as Jews and lesbians to pity and not respect ourselves. It also fosters comparisons of oppression. Despite our best efforts to avoid doing so, we focus on the ways in which our suffering compares with that of others. The problem is most clearly illustrated by Jews today in North America who live in relative comfort, free from oppression. We still cling to images of the Holocaust and claim the status of victim. We are wounded deeply by any and all expressions of anti-Semitism. No doubt, hatred of Jews is very real in the United States. But we often focus our energies claiming our victimization and ignore our own responsibility in the world for doing justice.

Ashkenazi Jewish lesbians forget the ways in which most of us are privileged because of the color of our skin in this country. We may be so engaged in seeing our own victimization that we forget the ways in which we contribute to the victimization of others. We cannot build coalitions if we do not acknowledge the difficult relationships between us. We also cannot build coalitions based on oppression alone; they must be built on a common view of a just society, of asot mishpat.

We need new categories to think about the possibilities for justice. In rethinking these questions, we may be able to put an end to the self-fulfilling prophecy of victim status and create new understandings of the way in which groups in a multicultural society interact. We can maintain our integrity as diverse groups and at the same time begin to work together to end injustice for all. It is time to stop viewing this world through the lens of oppressor and victim, for it has not enhanced our ability to do justice in the world.[11]

Instead we should look for opportunities to build coalitions with others whose goal is to create a just society and to challenge injustice for others within the Jewish community. When we work for justice, we do it as Jewish lesbians. It is important that we maintain our cultural heritage and identity and bring the wisdom that this heritage provides into our work in the world. We cannot neglect our own rights while we work for the rights of others. Of course it is easier to focus exclusively on our own problems and tempting to argue that no one will address our concerns if we do not take up our own cause. But the goal of doing justice is to be present for others and, by example, support the principle of working together toward the goal of a just society. Of course there cannot be a just society unless all groups are treated fairly. So in this model, Jewish lesbians must have our needs met as well as supporting the needs of others.

Supporting the needs of others means paying attention to those in the Jewish community who are also treated in a negative manner because of their sexuality. As Jewish lesbians, we must strongly support the rights of those people who define themselves as queer to find a place in the Jewish community.

Because the acceptance of gay men and lesbians into the Jewish community has been predicated on emphasizing the ways in which we are similar to other Jews, Jewish lesbians have demonstrated little interest in thinking about the perspectives of those who define themselves as queer, bisexual, and transgendered. Yet if we demand inclusion based on our differences, we must also consider how we include others whose difference is related to their sexual identities.

Like other identities, bisexuality does not describe a single phenomenon. A woman may define herself as bisexual for a number of reasons. She may be in transition between identifying as a heterosexual and coming out as a lesbian. She may have been in lesbian relationships and is now is involved with men but does not want to give up a connection to her lesbian past. She may be involved in relationships with women and men simultaneously. Or she may be involved in relationships with men and women at different times in her life. Like lesbians who claim that our sexuality is based on choice, bisexuals highlight the reality of a sexual identification based on choice. And bisexual identification may also involve non-monogamy. For these reasons, the Jewish community is resistant to bisexuality.

Jewish lesbians have our own disagreements with bisexuals.[12] Nevertheless, we need to be cognizant of the fact that bisexuality has been an important part of the lives of many Jewish lesbians and that we need to be in alliance with others in the Jewish community whose differences are similar to our own.

"Transgendered" is a term that includes a variety of phenomena. Transgendered people include cross-dressers, pre- and postoperative transsexuals and others whose gender identities are fluid. The phenomenon of transgendered identification complicates notions about sexual identity. Some transgendered people identify as either women or men and have a sexual identity based on their gender. Others do not, thereby throwing the whole question of sexual identity open. (Is the woman who takes male hormones and dresses like a man, who is in a relationship with another woman a lesbian? There is no simple answer to that question.)

Transgendered people raise important questions that do not have simple answers. Gender blending is problematic for the Jewish community because Judaism perpetuates rigid gender roles, even among liberal Jews. The Jewish community must question any concept of justice that limits human expression and has no rational basis. Lesbian Jews can begin to raise questions about welcoming transgendered Jews into our community. Lesbians also need to be open about the ways in which we confuse and complicate gender roles ourselves, even though that reality makes us look "queer" in the eyes of the Jewish community and threatens our acceptability. Jewish lesbians cannot afford to ignore the needs of other outsiders in the Jewish community because their issues threaten our status. If we are demanding that the Jewish community embrace those who are sexually different, we must make every effort to do so ourselves, despite the discomfort it may cause us.

All of these issues lead to the conclusion that asot mishpat requires the Jewish community to question its assumption that heterosexuality is normative and desirable for everyone. Rather, heterosexuality should be seen as one among many options, not the standard by which all else is judged. Acceptance of lesbians and gay men cannot be predicated on ignoring our sexuality, assuming that we do not choose our sexual identities, and denying differences such as bisexuality and transgendered existence. A rigorous and serious look at heterosexuality and its meaning within the Jewish community is the next step in dialogue.

But issues of justice inside the Jewish community are not the only ones that concern us. Jewish lesbians have models from our own community that have begun the process of coalition building and challenging unjust structures outside the Jewish community. The work of secular Jewish lesbian feminists provides an excellent example. Their focus on Jewish identity began when they noticed that their Jewishness was invisible in the lesbian feminist context. Their primary goal in exploring Jewish identity was to challenge the broader lesbian feminist movement to pay attention to the difference in its midst.[13] But they also wanted to open a dialogue with the rest of the Jewish community.[14]

In the process, these Jewish lesbians reconnected to Judaism and as a result have made significant contributions to Jewish life. Rather than focusing exclusively on their own oppression, they have worked on other issues facing the Jewish community, including building coalitions between Israelis and Palestinians and between African Americans and American Jews. Secular Jewish lesbian feminists moved on from naming their own oppression to dealing with other dimensions of oppression and doing coalition work.

One of the strongest contributions of secular Jewish lesbian feminism has been its focus on building coalitions with other marginalized groups. As Adrienne Rich has suggested, we must add another dimension to the famous words of Rabbi Hillel, "If I am not for myself who will be for me? But if I am only for myself, what am I? And if not now, when?" To this, Rich added "and if not with others, how?"[15]

Jewish lesbians have built coalitions between themselves and African-American lesbians. *Yours In Struggle*, a book of three essays by Jewish lesbian feminist Elly Bulkin, African-American lesbian feminist Barbara Smith, and white Christian lesbian feminist Minnie Bruce Pratt explores these connections. Bulkin emphasizes the ways in which anti-Semitism and racism are often used to divide Jewish and African-American communities. She suggests that while we must begin with identity politics, it is crucial that we transcend those boundaries, breaking down the divisions between "us" and "them." Rather than choose between oppressions, we must work on both.[16] What enables Bulkin, Smith, and Pratt to begin to talk together is their shared identity as lesbians. This commonality also undergirds a remarkable dialogue on identity by Jewish and African-American feminists in the lesbian feminist journal *Conditions*. For these women, survival as lesbians in their respective communities is the common thread that permits dialogue to begin.[17]

In a similar vein, Jewish lesbians have focused energy on Palestinian/Israeli dialogue. The Middle East often surfaces as an issue in African-American/Jewish dialogue, because many African Americans identify with the Palestinians and because of the intimate link between American Jews and Israel. Ironically, the publication of *Nice Jewish Girls* coincided with the 1982 Israeli invasion of Lebanon. Klepfisz noted how painful it was for her to claim her pride in being Jewish at the same time that Jews in the Middle East were oppressing others.[18] Many Jewish lesbian feminists devoted much of their energy to working to end the Israeli occupation. Their efforts included creating dialogue groups, making films, producing radio programs, and organizing protests.

These efforts are but a few examples of the possibilities for coalition building. Seeking justice as part of a Jewish lesbian transformation of Judaism means taking the opportunities to remind our community about looking outside its confines and connecting to others who need our help and support.

Guided by Micah's precept we have a set of goals to work toward: begin with self-acceptance, continue with love within our close communities, and reach beyond ourselves to demand and create a world within which there is justice for everyone. These goals are not for lesbian Jews only. This is a model for the transformation of Judaism from a lesbian perspective that derives from our interpretation of biblical text.

Seven

Modern Texts:
Jewish Lesbian Sexuality

New interpretations of ancient texts make it possible to envision Judaism transformed through a lesbian perspective. A second dimension of this project is calling attention to other, later texts that have gone unnoticed but that are an important part of constructing a lesbian Jewish past. The effort to find texts about Jewish lesbians in the past requires including sources that have not previously been considered part of a Jewish textual tradition. Unlike the ancient texts I have discussed in previous chapters, these modern texts explore the real lives and literary representations of Jewish lesbians in the one hundred years prior to Stonewall and the second wave of feminism, which marked the beginning of the current era of feminist and gay liberation. Our textual traditions must be broadened to incorporate texts that provide insight into Jewish lesbian life throughout the later part of the modern era. Finding textual traces of a Jewish lesbian existence corrects the inaccurate perception that there were no Jewish lesbians until the present and expands our notion of sacred texts to incorporate stories and histories that have been left out of the record.

Although I would have liked to include earlier materials, all of the sources that I discuss here come from the twentieth century. This is not surprising, given that female homoeroticism in earlier eras is much more obscure and that love between women only became a public issue in this century, as new understandings of lesbianism developed.

As lesbian culture has evolved, lesbians have come to understand the importance of having a history, having sacred texts of our own to tell our story.[1] The concept that there are lesbian texts has itself been challenged. Sexuality was not, until recent times, a subject of historical research. Lesbians were not identified as a group or class, so no effort was made to include lesbians in historical accounts. Rather, lesbianism was discussed as a pathology related to gender nonconformity.[2] Over the past few decades, sexuality has become an important subject for historical discourse.[3] While relatively easy to reconstruct a history of male homosexuality through texts,[4] the history of sexual relations between women has remained more obscure.[5] Research on female homoeroticism in the past is complicated by the limited textual references to women in general,[6] and by what historian Blanche Wiesen Cook describes as an:

> historical denial of lesbianism which accompanies the persistent refusal to acknowledge the variety and intensity of women's emotional and erotic experiences. That denial involves the notion . . . that physical love between women was experimental masturbation, studious preparation for marriage [and] . . . that erotic and sexual pleasure without male penetration is not erotic and sexual pleasure.[7]

Recent studies of lesbian history have not focused on the precursors to contemporary Jewish lesbian existence. It is imperative for several reasons that Jewish lesbians begin to find our own texts and reconstruct our own history. Jewish lesbians have made unique contributions to Jewish culture, and these stories should be told. Information about Jewish lesbians in the past should be transmitted as part of a standard Jewish education. Jewish lesbians should not have to grow up thinking we are the only ones who "are different"; we should know that we have models and stories of Jewish lesbians who lived in the past. Many of the sources from which I have constructed a modern Jewish lesbian textual tradition are lit-

erary texts written by men. Others are based on the lives of twentieth-century lesbians who associated with the Jewish community.[8]
Taken together, they form a picture of Jewish lesbian existence in
the recent past. This picture is however by no means exhaustive.
We are only beginning to find texts that are part of the hidden history of Jewish lesbians.

In this chapter I concentrate on texts that look at Jewish lesbian
sexuality to see how past generations interpreted the sexual status
of lesbians in the absence of an outright prohibition against lesbian
sexual behavior. It is possible to see the same forces in these texts
as those at work today among Jews coming to terms with lesbianism. The texts exoticize lesbian sex, psychologize it as immature
sexual behavior, and contribute to lesbian invisibility. Yet read
against the grain they form the basis for a reconstruction of a
Jewish lesbian textual tradition.

The Works of Sigmund Freud

Sigmund Freud's work had a significant impact on bringing lesbian
sexuality to public consciousness in Western society. In addition,
Freud has had a particularly strong influence on the thinking of
Jews.[9] Because Freud's influence was far-reaching, his ideas about
women in general, and lesbians specifically, have had a major
impact on the way lesbian love has been understood during most of
the twentieth century.

Freud thought that all human beings are born with the capacity
for bisexuality. He viewed lesbianism as a natural phenomenon.
Freud did not believe that lesbian orientation could be changed and
suggested that lesbians should be helped to lead productive and
happy lives despite their homoerotic attractions. He did not consider lesbianism to be an illness but thought that the repression of
lesbian feelings and attractions could result in psychological
trauma. He also defined lesbianism in relationship to a child's pre-
oedipal desire for the mother.[10]

Despite Freud's openness to lesbian sexuality, he missed its crucial role in one of his most famous cases, that of Ida Bauer to whom
he gave the pseudonym of Dora in his writeup of the case,
"Fragment of an Analysis of a Case of Hysteria." Ida's brother was

Otto Bauer, a noted socialist politician, and the Bauers were a prominent Jewish family in Vienna. Ida Bauer never identified her homoerotic feelings during her lifetime, and Freud did not raise the issue of such feelings during the course of her brief (eleven-week) analysis. Ida did marry, although unhappily. Another psychiatrist who later treated Ida reported that Ida complained bitterly about married life and men in general and that she exhibited a "disgust with heterosexuality."[11]

In his discussion of the case Freud was highly self-critical for not taking her lesbianism more seriously; yet he never pursued this question in the case analysis even after he recognized it.[12] This despite the fact that during the course of the analysis, Dora introduced her erotic attraction for a friend of the family, Frau K, who was having an affair with her father. She mentioned that they shared a bed when Dora came to visit the K's and that they read popular erotic literature together. She made reference to Frau K's "adorable white body" and never expressed anger and resentment toward her, despite Frau K's affair with her father and despite Frau K's later betrayal of Dora.

That Freud never considered the possibility that Dora's dreams and memories could have been erotic to her (or to Frau K herself) makes clear his limited interest in exploring the dimensions of lesbian sexuality that were unrelated to men and their lives. Like the rabbis, Freud showed little concern about what women did in private.

According to Freud, all children experience an erotic attraction for their mothers. During adolescence it is perfectly natural for girls to transfer that attraction to others of the same sex. But the psychologically mature woman sublimates that desire and becomes an adult by developing a heterosexual attraction. Lesbian women never complete the maturation process, thus, in Freud's view retaining an immature sexuality.

In recent years this conceptualization has been challenged by lesbian feminists. Adrienne Rich questioned the notion that heterosexuality is the ultimate goal and asked why, if Freudian psychology assumes that both men and women begin life with an erotic attraction for the mother, only women must renounce their desire for the mother by choosing a man as their object of sexual desire in order to reach maturity.[13] This question also suggests that while

Freud claimed to view bisexuality as normal, the theories themselves suggest that he still treated heterosexuality as the norm. By defining lesbian attraction as immature, and grounding it in infantile attraction to the mother, or in his terminology the pre-oedipal phase, Freud's work also pathologized lesbianism.

This perception hampered Freud's ability to understand lesbianism, as is illustrated by his handling of Dora's case. Many feminists have criticized Freud for his failure to take the attraction between Dora and Frau K seriously. Mary Jacobus suggests that Freud failed in this case because he focused on the oedipal desire (assuming Dora loved Herr K as a substitute for her father) and missed the power of the pre-oedipal desire (Dora really loved Frau K who was a substitute for her mother).[14] Here Jacobus follows Freud's own reasoning, seeing lesbian attraction as rooted in love of the mother.

Feminist critic Maria Ramas argues that the case has deep implications for same-sex love between women.[15] She states that Dora's case "encompasses issues beyond the thesis that Ida Bauer was a lesbian . . . at the deepest levels of meaning, Ida Bauer's hysteria was exactly what it appeared to be—a repudiation of the meaning of heterosexuality."[16] Ramas goes on to argue that Freud in fact assumes the naturalness of heterosexuality rather than bisexuality. Otherwise he would not have arrived at the conclusion that Dora was attracted to Herr K rather than to Frau K. Ramas argues that Freud's view is phallocentric and Dora's dreams and memories could have been interpreted differently. Freud never considered the possibility that the intimacy between Frau K and Dora was erotic to them both. As Ramas interprets the story, Dora's father's and Herr K's actual roles were to mask the homosexual desire between the two women. In this interpretation both Dora and Frau K are repressing lesbian desire. This interpretation makes plausible both Frau K's betrayal of Dora when confronted with their sexual secrets and Dora's inability to repudiate or condemn Frau K.

According to Ramas's interpretation, Dora's lesbianism was a rebellion against the patriarchal system in which she found herself. It is the repression of those lesbian tendencies, and their later betrayal by the woman she loved, that led to her hysterical symptoms.

By studying the text of Dora's case, it is possible to begin to understand some of the problems facing lesbians in the earlier part of this century. Freud's inability to see lesbian desire as a mature form of loving detracts from his positive assessment of it. This understanding of lesbian love as based in pre-oedipal attraction for the mother has influenced Jewish representations of lesbianism and has detracted from a Jewish acceptance of lesbian sexuality. The image of the lesbian as immature woman needs to be highlighted as part of the problematic picture of the role of lesbianism in Judaism.

Viewing lesbianism through the lens of women's attractions for their mothers and therefore defining lesbian sexuality as immature behavior were major factors that contributed to the trivialization of lesbians in the period I am examining. As lesbianism was seen as immature behavior, feminists wanting to support the cause of women's equality avoided labeling the women that they were studying as lesbians, for fear of making them seem to be immature women, incapable of handling adult problems. This desire not to depict women as immature contributed to later writers' efforts to ignore lesbianism in that period, or to downplay female homoeroticism when they found manifestations of it.

The Life of Lillian Wald

This attitude is in evidence in Doris Daniels's feminist study of social reformer Lillian Wald. Lillian Wald grew up in Rochester, New York, in a wealthy German Jewish family. She showed no interest in living a traditional life, which would have meant remaining in Rochester and marrying. She applied to Vassar College at age 16 but was rejected because of her youth. After living the life of a socialite for several years, Wald decided to become a nurse and move to New York City. There she met and moved in with Mary Brewster, a classmate at nursing school. Both resolved that their life's work would be to improve the lives of the new, predominantly Jewish immigrants to New York City, helping them obtain health care and social services. To that end, Wald created the Visiting Nurses Association, so that tenement dwellers could receive nursing care in their own homes.

With the help of noted Jewish philanthropist Jacob Schiff, Wald and Brewster founded the Henry Street Settlement, which Wald and many other women working among the poor on the Lower East

Side made their home for the next fifty years. The settlement house was part of a national movement of middle-class, college-educated women—the best known of whom was Jane Addams, Wald's counterpart in Chicago, who started the famed Hull House there—who lived and worked among immigrants and the poor. During the course of her lifetime Wald was involved in many other causes. She was active in the suffrage movement and helped to found the Women's International League for Peace and Freedom as well as the American Union Against Militarism, the precursor of the American Civil Liberties Union.

Wald's work was intimately connected to the Jewish community. Raised as a Reform Jew, she did not maintain any affiliation with organized religious activity. But the focus of her life's work at the settlement house was with Jewish immigrants, and her knowledge of German was most helpful in communicating with them in their native Yiddish. Her main sources of support were Jewish philanthropists. These men were deeply committed to Jewish life and viewed the settlement movement as a crucial factor in the assimilation of the Jewish immigrants from Eastern Europe to the American Jewish way of life.

Nonetheless, Wald did not identify strongly as a Jew and was surprised when others saw her in this way. Wald's German Jewish background may explain this. Although a vibrant German Jewish culture existed in the United States, late nineteenth-century German Jews themselves were not comfortable with the word "Jew" and its associations with the world of the new Eastern European immigrants. In addition many were also uncomfortable associating with their Eastern European coreligionists. German Jews saw themselves as a group apart and preferred to refer to themselves as Hebrew, Israelite, or "of the Mosaic religion," a pattern reflected in the names of their institutions: the Union of American Hebrew Congregations, for example.

Wald's work and her associations made her part of the Jewish world, however. Later in life Wald was asked to be part of a project on biographies of Jewish women, and the Jewish community claimed her as a role model.[17] While no one considers it problematic to identify Wald as part of the Jewish community, despite her lack of strong identification with that community, claiming Wald as part of lesbian history has been strongly contested by historians, including feminists.

There is no evidence that Wald had a single lifelong companion. But she did have a strong support group consisting of the women who lived at the settlement house. It was with these women (Mary Brewster, with whom she lived prior to finding 165 Henry Street, Lavinia Dock, Yssabella Waters) that Wald made a life, traveled, and worked. She also had close working relationships with Florence Kelley, with whom she worked on child welfare issues and with settlement leader Jane Addams and the women of Hull House.

In addition to her settlement house coworkers, there were other women with whom Wald was intimately involved. Among these was a group of younger, affluent women who looked up to Wald in admiration. She also spent time with a group of society women who were more interested in Wald as a person than in the settlement work.

On the basis of her homosocial lifestyle, Blanche Wiesen Cook claims Wald as a lesbian. Her analysis focuses on Wald's relationship with two women, Mabel Kittredge and Helen Arthur. For a number of years, Kittredge lived at the settlement house and was both demanding and jealous of Wald's time. In one letter to her, Kittredge wrote: "No wonder I am called 'one of your crushes' . . . It is kiss and run or run without kissing—there really isn't time for anything else."[18] Kittredge also wrote of her doubts about Wald's affection toward her, but then corrected herself: "And yet you love me—the plant on my table tells me so . . . and a look that I see in your eyes makes me sure."[19] After a while Kittredge tired of seeking Wald's affection, and soon thereafter Wald developed a similar relationship with Helen Arthur.

Wiesen Cook concludes that Wald lived in a

> homosocial world that was also erotic. Her primary emotional needs and desires were fulfilled by women . . . Insistence on genital evidence of proof for a lesbian identity derives from a male model that has very little to do with the love, support and sensuality that exists between women.[20]

Wald's biographer, Doris Daniels, disagrees with Cook's interpretation of Wald as a lesbian. Nonetheless, Daniels compiled evidence in her brief biography that supported Cook's conclusion. She devoted a chapter to Wald's relationships with other women and provided evidence concerning Wald's primarily homosocial world. The segments of Wald's letters quoted by Daniels powerfully evoke the romantic nature of the friendships at Henry Street; for example, Wald wrote to Yssabella Waters, one of the women who lived there with her:

> It seems too odd to have you an up-towner. I cannot visualize you in the dining room of the hotel, though it is not so hard to see you in a bedroom there.
>
> You may be sure that I know how fatigued and strained you are, and I wish to heavens that it were in my power to give you refreshment of soul and body.[21]

Daniels also made reference to letters from women such as Mabel Kittredge and Helen Arthur. But she argued vigorously against concluding from this evidence that Wald was a lesbian:

> Is it not possible for heterosexual women to love other women and to seek emotional support from them? Do all intimate relationships between women have a sexual component and should such relationships be called lesbian if that erotic dimension is absent or unprovable?[22]

Daniels chose to mark the boundary between lesbians and heterosexual women at the point of genital sexuality. She begins as Wiesen Cook suggests, with a male model of sexuality. From that perspective erotic love between women also must involve genital contact to count as sexual. Wiesen Cook's view incorporates the sensual, erotic, and romantic dimensions of women's relationships into a framework she defines as lesbian.[23] What is at issue here is not what Lillian Wald herself did or did not do but how lesbianism is defined.

Daniels argues further that even the language expressed in Wald's letters is not indicative of romantic feelings, because such expressive letters were common at the time and meant nothing. She claims that women like Wald sublimated their sexuality for a "higher purpose." Wiesen Cook argues that Wald did not need to sublimate sexuality, that it was present in the erotic, homosocial world in which she lived.

Daniels's arguments are predicated on seeing lesbianism as a stigmatized identity. She does not want to call Wald a lesbian, because doing so is to cast aspersions on her. For those of us to whom calling someone a lesbian is a matter of pride, a respite from hiding, and an opportunity to challenge the way history has been written, Lillian Wald's lesbianism is a positive addition to understanding her life. I view her not as a lonely spinster but as a woman who was fulfilled by her love of other women.

For Daniels, Wald's "sexual preferences are [not] essential to an understanding of her public career in social reform and feminism."[24] I disagree. I see her personal life choices as part of her feminism and essential to her work as a social reformer—to live a happy, creative, and fulfilling life with other women.

From a historical perspective I wish to claim Lillian Wald's life as a text for Jewish lesbian history. As Daniels notes, Wald did not recognize herself as a Jewish role model, nor did she take her Jewish identity seriously. Nevertheless, the Jewish community's claim to Wald as a role model is uncontested, and she appears in many Sunday School textbooks as an exemplary Jewish figure. I think those same textbooks might also represent Wald as a lesbian.

Lesbian Sexuality in the Writings of Sholom Asch

The most explicit presentation of lesbian sexuality from a Jewish perspective is found in the 1907 play by Yiddish playwright and novelist Sholom Asch, *The God of Vengeance*.[25] Although bolder in its frank depiction of erotic love between women than ancient sources, the play's point of view is similar to earlier rabbinic texts: a lesbian relationship is not a serious cause for concern.

Asch's play is about Yekel, a man who owns a brothel in Poland at the end of the nineteenth century. Because his young daughter, Rivkele, resides in an apartment above the brothel, he takes special precautions so that none of the patrons of the establishment will come upstairs to seduce her. To this end, he buys a Torah scroll and keeps it in the house. To commission the writing of a Torah scroll is an act of extreme piety. To keep the scroll in the house renders the home "kosher" (acceptable) in distinction to the "treif" (forbidden) brothel below.

While no men enter Yekel's home, Rivkele does come into contact with the people in the brothel. Unbeknownst to Yekel, Manke, one of the prostitutes, has become a regular visitor upstairs. She was invited there by Sarah, Rivkele's mother, who brings Manke into her home to teach her daughter embroidery. Manke helps Rivkele create a Torah cover for the new scroll, and in the process their relationship has grown to something more than friendship. In the opening scene, Rivkele sings Manke's praises to her mother. She suggests that Manke could come upstairs to comb her hair: "She does it so beautifully. She makes my hair so smooth . . . And her hands are so cool."[26] Sarah warns Rivkele that her father will scold her if he knows that Manke has been in the house. Manke is part of the "treif" world that Yekel wants to keep away from his daughter.

Yet Manke and Rivkele do meet again, in two very powerful scenes depicting lesbian love that include passionate kissing, fondling breasts, combing hair, and romantic dialogue, echoing the erotic dialogue between lovers in the Song of Songs. Asch's stage directions for their first meeting indicate the nature of their relationship. As Rivkele talks to her mother, Manke "appears in the doorway at the rear. First she thrusts in her head, shaking her finger playfully at Rivkele; Rivkele goes over to her, walking cautiously backwards, beckoning to her as she does so. The room is fast growing dark." At this point, Rivkele "falls into Manke's arms . . . Manke kisses her passionately."[27]

Later, Manke returns to the apartment, and the women steal off in the rain. Manke speaks:

Nestle close to me, Ever so close. Warm yourself next to me . . . Now rest your face snugly in my bosom . . . And let your body touch mine. It's so cool as if water were running between us. I uncovered your breasts and washed them with the rainwater that trickled down my arms. Your breasts are so white and soft. And the blood in them cools under the touch. Like white snow,—like a frozen stream. And their fragrance is like the grass on the meadow.[28]

The two make plans to go off together:

Manke. Then we come closer to one another, for we are bride and bridegroom, you and I. We embrace. (*She puts her arm around her*.) Ever so tightly. And kiss, very softly, like this. (*They kiss*.) And we turn so red, we're so bashful. It's nice, isn't it, Rivkele?

Rivkele. Yes, Manke, yes.

Manke. (*Lowers her voice, whispering in her ear*.) And then we go to sleep together. Nobody sees, nobody hears. Only you and I. Like this. (*She presses Rivkele to her*.) Do you want to sleep with me tonight like this? Eh?

Rivkele . . . I do, I do.

Manke. Come, come.[29]

The two go back to the home Manke shares with another prostitute and a procurer. The procurer returns Rivkele to her father's home, and the father is distraught. When he asks her if she's still a chaste Jewish girl, she replies "I don't know." The father then sends her down to the brothel, where he assumes she now belongs.

The parallels to the treatment of lesbian sexuality in classical Jewish texts are not coincidental. Like the author of *Sifra*, Manke sees this relationship in terms of a marriage. She speaks of sleeping in the same bed, which was the issue in question in the passage in the Talmud concerning Samuel's daughters. Rivkele's father questions her about her chastity, raising the same issue discussed in the Talmud: Is a woman who has performed a lesbian sex act considered a virgin, and therefore eligible for marriage? Yekel seems to agree with the minority opinion expressed in the Talmud that says that she is no longer a virgin. The daughter/wife (the woman in direct relationship to the male protagonist) is punished with a change in her status, but the prostitute who initiated the encounter is not. The love between Rivkele and Manke has the potential to endanger both the Jewish people and the integrity of the family.

Although lesbian behavior is not compatible with the norms of Jewish life in this play, it is not treated with extreme negativity, fear, or anger.

Asch does not portray religious tradition in opposition to the lesbian relationship. In fact, that very relationship is the instrument that teaches Yekel that he cannot use the Torah as a magical protection from his own connections to the sexual underworld from which he derives his living. By depriving him of a daughter "The God of Vengeance" punishes Yekel more severely than Rivke and

Manke, who are permitted to continue their relationship. Rivkele still lives under her father's roof, even though she is now downstairs with the other "treif" Jews who are sexual transgressors.

The love between the women is depicted sympathetically, as both tender and erotic. Asch was distressed at the negative reactions to the 1923 English language premiere of *God of Vengeance*. At that time, he discussed his interpretation of the relationship between Rivkele and Manke:

> As to the scenes between Manke and Rivkele, on every European stage, especially in Russia, they were the most poetic of all . . . This love between the two girls is not only an erotic one. It is the unconscious mother love of which they are deprived.[30]

While acknowledging the sexual nature of the love between the two women, Asch also provided this psychological motivation to explain the women's passion for one another. This idea of lesbianism as "unconscious mother love" made it safe. In adding this explanation, Asch shows that he regards the attraction between Manke and Rivkele as something both erotic and trivial.

Reading this text today through a lesbian lens, we feel delighted with the passion depicted on stage between the two women. And we could certainly write our own midrash about their life together, perhaps after their escape from the brothel. This play is a powerful text that models sexual love between Jewish lesbians.

Lesbian Sexuality and Isaac Bashevis Singer

This openness to lesbian sexuality is also manifested in the writings of Isaac Bashevis Singer. Singer's short story "Zeitl and Rickel" also illustrates the notion that there is nothing in the Jewish tradition that is opposed to lesbian love. It is only the prejudice of the Jews in the story that prohibit the lesbian protagonists from living in peace. Both Asch and Singer seem to be mocking the societal attitudes, manifested in the Jewish community, which revile lesbian behavior.

In Singer's tale of lesbian love, tradition, as exemplified by the local rabbi, is sympathetic to the lesbian couple. Zeitl and Rickel also expect their dead parents to welcome them in the afterlife. And the relationship between the women is depicted as both mutual and equal.

Zeitl and Rickel ignore the townspeople who are aghast at their behavior. The women go out for walks holding one another, are seen by the nightwatchman kissing each other on the mouth, speak romantically to each other, and live alone together. When people complain about them to the rabbi, he suggests, "There is nothing in the Torah to forbid it. The ban applies only to men. Besides, since there are no witnesses, it is forbidden to spread rumors."[31] The rabbi sees no reason to respond to the complaints. In fact, he charges the complainants themselves with a more serious violation of the ethics of Torah, lashon hara, spreading rumors.

The story ends with Zeitl and Rickel's preparations to end their discomfort in this world. They fast, do penance, and shave their heads as if in preparation for marriage. They become intensely pious, have a special meeting with a visiting rabbi, and even worship in the men's section of the synagogue. These activities are in preparation for a suicide pact, which they ultimately carry out. When Zeitl explains to Rickel that everyone is there waiting for them in heaven, she says, "We shall get married up there, too. In heaven there is no difference between men and women."[32] Their actions shock and dismay the people of the town, who refuse to bury them in the cemetery. The house they lived in is said to be haunted by their ghosts.

Zeitl and Rickel's fate is not unlike that of lesbians of earlier eras who received no acceptance from society and often were led to take their own lives. Yet there are elements in this story that can be a valuable resource for Jewish lesbian textual transformation. For example, we can interpret their suicide as not born of despair but of hope. In Singer's view it is the community that perceives them as dangerous. But Jewish tradition (in the guise of the rabbi, their own religious behavior, and the plans they had for the afterlife) is accepting of them. They lived outside the community's expectations, but within their own understanding of their faith. What is unusual in this story is their faith and connection to Jewish tradition. Their willingness to die is predicated on the belief that in the eyes of God and their ancestors their love is good and pure.

This is also an unusual portrayal of a lesbian relationship as both partners adopt masculine behavior and dress. That both women are "masculine" indicates that Singer did not make the assumption common to the period that lesbian love was only an imitation of heterosexual attraction between active and passive partners.

But however we may read these texts, they view lesbian sexuality through the perceptions and values of Jewish men—trivialized, exoticized, or pathologized. Because lesbian behavior was viewed in these ways, the historical record does not include much—if any—information about women who lived lesbian and Jewish lives in the earlier part of the twentieth century. The paucity of examples of Jewish lesbians from this period is also attributable to the attitudes prevalent in European and American cultures that pathologized lesbian behavior and forced women who wanted to make their lives with other women to do so in ways that would not make their lives together public.

The Life of Pauline Newman

Scholars of lesbian history are now discovering a great deal about women who lived as lesbians in the earlier part of the century. Pauline Newman (1889–1986) is one such woman. The story of Newman's life opens up a world that has been previously hidden from public view but deserves a place in Jewish history; it becomes one of the missing Jewish lesbian texts.

Newman lived openly as a Jew and in a committed relationship with Frieda Miller, with whom she raised a child. Newman divided her professional life between commitments to the world of Jewish socialism and the movement to gain rights and protections for women.[33]

Newman was born in Kovno, Russia. She was raised there by parents who embraced Jewish tradition and who made her aware of anti-Semitism in Russia and abroad. As historian Annelise Orleck recounts it, Newman always remembered the tension in her home as her father read about the Dreyfus trial. Her father taught Talmud and educated his daughter to be literate in Hebrew. Her contact with the religious world, even at an early age, taught her to be skeptical. She recalled a discomfort with the segregation of men and women in worship that fueled her fight against sex discrimination in later life.

Newman's socialist vision was also derived from her Jewish roots. She spent her professional career working to gain rights for workers. She began her career at age sixteen, organizing Yiddish-speaking women workers on New York's Lower East Side. She began publishing stories and commentaries in the *Jewish Daily Forward* about the bad working conditions in the factories, and in 1907 she organized a rent strike. The strike was unsuccessful in its immediate goals but had profound repercussions. It galvanized the energies of many women on the Lower East Side, initiated a discussion of rent control, and drew the attention of the leaders of the settlement movement, including Lillian Wald. As a result of this strike Newman began to achieve recognition as a young activist.

Newman took to the road as an organizer for the International Ladies Garment Workers Union (ILGWU). Traveling all over the country, she educated women workers on behalf of the union. While she was on the road, the tragic Triangle Shirtwaist Fire took the lives of many of Newman's old friends and concentrated her energies even more dramatically.

During this time Newman struggled over her "deep confusion about her intense friendships with women and unsuccessful romances with men."[34] Although she worked well with the Jewish working-class men in the union and always felt at home with them, she also needed the company of women in her life. She decided to pursue her work for a better standard of living for workers in the context of the women's movement. However, Newman would always manage to live in two worlds. She never abandoned her ties to either Jewish socialism or working women.

Newman went to work with the Women's Trade Union League (WTUL), an organization of upper-class and working-class women who supported the worker's movement. In 1916 she agreed to organize a chapter of the WTUL in Philadelphia and settled there for several years. In 1917, during the course of her work, Newman met Frieda Miller, a research assistant in the Economics Department at Bryn Mawr College who had been raised in Wisconsin, the daughter of a wealthy manufacturing family. Newman and Miller fell in love, moved in together, and from that point on ran the Philadelphia WTUL together, with Miller serving as secretary.

In 1923 Miller and Newman left the Philadelphia WTUL and traveled to Vienna for the Third International Congress of Working Women. Their European trip had another purpose; they stopped in Germany and told the world that they had adopted a war orphan, Elisabeth. In fact, Miller had become pregnant as a result of a relationship with a married man, and the trip was made in part so that she could give birth away from home. Elisabeth did not know that Miller was her birth mother until she was a teenager. Upon their return to the states, they moved to New York and took up residence in the West Village, where they could live together publicly and comfortably.[35]

Upon their move to New York, Newman returned to work for the ILGWU as the Education Director for its newly opened Health Center. She remained in the post for sixty years. Miller, due in part to her connections with other upper-middle-class activists, began a career as a leading expert on labor issues, working in Albany and ultimately in Washington as head of the Women's Bureau under Franklin Roosevelt. Miller often relied on Newman as a consultant, and both worked effectively in the world of politics. Through her connections to upper-class women, Newman was instrumental in developing legislation to meet her original goals for safe working conditions for American workers, men and women.

Newman was able to live in two worlds—the Jewish world of socialist union organizers by day, and Miller's upper-class world at home. While their daughter Elisabeth called Miller "mother," Newman did much of the child-rearing. Newman did not keep these worlds completely separate. Her male coworkers and all her friends knew about her family life; she kept a photograph of her daughter on her desk. All correspondence to her sent regards to Frieda and Elisabeth. Orleck suggests that much of Newman's success was based on her ability to live in two worlds. The union men expressed happiness that she had a home life because it kept her from being a sexual threat and in a traditional, if unusual, woman's role. Her ties to Jewish socialism allowed her an arena where she could exercise independence from the upper-class world of politics that she shared with Miller.

In 1949 Miller left her position in government, and the two women traveled together to investigate working conditions for women in Germany. Miller continued to desire to travel and be involved in politics. Their different paths led them to separate for six years, from 1958 to 1964. They were reconciled in 1965 and continued to live together in their Twelfth Street home until Miller's illness required that she live in a nursing home, where she died in 1973.

Newman lived until 1986, first in the home she and Miller had shared and later in the home of her daughter, Elisabeth Burger Owen. Newman was often asked to speak for the ILGWU and had frequent requests from feminists for interviews in the 1970s. She was reportedly uncomfortable with their interest in her personal life and feared that her life would be sensationalized by their accounts. She threatened to sue when one feminist published an article that suggested that Newman and Miller were lesbians.[36] Her discomfort with the new generation of feminists was not uncommon; many women who had lived in longtime companionships, or who had been part of the underground lesbian culture in the 1950s were skeptical of the motives of the lesbian feminist movement of the 1970s. These women saw the private world as a separate sphere and did not see any political implications in the way they lived their lives.

As Orleck points out, Newman did not hide her personal life at any time. Her contemporaries knew about and respected her relationship with Miller. In her nineties she left her personal papers, including passionate correspondence with Miller, to the Schlesinger Library at Radcliffe College. While she was reluctant to talk about herself, Newman did not hide. She successfully lived in two worlds, the Jewish world of the socialist labor movement and the women's world of romantic involvement and women's politics. But she never brought the two together.

Newman would be an important addition to Jewish textbooks, where she is rarely, if ever, mentioned. The Jewish labor movement was an important part of American Jewish history, and Newman's long and crucial role in it should be studied and remembered.

The writings of Asch, Singer, and Freud and the stories of Lillian Wald and Pauline Newman are all textual resources for a lesbian transformation of Judaism. The lesbians in these texts were all at least depicted as women, even if as immature or misguided. More complicated for Jewish lesbian existence today is the correlative view of lesbians not as women but as a third sex. This aspect of lesbian existence raises issues of gender nonconformity that are deeply threatening in Jewish life and are the main source of difficulty surrounding a later acceptance of lesbianism in Judaism. Nevertheless, some of the stories we find of gender nonconformists are powerful texts for contemporary Jewish lesbians who seek to challenge assumptions about gender in Judaism.

Eight

Modern Texts:
Lesbians as Gender Nonconformists

As I discussed in the last chapter, some Jewish sources in the early twentieth century viewed lesbians in a nonthreatening light primarily because the choice to love other women was seen as a sign of psychological immaturity and not as a danger to the primacy of heterosexuality. However, the most common view of lesbians at the time was that they were "inverts"—members of a third sex, not really women but something entirely other.

These gender nonconformists were very problematic for Jewish sensibilities for two reasons. Traditional Jewish values prescribe a rigid division of gender roles, and any confusion or blending of genders is seen as a threat. Second, much anti-Semitic rhetoric questioned the masculinity of Jewish men. So any hint that Jewish women were not "real women" threatened the integrity of Jewish masculinity. The stories of lesbians as gender nonconformists that I examine in this chapter can be read as stories of women who challenged Jewish norms and raised important questions about gender in Jewish life.

Defining Gender Nonconformists

In the late nineteenth and early twentieth centuries, the works of the sexologists (most notably Richard von Krafft-Ebing and Havelock Ellis) brought the existence of love between women in Western cultures to public attention.[1] Ellis and Krafft-Ebing studied groups of working-class women in Britain and Germany and concluded that they were "sexual inverts": women who were born with the soul of a man in the body of a woman. The sexologists defined sexual inversion as mental illness. They had little interest in women who had erotic attractions for other women but whose sexual desires did not also incorporate behaviors that were outside of traditional gender roles. Their attention was focused on the women who appeared to be different, who were thought to possess "unnatural" attributes that made them dissatisfied with being women in the world, and compelled them to desire to be like men: to adopt male prerogatives in dress, comportment, work, and choice of sexual partners. The sexologists' concerns with these "unnatural women" form a contrast to traditional Jewish texts, which were more concerned about the wives of men who engaged in *mesolelot* than with their (presumably "unnatural") sexual partners. Modern Jewish texts, however, have much to say about women who were born "with the soul of a man."

The Maid of Ludmir

There are many examples of gender nonconformist women in early twentieth-century Jewish writings, all of whom were described as possessing "men's souls in women's bodies." Samuel Horodetzky wrote about one such woman, Hannah Rachel Webermacher, the Maid of Ludmir.[2] As a child, Hannah Rachel was interested in studying Jewish law and did so, although study was prohibited to women. It was said of her that she prayed like a man. Plans were made for her marriage; she was betrothed to a man but not allowed to meet him. During the time of the betrothal, Hannah Rachel's mother died. At this point, Hannah Rachel fell ill, going out only to visit her mother's grave and, according to Horodetzky's version of the story, "to cry her heart out."[3]

One day, when visiting her mother's grave, she fell asleep. When she awoke, she returned home and announced, "I have just been in Heaven at a sitting of the highest court . . . and there they gave me a new and sublime soul."[4] From that time on, she conducted herself as if she were a man. She dressed herself in men's garments, including the traditional male prayer garb of tallit and tefillin. At first she was an itinerant scholar, and she developed a considerable following. When her father died she built herself a bet midrash (house of prayer) from her inheritance and taught from a locked room. Her male followers listened to her teachings from an adjoining area because Jewish law prohibited men from looking upon a woman.

Rabbis in the region were threatened by Hannah Rachel and made efforts to force her to marry and return to acting like a woman. She ultimately relented and married a well-known Hasidic leader, Mordechai of Chernobyl. They did not, however, have sexual relations. Mordechai thought he could "awaken her womanly feelings" but eventually gave up and gave her a divorce. He analyzed the situation as follows:

> We do not know whose soul, the soul of which great Zaddik, is dwelling in this woman, but it must be very difficult for the soul of a Zaddik to find peace in the body of a woman.[5]

Mordechai concluded that Hannah Rachel's lack of sexual interest in him was connected to her usurpation of men's roles as teachers and leaders. He saw her not as a traditional woman but as a member of a "third sex," a man's soul in a woman's body.

The failed marriage gave the Hasidic leaders an opportunity to discredit Hannah Rachel as a teacher, and she no longer had a following amongst the Hasidim. As historian Ada Rapoport-Albert points out, this is certainly no feminist tale—it shows only that Hasidim were willing to accept the words of a woman if she were not in a traditional female role and that the Hasidic leadership did everything they could to discourage her followers.[6]

Hannah Rachel's reason for taking on men's dress and roles is obscure. It is impossible to assume anything from Horodetzky's text; his motives for including her story were to prove that there were women leaders in Hasidism. Even if he had known other details about her life, he might have chosen to omit them, or may in fact not have been able to interpret them. But the comment of Mordechai of Chernobyl places Hannah Rachel Webermacher in the tradition of gender nonconformists and as one of those women whom sexologists defined as lesbians.

Gender Nonconformists in the Stories of I. B. Singer

The Maid of Ludmir's masculine identification became a model for Isaac Bashevis Singer's fictional character Yentl. Singer discusses the relationship in his autobiographical novel, *Shosha*. In *Shosha* the protagonist, Aaron Greidinger, is a Polish playwright. He meets an American actress, Betty Slonim, whose "voice was that of a boy." She wants to act in his play, which he tells her is about

> The Maiden from Ludmir. She was a girl who wanted to live like a man. She studied the Torah, wore ritual fringes, a prayer shawl, and even put on phylacteries. She became a rabbi and held court for Hasidim. She covered her face with a veil and preached the Torah.[7]

Yentl, too, wants a man's life. At a young age, she secretly dresses in her father's clothes. Singer describes her as

> unlike any of the girls in Yanev—tall, thin, bony, with small breasts and narrow hips. On Sabbath afternoons, when her father slept, she would dress up in his trousers . . . and study her reflection in the mirror. She looked like a dark, handsome, young man. There was even a slight down on her upper lip . . . Secretly, she had even smoked her father's long pipe.[8]

Her father points out that she (like Hannah Rachel) "has a soul of a man in the body of a woman." When Yentl asks him why, he suggests that even God makes mistakes. Also like Hannah Rachel, a parent's death marks a turning point for Yentl. At her father's death, she assumes the identity of a man (Anshel—perhaps a mixing of the letters for the Hebrew of women [nashim] and man [enosh]) and moves to another town. During the time of Yentl's masquerade as Anshel, Singer never lets the reader forget that she/he has a double identity as man and woman.

Yentl disguises herself as Anshel so that she may study Torah. While masquerading as Anshel she falls in love with Avigdor, her male study partner. Singer wants his reader to see Yentl/Anshel as maintaining both her male and female identities during this process. So it is both as a man and a woman that Yentl/Anshel also shows interest in Hadass, the woman she/he intends to marry. When they first meet Yentl/Anshel contemplates Hadass's beauty:

> Anshel looked at her as she stood there—tall, blond, with a long neck, hollow cheeks, and blue eyes, wearing a cotton dress and a calico apron. Her hair, fixed in two braids, was flung back over her shoulders. A pity I'm not a man, Anshel thought.[9]

And again, when Anshel/Yentl proposes:

> "I, too, want you."
> Anshel was astonished at what she had said . . .
> Hadass turned to go, her high heels clattering. Anshel began hunting for beans in the soup, fished one up, then let it fall. Her appetite was gone; her throat had closed up. She knew very well she was getting entangled in evil, but some force kept urging her on.[10]

And finally, in the scene on their wedding night:

> Anshel had found a way to deflower the bride. Hadass in her innocence was unaware that things weren't quite as they should have been. She was already deeply in love with Anshel.[11]

Part of what Yentl discovers is that she can feel attraction toward women, as Singer indicates by describing her desire for Hadass: wishing that she were actually a man so that she could have her and then boldly going ahead with their marriage and sexual encounter.

Isaac Bashevis Singer often wrote about the intricate relationship between Jewish tradition and sexuality. In *Yentl* he was asking about the relationship between gender and sexuality as it is played out in the context of Jewish tradition. Singer addressed what can

happen when individuals blur the rigid gender boundaries set by
the tradition. Singer knew the work of the sexologists, and brought
the ideas they were raising about the relationship between sexual
differences and gender into a Jewish context.

Ironically, a contemporary feminist reading of this work elimi-
nates the gender nonconformity and female homoeroticism that is
explicit in the original. When Barbra Streisand made a film of
Yentl, it was clear that Yentl loved Avigdor as a woman not as a
man. Because the viewer could see so clearly through Yentl's dis-
guise, there was no possibility of entertaining the notion that when
posing as Anshel, Yentl would feel any attraction to Hadass. Barbra
Streisand's film adaptation of the Singer story read *Yentl* as a
progress narrative, the story of a woman who would do anything
to study the holy tradition, including dress as a man.[12] For
Streisand's Yentl, dressing like a man was only a masquerade in the
service of another goal. She never became confused at all about the
object of her attraction nor about who she *really* was.[13] But this
reading misses much in Singer's story. Yentl is a story of a woman
who not only takes on men's prerogatives but in the process discovers new dimensions of the self, including sexual ones. In Singer's
story, Yentl's awareness of being different dates from her childhood
and part of what she later discovers, when she has the freedom to
do so, is that she can feel attraction toward women. Singer's *Yentl*
is an important text for the lesbian transformation of Jewish tradition.

Deborah Brown's Gender Nonconformity

A novel with Jewish lesbian themes published in 1946 used the psychological perspective to underscore the acceptability of lesbian
sex. A first novel by Jewish author Ruth Seid,[14] written under the
pseudonym Jo Sinclair, *Wasteland* tells the story of Deborah
Brown, a Jewish lesbian who has come to terms with her identity
and sexuality through psychotherapy. The story is narrated
through the eyes of Deborah's brother Jack, who is dealing with his
own feelings about her sexuality in therapy. The book tells of Jack's
slow process of accepting both his sister's sexuality and his own
Jewish identity.

Much of Jack's struggle over his sister's identity consists of coming to terms with the fact that he perceives her as somehow masculine and therefore not a woman. Deborah is the youngest of five children. When Jack first describes her, he emphasizes not only her difference from the rest of the family but also her similarities:

> And then look at Deborah. As if she didn't belong to any of them . . . Yes, she looked a lot like them, except she was more blond, her eyes much more blue . . . But what resemblance was there between her brain and theirs? Her—all right, her soul! . . . She was a book person, a music person . . . Yes, he'd always felt funny about her. He thought that was a feeling of shame, too. The way she looked like a boy, her hair cut short that way . . . She talked Yiddish to Ma and Pa, sure, and she liked those Hebrew things the old man sang on holidays. But she looked just like a gentile boy.[15]

Her brother's sense of shame around Deborah's lesbianism is expressed in terms of her looking like a boy. While Jack is uncomfortable with his sister's difference, it is clear that he also admires and respects her intellect and her "soul." In an interesting variation of the pattern defined by Yentl, this Jewish lesbian has the soul of a Jew in the body of a gentile boy.

The most difficult issue Jack must deal with is his discomfort with Deborah's masculinity. In therapy Jack recalls how Deborah was a tomboy while growing up and how much discomfort her looks and behaviors had caused him. Her parents, on the other hand, gladly accepted her as the one who would be responsible around the house, would take care of things. The doctor helps Jack to see that he is jealous of Deborah because she has taken his place in the family. He asks Jack pointedly: "Do you feel sometimes that she is encroaching on your territory? Do you feel sometimes that she, as a woman, is stealing what belongs to men?"[16] And, pushing further: " 'Do you feel sometimes,' the doctor went on, 'that she, a woman, has no decent right to another woman?' "[17]

While the doctor probed the sexual issue, the symbolic stealing of the son's place in the family is really focused, for Jack, in a Jewish context. Jack could not get angry with Deborah for behaving "like a man," which he defines as including being clean, dependable, dressing and cutting her hair in a masculine style, being an intellectual, caring for her mother, and standing up to her father. But he did feel rage at her when she usurped his position at the family Seder by asking the Four Questions in his absence. Then, Jack did experience Deborah as stealing his place.[18]

Jewish identity becomes the locus of the struggle over Deborah's lesbianism. What is necessary for Jack's cure is that he understand that Deborah's lesbianism is acceptable and that it is not her fault that she wound up in the role of protector of the family. In fact, Jack must take responsibility for Deborah not having the opportunity to be the baby sister. Jack finally, after much struggle during his therapy, concludes:

> The way Debby is now. The way I used to hate so much, and be so afraid of . . . I mean, I used to think it was like being crippled, or sick! But it isn't . . . And she used to feel that way about herself! But it's Debby, it's her, the way she is.[19]

The resolution of Jack's problem is also based on his ability to see Deborah as a woman. At the end of the novel, when Debby and Jack are sitting together, he thinks to himself: "She was wearing slacks and a blue, pull-over sweater that showed her small breasts, and she looked a lot like a tall, slim boy but you knew she was a woman all right, and your sister."[20]

In Ruth Seid's work, the Jewish man manages through psychotherapy to resolve his problems with his masculine sister who has usurped male prerogatives. But the resolution to this problem has not always been so easily handled. There is still great discomfort around lesbians who refuse to conform to stereotypical gender roles.

Jewish Problems with Gender Nonconformity: Freud's Dora

Historian Hannah Decker's important work on the role of Jewishness in the encounter between Freud and Dora suggests a possible reason for this discomfort. According to Decker, Freud's failure to understand Dora is related to their mutual difficulty with accepting their Jewishness. Decker focuses primarily on the anti-Semitism of turn-of-the-century Vienna and on the anxiety that both doctor and patient must have experienced in their roles as Jews in that society. Decker suggests a correlation between hatred of women and hatred of Jews in that culture, a connection that she argues cannot be ignored as a factor in Dora's expression of her illness. According to Decker, "Jewishness intensified feelings of powerlessness and repressed anger that places human beings at risk for hysteria."[21]

Ida Bauer suffered from hysteria, a malady commonly ascribed to young women. From the Greek root word for womb, "hysteria" implied a fundamentally female disorder. Both Decker and Sander Gilman point out that hysteria was also understood to be the disease of the Jewish male who was often depicted in anti-Semitic literature as effeminate and androgynous.[22] Dora becomes the site of this disorder of women and of Jewish men, whose identities coalesce as the Jewish lesbian who has the "body of a woman and the soul of a man." Hysteria is the maladaptive response to the forced repression of both Jewishness and lesbianism that was fostered by the society in which Ida Bauer lived.

Freud's Dora represents the way in which the problem of lesbianism was understood in Jewish circles beginning in the twentieth century. Homoerotic behavior was not itself considered to be a problem. But once it was linked in the scientific and popular imagination with the idea that lesbians had women's bodies and men's souls, lesbianism became problematic. I would argue that it was not only the male soul trapped in the female body that was of concern. It was the corollary, that Jewish men had the souls of women in the bodies of men that was really the problem for Jews dealing with lesbianism as sexual inversion. To avoid dealing with this conundrum of gender, lesbians had to disappear, to become invisible. The recovery of information about some of the lesbians whose lives were hidden because of this prejudice has only just begun.

The Story of Charlotte Wolff

Charlotte Wolff (1897–1986), a self-described lesbian in the early twentieth century, reemerged in her later years to become part of the lesbian-feminist movement. Her memoirs are an important part of Jewish lesbian textual history. Wolff's biography reveals the story of a woman who identified as strongly masculine and who was comfortable, in a Jewish context, with her identity. Wolff's work on the subject of lesbianism in the 1970s played an important role in the changes in the status of lesbians in society.

Charlotte Wolff was a prominent Jewish physician in Weimar Germany. A refugee from the Nazis, she gained fame after World War II in her adopted country, Britain, as a chirologist (hand reader), psychologist, and, after 1970, a leading researcher and author on the subjects of lesbianism, bisexuality, and gay history.

In her autobiography, *Hindsight*, she talks at length about what it meant in her childhood to be Jewish and to have a stereotypically masculine appearance.[23] She was born in a small town in Eastern Germany, Westpreussen, near Danzig. It was her impression that at the time of her birth, Jews in such towns were completely unaware of anti-Semitism. She and her family were liberal Jews who saw themselves as "German citizens of the Jewish religion,"[24] who lived at ease with their neighbors.

Her parents were comfortable with Charlotte's unconventional gender and sexual identity. From her birth, her family behaved sympathetically toward her preferences for boy's clothing, making comments such as "You have always been a camouflaged boy."[25] She claimed never to have a preference for being male, except on occasions in her teens and early twenties when "the girls and women I loved were attracted to men."[26]

Wolff attributes her family's acceptance of her sexual difference to the fact that liberal Jews in Germany at the time were comfortable with all forms of sexuality, although she provides no evidence of the toleration of others outside her family and circle of friends.[27] She did have some positive feelings toward her family's Jewish rituals, especially the celebration of Shabbat at home on Friday evenings.[28] But she deeply disliked the synagogue and its rituals. She felt suffocated by High Holy Day services. Despite her family's liberal bent, the synagogue they attended had separate seating, and Charlotte deeply resented being stuck in the balcony. "I accepted neither the discrimination between the sexes nor the hollow holiness of the religious service."[29] At sixteen, she refused to return to the synagogue.

She also makes it clear that in her youth she was always "drawn to Jewish girls,"[30] and most of the love relationships and crushes she describes were with Jewish girls and women. Her first was with a young classmate:

> Neither Ida nor I had ever heard of the term homosexuality, nor did we know anything about love between people of the same sex. We experienced our attraction without fear or label, and had no model for love-making. We just loved. Kissing produced the greatest excitement, and we kissed at any hour. When we slept together our legs were entwined, while our two mouths moulded into one. These were probably the happiest nights of all my days . . . Later on I realized that my parents knew of my love for women. They never questioned me about it, but accepted me as I am. Their attitude was contrary to everything the Old Testament and the Talmud teach about unorthodox sex . . . But liberal Jews had, already then, quite a different attitude.[31]

In 1917 Wolff began her medical studies and had no time for a serious relationship during this period. Yet living in Berlin in the 1920s, she had an opportunity to become part of the underground lesbian life that existed there.

Wolff frequented the lesbian clubs in Berlin's West End.[32] She described the climate as "erotic . . . exciting . . . [it] gave me the feeling of being alive."[33] Yet she didn't view the clubs as opportunities for casual sex. Although Wolff openly stated her positive feelings about sex between women, she was of the opinion that the emotional component of the relationship was far more important than what she termed "technical acrobatics."[34]

From 1924 to 1933 she practiced medicine (family planning and physical therapy) and lived a settled life in Berlin with her Christian lover, Katherine. She had no sense until the early 1930s that she might have to leave Germany because of the rise of the National Socialist Party. Only later did she discover that one of her progressive medical colleagues was in fact a Nazi spy.[35] And then in 1932 Katherine left her, at the urging of her father who thought it unsafe to associate with Jews.

At this critical time in Wolff's life, being persecuted as a Jew and as an "invert" coincided. Several months later in February 1933, Wolff, like all Jews, was dismissed from her job. The next day, when she was returning to the clinic one last time to say good bye to her colleagues, she was arrested by a member of the Gestapo. When she asked him the reason, he said, "You are a woman dressed as a man, and a spy."[36] The guard at the police station was the husband of a patient who recognized her and embarrassedly dismissed the charges. A few days later, her apartment was searched. It was then that she finally decided to leave and the same day obtained a passport to Paris.

In the late forties Wolff settled in London. Unable to practice as a physician, she worked as a psychologist and chirologist (hand reader). She published three books on the meaning of gestures and psychological interpretations of the anatomy of the human hand. At this point in her career, Wolff's research on hands was characterized by racial theories and stereotypes. Although her work did not include references to stereotypical Jewish gestures, she judged the hands of homosexuals in racialized terms. She attributed a preponderance of left-handedness among homosexuals to the notion that the "whole left side of the body . . . expressed characteristics of the opposite sex."[37] Wolff was here following the theory that homosexuality is congenital inversion, an idea she later repudiated. She concluded:

> It would mean that in "masculine" men and "feminine" women the irrational side and its expressions come from his or her opposite sex tendencies. We may further conclude that in all ill-balanced people these tendencies are accentuated and that it is their homosexual component which deepens and widens their emotions but also leads to neurotic responses and disintegration.[38]

During these years Wolff did not have the kinds of lesbian relationships she had pursued in Germany. Perhaps the political climate was not conducive, or perhaps she was then uncomfortable with the underground lesbian culture she might have been involved with, given her public presence as noted psychotherapist and researcher. However, most of her friendships were with women in same-sex couples who despite living alone together in a longtime companionship did not think of themselves as lesbian.

For many years she lived the same existence as her friends the hidden lesbians. In *Hindsight* she reflects that "labels like 'lesbian' . . . were out of place in my world. Even after I had studied the works of Krafft-Ebing . . . I never applied them to myself."[39] Wolff did not identify as a lesbian, even to herself, prior to her dramatic shift of consciousness that began in the early 1960s. Her comment illuminates the situation of women who were not comfortable with the label lesbian.

Wolff was seventy-four years old when her first book on lesbianism, *Love Between Women*, was published in 1971. Wolff continued to grow and change. She was positively influenced by the feminist movement in England and put all her efforts into dealing with the lesbianism that had been an important part of her personal life since birth but that, prior to this time, she had never discussed publicly or professionally.

Wolff began her research in 1967, upon the publication of *On the Way to Myself*, her first set of memoirs. She admits to having read little about female homosexuality before she wrote her memoirs. She did have a friend who joined the first lesbian collective in Britain, the Minorities Research Group, which was founded in 1963, so she knew of their activities. Her early thoughts on lesbian community reflect the thoughts of many of her generation:

> I was probably rather prejudiced against lesbian groups which, in my view, were bound to lead to a ghetto. And nothing was more alien to me than a "professional lesbian"—the likely result of forming groups of this kind. It seemed to me insensitive and uncivilized to make a focal point of a perfectly natural way of loving and living. On account of such reflections and sensibilities, I do not believe that the then existing lesbian movement can have had much to do with my own inclination to know, rather than feel, something about love between women.[40]

Wolff does not give adequate credit to these groups for their role in creating a social climate in which she could carry out her research without stigma. She does credit them with helping her obtain a database of lesbians who were willing to participate in her study.[41]

Her conclusion from this study was that lesbians are like all other women, with one difference: they are more independent.[42] She also asserted that social and biological factors go into making up lesbian identity, taking a neutral position on the debate about the origins of female homosexuality.[43]

Wolff theorized that ideal lesbian love has its core in "emotion and romanticism" and that the sexual expression, while important to many lesbians, is not "a goal or a necessary outlet." She suggested that "many lesbians, particularly in the older age groups . . . have lived happily . . . without any sexual acts."[44] Wolff was still not comfortable with the lesbian label and suggested another name for women loving women: homoemotional. This term echoes the concept of romantic friendship. Nonetheless, because of convention, she used the terms "lesbian" and "homosexual" in this and all of her subsequent works.

Her most important conclusion was the one she alluded to in *Hindsight* where she stated:

> Lesbians possess, through their very nature, a labile gender identity which might be interpreted as a sign of immaturity or arrested development. I do not share this view—quite the opposite. *The retention of the capacity to change feminine into masculine feelings and attitudes, and vice versa, is one of the assets of female homosexuality, because it makes for variety and richness in personal relationships.* (Italics in original.)[45]

In 1971 this was a bold challenge to the psychiatric establishment, which, until 1973, had defined homosexuality as illness. Wolff's research was an important weapon in the battle to change that diagnosis and to end the idea of causal connection between sexual inversion and love between women.

The publication of *Love Between Women* changed Wolff's life. Women in conflict over their lesbianism began to go to her for psychological counseling and treatment. She also began to understand the contemporary prejudice and hatred against lesbians. And she became conscious of the important role that feminism was playing in bringing these issues to light.[46]

But more important to Wolff's research was her notion about the underlying bisexuality of lesbians, which led her to pursue research on the subject of bisexuality. Modeling her theory on the ideas of Freud, Wolff posited the original bisexuality of all human beings and argued that only life circumstances will determine whether individuals will become homo- or heterosexual. Her study of bisexuals led her to the conclusion that this group of people is the most beleaguered of all, being unacceptable to homo- and heterosexuals alike.

Later in life, Wolff abandoned biological notions of homosexuality, arguing that we must all accept the essential bisexuality of the human race as a necessary step in a cultural revolution. She emphasized in all her subsequent works that we must work toward a society in which all sexual orientations are acceptable, and that so doing would bring about a world free from evil.[47] This utopian vision led Wolff to argue further that there should be only "one human sexuality with manifold expressions", and to call for an end to categorizing people by their sexual orientation.[48]

Through the process of her research into lesbianism and bisexuality Wolff became radicalized. She realized that it was feminism that led her to pursue her research about female homosexuality. She began to describe lesbianism as the foundation of feminism and called upon heterosexual feminists to make alliances with the lesbian cause.[49] She also came to the understanding that until a utopian future came about where sexual orientation would not be an issue, lesbians needed a community in which they were free of persecution.[50] Her research stimulated her to join lesbian organizations and to become a public advocate for lesbian rights.

As Wolff developed a lesbian identity and consciousness in the 1970s, she became an important public figure in the gay rights movement in Britain. Inevitably, German lesbians learned about her; her books were translated into German, and she was invited to speak in Berlin. These circumstances compelled her to come to terms with her identity as a German Jew. Her new understanding of the importance of subcultures in fighting oppression led her to confront German anti-Semitism openly.

Wolff had a strong need to come to terms with her identity as a German Jew. She accomplished this goal in two ways. One was through her writing; this time, a biography of Magnus Hirschfeld, her last work before her death in 1986. The other was by returning to Germany as a guest of the German lesbian feminist movement and confronting movement members on their anti-Semitism.

Wolff's biography of Hirschfeld examined his commitment to his gay and Jewish identities. She criticized Hirschfeld and his coworkers for ignoring the existence of the Jewish feminist movement and remarked on her own dismay at never having encountered the Jewish *Frauenbund* in the years before the war, only finding out about them by reading Marion Kaplan's 1979 work *The Jewish Feminist Movement in Germany*. She argued that the movement was still unknown because of "Germany's shame about the Hitler period and a still prevailing fear of feminism."[51]

Hirschfeld was, in the end, exiled from Germany as a Jew and not as a homosexual. Like Wolff herself, "exile had profiled his own Jewishness."[52] Hirschfeld's response to his ouster was to write a book entitled *Racism*, which refutes Nazi concepts of eugenics.

While Hirschfeld chose to write a direct challenge to Nazi ideology, Wolff would wait until her return to Germany to raise questions about German anti-Semitism. As her work on lesbianism came to be known in Germany in the 1970s, there was great interest in having her come and speak. These visits provided an opportunity for reconciliation. She met women who risked their lives to save Jews.[53] And she found opportunities in her public presentations to challenge German anti-Semitism, although she often met with hostile, silent responses. When one woman asked why and how she left Germany, Wolff replied:

> This was the moment when I rose to the occasion as I had wanted to. I told them how I felt about Hitler and the Nazis, and about my estrangement from Germany. I said (passionately by then) that I had been one of the lucky people who had not only survived, but had found a new life of such possibilities as I could never have met with in Germany. And I continued: "I have been grieved that your great country was put into the abyss of sadism and inhumanity by that madman Hitler. You lost half your land, and the Jews lost six million people— all through the madness of one man."[54]

At another lecture Wolff issued a warning to German lesbians that they needed to be willing to "fight political oppression collectively otherwise they might one day be in the same position as the Jews were under Hitler."[55] The audience responded with hostility to her confrontational remark, claiming that their situation was not similar. But she remained obdurate and continued to make efforts to get her message across—both about Jewish suffering in Germany and about its relationship to the sufferings of gay people.

In many instances in her speaking and writing, Wolff made comparisons between the fate of the Jews and the fate of homosexuals under Hitler, drawing the lesson that it could happen again, to either group or to both. She argued publicly with the Bishop of Gloucester, who presided over a discussion on the report of the Church of England on homosexuality in the mid 1970s. The Bishop recommended tolerance, and Wolff replied: "Don't speak of tolerance, Bishop. Tolerance is condescension . . . homosexual people . . . might answer you 'Go to hell.' Jews would feel similarly offended if treated in a diminishing fashion."[56]

In *Love Between Women* she suggested that like the "wandering Jew" the "homosexual woman . . . is nowhere really at home." Wolff experienced this sense of rootlessness as a Jew and a lesbian, never finding a supportive community. Continuing to find analogies between Jews and lesbians, she also suggested that the groups are similar in that they "are found in all parts of the world, and both are made to feel . . . that they are out of place."[57] Yet she concluded that the lot of lesbians is worse because they are rejected by society at a more profound level.

Wolff's final contribution to the development of a Jewish lesbian sensibility was to remind gay men and lesbians that they have a history.[58] The Hirschfeld biography was a contribution to a history of gay and lesbian Jews. Her own story is also an important chapter of Jewish lesbian history. Charlotte Wolff is a bridge between the era in which she grew up, when feelings remained unnamed or lesbians were identified as sexual inverts, and the era in which she grew old when lesbians were able to articulate our identities and establish community.

Wolff's life, the stories of the Maid of Ludmir, and the fictional characters of Yentl and Deborah Brown are key resources in the development of a Jewish lesbian textual corpus. As women who did not conform to gender expectations, they are models for all contemporary Jewish women who oppose rigid gender roles. As women who combined their differences with the act of loving other women, they are models for contemporary Jewish lesbians.

Nine

Contemporary Jewish
Lesbian Fiction

Reinterpreting ancient texts and incorporating modern texts are crucial steps toward claiming a place in Jewish tradition for Jewish lesbians. But there is also another method we need to consider. As Jewish lesbians we must ourselves take the opportunity to make our own lives part of this story. Our need is not only to transform traditional texts but also to transform our understanding of the sacred. Like Jewish feminists we insist that our lives themselves are text. It is not only stories from the past that make up the sacred canon of the Jewish people. The stories we are creating in our lives today are part of the ongoing drama of the Jews. In books such as *Nice Jewish Girls*, *Twice Blessed*, and *Lesbiōt*, contemporary lesbians have shared their coming out stories and oral histories. Incorporating, reading, and interpreting these real life stories into Jewish textual tradition is a critical part of the process of transforming that tradition. In addition, writers of Jewish lesbian fiction are also creating texts that can be added to this process. This chapter focuses on Jewish lesbian fictional characters who can stand alongside Ruth and Lilith and become part of the textual tradition of the Jewish people.

Fiction plays an important role in the lesbian transformation of Judaism. These stories are just that: stories. They do not describe our lives as they are but as we see them and as we want them to be. They help us imagine a Judaism into which we fit—in the present day, and also in the past and future. Like the midrashim we have created, they represent our dreams about what it might look like if Judaism were seen through a lesbian lens.

Jewish lesbian fiction presents a variety of options for reconceptualizing the story of our people. The writers of this genre have created role models for the Jewish lesbian: interpreter of tradition, skeptic, and prophet. They have also developed new ways of looking at sacred Jewish space and time.

Redefining Sacred Space and Time

The Mikveh

Sacred Jewish spaces look different through a lesbian lens. Elisheva Rogin, the protagonist of Alice Bloch's novel, *The Law of Return*, transforms the sacred space of the mikveh. In the Orthodox community, the mikveh is a private place; women do not speak about their experiences there, and the ritual itself is closely tied to the menstrual cycle of married women that governs patterns of heterosexual sex. But for Elisheva, the mikveh becomes a location to explore her lesbian images and desires.

During the course of Elisheva's coming out, she has to come to terms with the knowledge that, as a way of avoiding her feelings for women, she wants to marry Daniel—who has revealed to her that he is gay. She prepares herself to read the letter in which he comes out to her by immersing herself in water. In her personal "mikveh" she expresses the desire for a "private revelation . . . not the same words that have been repeated for thousands of years." And she wants this Jewish experience to "emerge from her fingertips."[1] Her holy insight must come through her woman's body.

Elisheva's response to Daniel's letter is panic; she sees threatening possibilities for herself in his coming out. Her therapist is supportive of Elisheva coming to terms with lesbian desire, seeing it as a necessary step toward a mature heterosexuality.[2] But for Elisheva, it is more. She goes with her friend Miriam to the mikveh, and while she is there she imagines the sensual and loving relationships of traditional Jewish women in the Orthodox community and in the Jewish past.[3] As for many Jewish lesbians, the mikveh is transformed into a potentially erotic site of women bathing and bonding together over a shared experience of pleasure in their bodies.

The Synagogue

The synagogue is another space that is transformed in Jewish lesbian fiction. Usually the synagogue is understood as a place that is predominantly for men and their prayers. But Jewish lesbian fiction writers have reclaimed the synagogue through making it the location of some fantastic events, adding possibilities to what we might imagine when we enter there.

In Sarah Schulman's *The Sophie Horowitz Story*, Sophie is a writer for the underground newspaper *The Feminist News*, for which she is investigating a radical feminist bank robbery. The story is both mysterious and intensely humorous. Sophie's Jewish and lesbian identities are established at the outset. Her Jewishness is expressed through her name, her geographic location (New York, and a particular love of the Lower East Side), her passion for Jewish foods,[4] her use of Yiddish and Hebrew phrases, and her ironic humor.

In a brief and amusing plot diversion, Sophie tells the story of how she made her peace with Jewish tradition and in doing so transformed her relationship to Judaism: While writing an article on women, orthodoxy, and abortion, Sophie found herself doing "fieldwork" in an Orthodox shul. She brought along Muffin, her photographer, "another Jewish lez." The shammes seated them behind a curtain, "a heavy, dirty brown canvas," as would be expected. Alone in the women's section, Sophie had an idea, one that she assumed she was not the first to have: "as women before us must have realized . . . old men, praying to themselves, did not know or care what we were doing." What follows is a funny and erotic sex scene, which is interrupted as she and Muffin realize that the service is coming to a close and hurry to get their clothes on.[5]

By having her characters make love behind the meḥiẓah, Schulman infuses sacred Jewish space with a lesbian presence, thus transforming it. As Muffin and Sophie move their bodies to the "tune of the old men's prayers," their lovemaking is connected as a sacred act to the holiness of prayer. Schulman's parody makes the serious point that reclaiming sacred space is an important dimension of the transformation of tradition.

The synagogue is also the location of a lesbian transformation of Jewish space in the wedding scene from Judith Katz's *Running Fiercely Toward a High Thin Sound*. The protagonist, Nadine Pagan, is estranged from her family and is not invited to her sister's wedding. She goes to the wedding uninvited, and in a fantastic sequence hides herself in the ark among the Torah scrolls during the ceremony. She describes this act as "our mother's worst fear, my lover's best fantasy."[6] She was the "Lesbian Wedding Guest from Outer Space." Hidden in the ark, Nadine imagines herself to be the Torah. She fantasizes that the rabbi will

> open the Ark, take me out and cradle me in his rabbinical arms, walk with me among the congregants to be kissed and blessed blessed and kissed, how I wish someone would hold me up on the *bima*, untie me, unravel me, read my wisdom and stories out loud, bring blessings one to the other from inside of me, the holy teachings of Nadine.[7]

Nadine cannot contain herself in the ark. When Mickey, the groom, breaks the glass to end the ceremony, "an ages-old sorrow implodes," and Nadine bursts forth. Nadine reclaims the most sacred Jewish space. By her unorthodox actions she asks: What if Jewish lesbian "torah" were not hidden at Jewish weddings but exploded forth? Katz here expresses the lesbian desire that our lives be seen as powerfully connected to Torah.

This satirical account poignantly depicts the alienation of lesbians at weddings. But it is not only a rejection of tradition. Nadine also claims a new relationship to Jewish space and its symbols. Rather than in her alienation placing herself outside Jewish space, she enters the holiest of places and becomes the Torah herself. To Katz this is an ambivalent symbolic act: the lesbian's joyous fantasy is her Jewish mother's nightmare. But as Katz's narrative suggests, the sacred places of Judaism can only be reclaimed for Jewish lesbians if we dare to make ourselves visible in them.

At the end of Nadine's story she dreams of another event in a synagogue: a huge lesbian wedding. Hundreds of women gather in the main floor of an elaborate sanctuary with a balcony in which women did not have to sit. The women dance, hold a ḥuppah, and take turns being rabbi. Many women, dressed in all sorts of clothing, with all sorts of bodies and faces, are brides. Nadine is at the center, being carried by the brides like a Torah on Simḥat Torah. Nadine then steps to the center of the ḥuppah and plays magnificently on her violin. Then she breaks the glass with both feet, and everyone eats and dances.[8]

Through this wedding Nadine reconnects to Judaism and transforms it. She is the center of a wedding that celebrates community rather than coupling. Nadine can be and teach her own Torah; her life is a Jewish text. This celebration of Jewish lesbian life is what Nadine was yearning for when she made her presence felt at her sister's wedding. At the fantasy wedding Jewish symbols are no longer the source of pain and alienation. Rather, they become the vehicle for the transformation of sacred Jewish space.

The Home

The synagogue and the mikveh represent public spaces transformed through the power of Jewish lesbian fiction into places where we belong. A more difficult space to transform is the private space of the Jewish home. The Jewish home incorporates not only Jewish symbols but also the Jewish family with which lesbian Jews cannot always be reconciled.[9] Sophie Horowitz differentiates between her parents' rejection and her own feelings about being Jewish: "It's not the Judaism that bothers me, it really is the family."[10] It is our inability to deal with our Jewish families that makes transforming the textual tradition all the more important.

Frequently in Jewish lesbian fiction sacred space is represented in the context of a sacred time: the Passover seder. The seder is the location for conflict with Jewish families. Yet Passover is also an important symbol of liberation for Jewish lesbians, a time when many of us recognize the spirit of our own freedom from the bondage of a closeted life.

This conflict is played out in *Running Fiercely* when Nadine Pagan returns to her family during the seder. She comes in the door just as they are about to open it for the prophet Elijah. To Nadine, her reconnection to Judaism is the harbinger of the messianic future usually heralded by Elijah. Her family does not see it that way, however, and she is not a welcome guest. The seder degenerates to chaos and pandemonium. Everyone screams, and her sister Jane breaks the seder plate, a family heirloom. Nadine's reconciliation with Judaism does not easily translate into the desired reconciliation with her Jewish family.[11]

Rainbow Rosenbloom's story in *The Dyke and The Dybbuk* by Ellen Galford differs in its interpretation of the possibility for reconciliation at the Jewish table. Rainbow is an orphan. In the beginning of her story, she comes in contact with her Jewish family, her father's five sisters, once a year on Passover. After the seder, Rainbow invariably goes out for Chinese food. Her opposition to Judaism is her only connection to it. As the story ends, Rainbow is reconciled to her aunts who come to eat at her house. The story concludes by asking the question from the seder, "Why is this night different from all other nights?" It is different because on this night, "Rainbow's separate worlds collide."[12]

Images of the seder provide an opportunity to think about Jewish time and space and to transform them from the perspective of Jewish lesbian life. Although family relationships may be fraught with tension, Rainbow's experience suggests that we can create our own Jewish homes and bring our families into them, thus transforming the sacred space of the Jewish home into a place where we make ourselves welcome.[13] The stories we tell of our experiences of seder are texts that we need to transform Judaism into a world that welcomes us, where we are no longer like bread on the seder plate.

New Role Models

The characters created in Jewish lesbian fiction are powerful role models for lesbian Jews. Elisheva Rogin is an interpreter of Jewish texts and tradition and as such functions in the role of rabbi. Rainbow Rosenbloom functions in the role of the skeptic who questions Jewish antipathy toward lesbianism. Nadine Pagan acts as a prophet, naming what needs to change for lesbians to be at home in Judaism. In these roles the protagonists of Jewish lesbian fiction transform our images of Jewish lesbians from outsiders to the tradition to participants who are making a valued contribution to Jewish life.

The Interpreter of Tradition: Elisheva Rogin

The protagonist in Alice Bloch's *The Law of Return*, reinterprets Jewish traditional texts so that they have meaning in her own process of coming out. Elisheva Rogin takes a variety of opportunities to redefine and interpret Jewish text from a lesbian perspective. Elisheva's lesbian fantasies are inextricably bound to the Jewish tradition. While living in Israel, she takes a trip to Eilat and spends an evening alone with her sexual dreams and fantasies about Jewish women. The midrashic figure of Lilith appears to her, enticing her. Lilith sings the words of Song of Songs to her, "You have ravished my heart, my sister, my bride." Through Elisheva's lesbian lens, the women demons and love poetry of Jewish tradition take on new resonance, alluring her to a new life.

Later in the story, Elisheva returns to the United States with hopes of marrying Daniel—a convert to Judaism who comes out as a gay man—and banishing her lesbian desires. But Daniel rejects the idea of marriage. Elisheva comes to terms with this loss on Simḥat Torah. Although she does not go to synagogue, she recalls the words that are recited at the end of the Torah cycle, "from strength to strength we are strengthened." Based on the power she derives from these words, she is prepared to let Daniel live his life and pursue her own desires. And the words take on new meaning in the context of her own coming out.[14]

Elisheva and Daniel become friends rather than lovers, and he introduces her to the gay community. Together they become involved in organizing a gay switchboard. Through her political work, she is reunited with Deborah, a woman she met in Israel, and they begin a long-term relationship. Now that she is a lesbian, Elisheva compares herself to "the stone the builders rejected" (Psalm 118) but that has now come to life.[15] Making love with Deborah evokes for her images of mikveh and thoughts of the love poetry of the Song of Songs.[16] She imagines her lesbian relationship fulfilling a new interpretation of the commandment to "be fruitful and multiply":

> "There are many ways to be fruitful, many ways to increase, many ways to fill the earth." We are learning, Deborah and I, the meaning of this law, which is also a promise: You will be fruitful, you will increase, you will fill the earth.[17]

Finding Kol Isha, the feminist community in Jerusalem that also includes lesbians, is the final step for Elisheva in reconciling her Jewish and lesbian identities. The story ends with one more allusion to Jewish text, the story of the Israelites at the Red Sea: "They took a deep breath, and then, in a powerful gesture of trust, in the faith that someone who loved them would not let them drown, they stepped forward, toward the water."[18]

On the other side, the Israelites sang. For Elisheva, echoing the Song of Songs, "the time of singing has arrived" again. Through reinterpreting Jewish texts, she finds a way to unite her Jewish and lesbian identities.

The Skeptic: Rainbow Rosenbloom

Rainbow Rosenbloom plays a role more commonly ascribed to the Jewish lesbian—the skeptic or apikoros. But Galford defines Rainbow's skepticism as crucial to the development of Judaism. Rainbow's story suggests that without the skeptic, Judaism would have stagnated. The lesbian as questioning outsider provides challenge and growth for the tradition.

In *The Dyke and the Dybbuk* Rosenbloom is actually possessed by a dybbuk named Kokos, who narrates Rainbow's story of transformation. Kokos describes Rainbow as an outsider Jew. As a lesbian she is a "devotee of forbidden fruits," who has not been in a synagogue in twenty years and flouts the crucial obligation to "be fruitful and multiply." Rainbow is a film critic for *The Outsider*, a gay and lesbian newspaper. Her vocational choice is attributed to her "passion for graven images." In addition she drives a cab, which is "no job for a nice Jewish girl."[19] She has changed her name from Rosalind to Rainbow, further proof of her alienation from her Jewish family.[20] But Rainbow's life is changed forever when she is possessed by Kokos, who has taken her over because of a two-hundred-year-old contract that was the result of hidden lesbian love gone awry in the Eastern European Jewish community.[21]

At one point in the story, the dybbuk argues with Riva, a traditional woman who calls her an abomination. Kokos responds that while charismatic Jewish sects like the one to which Riva belongs only came into Jewish life in the eighteenth century, Rainbow and other "heretics and deviants and dissenters" have been around much longer.[22] When Riva suggests that is precisely why her group plays a vital role, keeping the law alive, Kokos responds: "And that's why there have to be heretics . . . To keep asking the questions that override your easy answers."[23]

This story brings us the insight that the presence of skeptics is as crucial to keeping Judaism alive as is the piety of the Orthodox. In fact, the relationship between belief and skepticism is what is necessary for the growth and development of Judaism; the tension between them makes possible its transformation.

Rainbow's story adds another dimension to the textual transformation of Judaism. Lesbians may have been hidden in the Jewish past, but they played a crucial role. Along with other heretics, they maintained the Jewish tradition of skepticism and disdain for easy answers. Now that Jewish lesbians are visible, we can bring our skepticism into dialogue with tradition and with its adherents, asking questions of the text that have not been addressed before.

It is important to retain an appreciation of the need for skepticism and even for heresy. A lesbian transformation of Judaism does more than incorporate lesbian sensibility: it demands the acceptance of difference. While we may dream of a time when identifying as lesbian is simply accepted as part of Jewish life, we must also remain aware that other differences will arise to challenge the Jewish community. Part of the lesbian transformation of Judaism includes a willingness to embrace those differences and to question our fear of them. There must always be room for the heretic and skeptic, for it is the people who don't feel at home who raise important questions for our self-understanding as a people. The lesbian as skeptic reminds us to remain open to that challenge.

The Prophet: Nadine Pagan

Nadine Pagan's contribution to this challenge is as a prophet who dreams of a Jewish world transformed and open to a lesbian vision, a world that does not yet exist. In *Running Fiercely Toward a High Thin Sound* Nadine struggles with internal demons and a family that does not support her. In her visions she imagines a better world for Jewish lesbians.

Like many ancient prophets Nadine suffers from bouts of mental illness. The story begins with Nadine setting fire to her head using the candlesticks (family heirlooms) on Shabbat, after which she is confined for some time to a psychiatric hospital and then sent to live at her grandmother's house. Nadine's madness is connected to her passion. She speaks little, but plays exquisite melodies that evoke past generations of Jewish music reminiscent of a "fiddler on the roof." This violin is Nadine's Jewish soul, and often it speaks for her.

When Nadine decides that she needs forgiveness for her sins of disrupting her family, she plans her own tashlikh ritual. Throwing her sins and herself into the river, she finds herself underground in another world. Here she becomes alternatively a little Jewish boy, with payis and ẓiẓit, and a healed version of herself, without the scar from the candle incident. She journeys through the Jewish past with four women who resemble her mother, sisters and her lover—Esther, Magda, Shula, and Etta. She makes love and experiences the Jewish past with them. Her prophetic role is to reclaim the Jewish past as a lesbian and to bring lesbian sensibilities to the stories of Eastern European Jewish life that she experiences in a dreamlike state.

After the lesbian wedding in the synagogue in which Nadine claims for herself a central role in the Jewish drama, her journey to the other world ends. She is transported back to the water and, like Moses, left on the banks of the river. She perceives herself as "new now, and ready to forgive"[24] her family for the pain they have caused her, and to be forgiven by them.

Despite the difficulties in communication she encounters at the seder, Nadine represents a new coming of the Prophet Elijah, looking for reconciliation and a new beginning for Jewish lesbians. The final scene, "Tikun," is her sister Jane's dream of wrestling with

Nadine. Like Jacob and the angel, Nadine and Jane reconcile as "true sisters" by wrestling and weeping together.[25] In this reinterpretation of the biblical story Nadine is again the prophetic figure, bringing the message of new possibilities for seeing Judaism through a lesbian lens: transformed.

As interpreter, skeptic, and prophet, Elisheva, Rainbow, and Nadine bring lesbian sensibilities into relationship with Jewish tradition. Their presence and the way their creators have conceptualized their roles open new possibilities for the lesbian perspective on Jewish religious life. As interpreters of text, Jewish lesbians make a contribution by shedding new light on old traditions. As skeptics, we can stand apart from that life and with good humor and insight bring a critique of the texts, looking at them from a perspective that has up till now been silenced. And as prophets, we can imagine the possibilities for change inherent in the traditions and texts of our people and our relationship to them.

These stories are not only models of ways into the text, they also have the power to change our lives. The stories that the writers of lesbian fiction share with us point us in new directions for a lesbian transformation of Judaism. They teach the lesson that our lives are the text. It is not enough to study the past and make new interpretations of it. It is not enough to use the texts of the past to rethink contemporary practices. We must be engaged in creating new texts that can be passed on to the next generation. In this way, we write ourselves into the Jewish story.

Ten

Visions for the Future

A Jewish lesbian transformation of Judaism is not yet a reality. In writing this book, I have sought to identify those elements in Jewish life that have begun to open up to the lesbian perspective, as well as those that need to be transformed in order to make Judaism more hospitable to lesbian sensibilities. I have suggested that in order for Jewish lesbians to be at home in the Jewish community our visions and stories must become part of the Jewish textual tradition. I have located many texts within the tradition to be confronted and reinterpreted, and suggested adding other texts that have not received sufficient attention. My goal is to bring a new understanding of Jewish sacred text, one that makes room for a lesbian perspective.

It is my hope that this new perspective will engage Jews in the process of transformation. The process begins with the texts, but the necessary changes cannot happen unless Jews make it happen. There is no Judaism without Jews, and it is up to the Jewish people to accomplish this transformation.

I also hope that those who have read this book will be interested in pursuing these ideas further, and in arguing about them. It is my wish that readers will now see the creation story and the passage in Leviticus that labels homosexuality an abomination in a new light. That they will reread the Book of Ruth and think about it from a lesbian perspective. That they will consider implementing some of the suggestions described as part of a new understanding of Micah 6:8. That they will read Asch and Singer, Freud and Jo Sinclair, or find out more about the lives and times of Lillian Wald and Charlotte Wolff. That they will suggest that their libraries carry works of contemporary Jewish lesbian fiction. And that they will understand all those activities as part of Torah study—the holy pursuit of Jewish knowledge.

The study of these texts is not an intellectual process alone. Real study involves the growth of the individual as a whole person, an experience of fellowship and community, and the opportunity for a spiritual experience. When we learn, we need to involve our whole beings. We must use the experience as an opportunity for growth and change. The information we gain in study is only the beginning of learning. True learning takes place when we are able to use what we know in our lives. What we learn, especially in a Jewish framework, should help us make decisions about the kind of people we want to be in the world and about the values that undergird the way we live our lives. A standard method of Jewish study is in ḥevruta, learning partners. Studying the texts that we have looked at in partnership with others will inevitably lead to new interpretations and to further study.

The ultimate goal of this book is to further the dialogue between lesbian Jews and other segments of the Jewish community who, working together, will bring a new kind of learning about Jewish lesbians into the fabric of Jewish communal life. Transformation depends on the willingness of both Jewish lesbians and the rest of the Jewish community to continue the process of dialogue, even when it is difficult to do so. And it assumes that Jewish life is amenable to this transformation: that someday lesbians in all our variations will be completely comfortable claiming and celebrating our lives as Jews in the Jewish community.

Some would argue that such full acceptance is a dangerous goal for cultural change. If lesbians became insiders we would lose our perspective; lesbian challenges to Judaism would in that case no longer be as thoughtful because lesbians would have become stakeholders in the very system we wished to change. But this argument denies the very possibility of cultural change. If the Jewish world responds to the lesbian critique, then it is a system capable of change and capable of including difference.

And lesbians are not alone in demanding change in the Jewish community. We share many of our concerns with other groups of Jews:

With heterosexual feminists we are engaged in the process of changing women's roles and place in Jewish life, questioning any limits that have been placed on what women can do;

With gay Jewish men we have created alternative structures for community and worship that are playing an important role in reconfiguring Jewish communal life;

With heterosexual intermarried couples we are raising questions about the importance of differences in loving relationships, and about ways of making relationships across differences holy;

With bisexual Jews we question assumptions about the way our tradition looks at sexual choices;

With transgendered Jews we challenge rigid gender roles in Judaism;

With those who can't or don't wish to raise children, we are finding new ways of thinking about and supporting the next generation of Jews;

With single heterosexual Jews we are questioning the nuclear family structure as the ideal to which all Jews must aspire;

With other Jews who have been uncomfortable with traditional prayer and observance, we engage in the process of making new rituals and ceremonies for our lives;

With Jews who find the Torah both fascinating and alienating, we are using our hearts and intellects to refashion our understanding of the words of our ancestors that we claim as sacred;

With other liberal Jews we are finding ways to create a Jewish life that is not based on halakhic (legal) precedent but is driven by a Jewish ethics that relies on values gleaned from the stories of our people—both ancient and those we are creating;

With progressive Jewish educators we are searching for new ways and models to teach children about the Jewish past, one that includes the stories of lesbian Jews;

With scholars of women's history, mysticism, and Mizrachi Jewish communities, we are searching for those parts of our past that have escaped scholarly interest and notice;

With Jews who are discouraged by the values of some in the Jewish community who care only if something is "good for the Jews," we seek to build coalitions with other groups who want to bring justice and peace to a troubled world.

Lesbian Jews find ourselves part of a broad coalition that is involved in transforming Jewish life. But while we share commonalities with other Jews, Jewish lesbians also make a unique contribution to that coalition. The lives we have created for ourselves overcome stereotypic notions about women's interdependence on one another and our dependence on men. Our presence in the Jewish community heightens awareness about the interplay of gender and sexuality. We look at Jewish texts from a completely new perspective, and the Jewish world is changed by the questions we raise.

For the transformation to be genuine, Jewish lesbians must retain our differences—those perspectives and practices that made us unacceptable to begin with. As we become part of the Jewish community, rather than becoming complacent, Jewish lesbians can influence attitudes towards other unwelcome groups. We may also be able to contribute a new perspective on other controversial questions the Jewish community faces. We may also enable the Jewish community to become a model for change in the larger society or other cultural contexts in which we as Jews or as lesbians are also marginalized.

All these efforts and ideas have the possibility to invigorate Jewish life, to make it accessible to those who have not found a place in it in the past. These efforts make possible new understandings of Jewish lesbian lives and open up the opportunity to experience being Jewish and lesbian as connected identities. The Jewish world looks different when approached from a lesbian perspective. Embracing these differences enriches Jewish life. This Jewish lesbian perspective is now beginning to infuse our understanding of being Jewish with new meanings, signaling a transformation of Judaism.

Jewish lesbian self-awareness grew out of anger about invisibility and oppression and moved forward to demands for acceptance. We have moved beyond wanting simply to make a place for ourselves, beyond the bread on the seder plate: we now seek to transform the Judaism we found when we reached that place. This book suggests that we continue the conversation between Jewish lesbians and others in the Jewish community through the medium of text. It is my hope that Jewish lesbians in particular will find this a useful perspective and an invitation to closer connection with Jewish life and heritage. To the extent that all lesbians and our gay, bisexual, transgendered, and feminist allies are interested in matters pertaining to lesbians, I would hope that those readers have found their voices reflected in these pages.

Finally, I hope this work will be a model of a dialogue for others (for example, gay Christians[1] or Latina lesbians) who seek to transform existing communities into places where they can feel at home.

Notes

1. Lesbian and Jewish: What's the Problem?

1. This story was told to me by the person who asked the question, Riki Friedman, in a telephone interview, April 16, 1996. I am indebted to Jane Litman, an organizer of the Berkeley group, both for connecting me to the source of this story and for her insightful comments about its meaning.

2. From *A Woman's Haggadah* (25–26), this version of the legend was written by Shifrah Lillith [Susan Fielding]. Shifrah remembers reading an article in a New York feminist newspaper in 1982 that told the story of a woman going to a rabbi in New York to ask him about the place of lesbians in Judaism. According to the article, he replied that lesbians have as much place in Judaism as bread does on a seder plate. Shifrah embellished the story for the Haggadah. (Personal communication, May 8, 1996.)

3. *A Woman's Haggadah*, 27.

4. Susannah Heschel, editor of *On Being a Jewish Feminist*, an early and influential anthology on Jewish women, takes credit for this innovation. (Personal communication, March 14, 1996.)

5. This story has also been attributed to Heschel, but she denies either changing the symbolism or having been the feminist who had this experience in Florida. Nonetheless, the story about women and oranges has appeared in print, in *Lilith* (Spring 1992): 2, in reference to seder plates

and in an alternative haggadah published in Berman and Waskow, *Tikkun*, 74.

6. Elsie Goldstein designed a seder plate with a place for an orange, as described in her letter to *Lilith*. I learned about the embroidery from Ellen Garvey. (Personal communication, October 5, 1994).

7. The history of the development of a lesbian presence in Judaism is told by Faith Rogow in her essay, "Why Is This Decade Different From All Other Decades?"

8. See Merkin, "A Closet of One's Own."

9. In the 1970s early Jewish feminist publications made no reference to lesbians. In the early 1980s Jacob Rader Marcus included two references to lesbians in his *Documentary History of Jewish Women in America*. *Lilith* ran a few articles about Jewish lesbians such as Evelyn Torton Beck and Batya Bauman, and about coming out in the Jewish community. *Lilith*'s editor, Susan Weidman Schneider, raised the issue of Jewish lesbians in her book *Jewish and Female: Choices and Changes in Our Lives Today*. But Schneider concluded that most lesbians in the Jewish community were more troubled by sexism than by any problems they encountered as lesbians. She concluded "they feel outraged not so much because of their invisibility as lesbians as because of their oppression as women" (315). This perspective marginalizes Jewish lesbian concerns.

Julia Wolf Mazow's 1980 anthology of Jewish women's writings, *The Woman Who Lost Her Names*, includes two lesbian stories, thus breaking the silence in the predominantly heterosexual Jewish feminist community. Susannah Heschel's anthology, *On Being a Jewish Feminist*, published three years later, also includes articles by Jewish lesbians Alice Bloch and Batya Bauman. While Bauman's piece looks at problems with patriarchy, Bloch's essay is a coming out story that conveys the difficulty of finding a comfortable place as a lesbian in the Jewish community. It was the first such complaint to which a broad Jewish audience was exposed.

The inclusion of one or two articles by lesbians was a breakthrough in the 1980s. But recently published Jewish feminist works continue the earlier pattern of token representation rather than full inclusion; this represents a problem. Given the number of Jewish lesbians who are visible in the community, it is hard to believe that our ideas have not been incorporated in collections of Jewish religious feminist writings in ways that are inclusive. Historical works have failed to include any more than scant references to Jewish lesbians. Anthologies have continued to include a token article or two on the subject of lesbianism.

10. When Napoleon emancipated the Jews of France in 1791, the French National Assembly granted the rights and responsibilities of citizenship to every individual Jewish male while at the same time revoking

all special privileges granted to the Jewish people as a nation. For example, Jewish divorces and weddings were no longer legally valid without an accompanying civil ceremony. As was true in other nation-states in Europe, the Jews gave up the right to self-govern in exchange for citizenship.

11. Dafna Hirsch, internet message, January 10, 1996.

12. See Beck, *Nice Jewish Girls*, xl.

13. *New York Times*, March 31, 1993, B2.

14. "Anti-Gay Group Targets Museum," *Jewish Week*, April 12, 1996. An ad hoc Committee for Holocaust Truth protested the inclusion of homosexuals in an exhibit on Nazi victims. Other protests have affected Yad VaShem in Israel and the Holocaust Museum in Washington, D.C.

15. Maggid, "Joining Together: Building a Worldwide Movement," 161.

16. See Kaufman, *The Woman in Jewish Law and Tradition*, 127–128.

17. The Reconstructionist Movement has been a place where gay and lesbian Jews have been able to find a home. Reconstructionists have prided themselves on their willingness to tackle unpopular issues, a legacy of their founder, Mordecai Kaplan. Welcoming gay and lesbian Jews was a slow process for the Reconstructionist movement. In 1978 an openly gay man sought application to the Reconstructionist Rabbinical College (RRC), but the faculty unanimously voted against admitting openly gay students. By 1984, when the issue was raised by another applicant, the college had both a new administration and a new faculty. Under the leadership of President Ira Silverman, and with the work of faculty members Rabbis Hershel Matt and Linda Holtzman, the RRC faculty voted to admit gay and lesbian students to the rabbinate.

Holtzman herself was an open lesbian who was the part-time director of Practical Rabbinics. She had previously been the rabbi of a Conservative congregation in Coatesville, Pennsylvania that was willing to accept her as long as she hid her lesbianism. Matt was a Conservative rabbi who was known for his progressive views on homosexuality and other issues, which were predicated on the notion that gay and lesbian identities were fixed and that there was no question of choice involved. This rationale was an important factor for the success of this effort.

In 1992 the Reconstructionist rabbis and congregations followed the lead of the rabbinical college and published a lengthy document in support of gay men and lesbians in Jewish life. The pamphlet emphasized the ways in which gay men and lesbians are like others in the Jewish community, who are involved in loving, long-term relationships.

The Reconstructionist movement gained much recognition as the first Jewish denomination—and one of the first of any religious groups in the

United States—to be open to lesbians and gay men. The movement has withstood many attacks on its position. (See Carol Towarnicky, "Accepting or Embracing.")

Reform Judaism has also been most accepting. It was the first denomination to give support to gay synagogues, and the vast majority of gay synagogues in the United States are affiliated with the organization of Reform congregations, the Union of American Hebrew Congregations (UAHC). In 1973 Reform leaders in Southern California sponsored the first gay congregation, Beth Chaim Chadashim (BCC).

In 1975 the Union of American Hebrew Congregations passed a resolution in favor of civil rights for gays and lesbians. In 1987 the UAHC began actively to seek gay and lesbian congregations for membership. In 1990 the Reform rabbinical training program, Hebrew Union College, passed guidelines stating that sexual orientation would not bar a candidate from admission to HUC. The rabbinic wing of the Reform movement, the Central Conference of American Rabbis, supported this policy, although its statement affirmed that heterosexual monogamy still stood as the ideal Jewish relationship. (See "Report of the Ad-Hoc Committee on Homosexuality and the Rabbinate.")

Many lesbian rabbis in the Reform movement have, like Reconstructionist rabbis, remained closeted or chosen to serve in gay congregations or in nonpulpit positions. Stacey Offner, the first lesbian rabbi in a traditional congregation to come out, was fired from her position as associate rabbi of Mount Zion Temple in St. Paul, Minnesota, in 1986. She subsequently started her own congregation, Shir Tikvah, which includes gay men and lesbians but is predominantly heterosexual. Beginning in 1994 several open lesbians have gained congregational positions in New York and Los Angeles.

The Reform movement has been outspoken on issues of justice for gay and lesbian Jews through their social justice organization, the Religious Action Center. The Stephen Wise Free Synagogue in New York City, under the leadership of Associate Rabbi Helene Ferris, organized a groundbreaking conference on Gay and Lesbian Jews in the Jewish community in 1986. Ferris's stated goal was to begin a dialogue between the Jewish community and its gay and lesbian members, and a tenth anniversary conference was held by that congregation in 1996.

In 1996 the CCAR voted to support gay and lesbian civil marriage. The issue of conducting religious ceremonies was left to a later date.

The Conservative Movement has included debate on the issue of gay and lesbian Jews in its journals, and leading Conservative rabbis have debated the issues. The congregational organization (the United Synagogue) and the organization of rabbis (the Rabbinical Assembly) have both endorsed civil rights for gays and offered workshops on gay and lesbian issues. But in 1992 the Rabbinical Assembly's Committee on Law and Standards promulgated a decision that gay men and lesbians could be rabbis only if they vowed celibacy and that they could serve as teachers and youth group leaders only at the discretion of local rabbis. Gay marriage ceremonies were deemed unacceptable.

18. See Faderman, *Surpassing the Love of Women*, for a full discussion of the concept of romantic friendship in the modern era.

19. Taylor and Rupp, "Women's Culture and Lesbian Feminist Activism," 32–61.

20. Faderman, *Odd Girls and Twilight Lovers*.

21. The pioneering work in this area has been done by Gayle Rubin in her classic article, "Thinking Sex," 267–319. The edited volume in which it appears is the product of the 1982 conference at Barnard College where issues about sexuality and gender were hotly debated. For radical discussions of lesbian sexuality, see Califia, *Sapphistry*; *The Persistent Desire*, ed. Nestle; and Hollibaugh and Moraga, "What We're Rollin Around in Bed With."

22. Warner, "Introduction" in *Fear of a Queer Planet*, vii-xxxi.

23. See Calhoun, "Separating Lesbian Theory from Feminist Theory," 558–581.

24. Taylor and Rupp, "Women's Culture and Lesbian Feminist Activism."

25. The most complete exposition of separatism is found in *For Lesbians Only: A Separatist Anthology*, ed. Hoagland and Penelope.

26. Reagon, "Coalition Politics," 359.

27. My Jewish lesbian critique of Judaism is based on the feminist model articulated in Judith Plaskow's *Standing Again at Sinai*. The notes to Plaskow's text provide a thorough bibliography of Jewish feminist writings to 1990.

28. Leviticus 18:22. This text is discussed more fully in chapter 2.

29. David Biale, "Who Was a Jew—Who Is a Jew?"

30. Silberstein, "Others Within and Others Without," 14. Many scholars have suggested that the Jewish community's own history of being outsiders has kept us from seeing the ways in which we have the power to define others as outsiders as well.

31. This definition is not broadly shared in the Jewish community, which generally defines inclusion based on birth or conversion. While I understand the dangers of my definition—it is too inclusive, anyone or any group can claim connection and define themselves as Jews—I am more concerned about the problems we encounter and the energy we waste setting up more rigid boundaries. I therefore prefer to make broad definitions

and to err on the side of inclusion in this process. For helpful discussions of boundary questions see "Negotiating Boundaries" in *The Reconstructionist* and *Jewish Identity*, ed. Goldberg and Krausz.

32. Collins, *Black Feminist Thought*, 21.

2. TROUBLING TEXTS FROM TORAH

1. Although in this context Torah refers specifically to the first five books of the Hebrew Bible (Genesis, Exodus, Leviticus, Numbers, and Deuteronomy), the term "Torah" is used generally about all Jewish teaching. This use of "Torah" includes all of the Hebrew Bible (which Christians have called the Old Testament). The Hebrew Bible is comprised of the first five books (Torah); Prophets (early historical books and the writings of the Hebrew prophets); and Writings (Psalms, Proverbs, later historical materials, and the stories of Job, Ruth, and Esther). The Hebrew Bible is often called the Written Torah, and later works are called Oral Torah. The Jewish texts to which I refer later in this chapter (for example, Mishnah, Talmud, Sifra, Rashi's commentaries, Tosafot, Emunot ve-Deot, Torah Temimah, Mishneh Torah) are all part of Torah in its more general sense. These texts, written over a two-thousand-year period, contain commentary on the Hebrew Bible as well as legislation, folklore, and theology.

2. See Anne Fausto-Sterling, "How Many Sexes Are There?" *New York Times*, March 12, 1993, A15.

3. See Bornstein, *Gender Outlaw* and Feinberg, *Stone Butch Blues*, for poignant descriptions of the discrimination experienced by those who refuse to define themselves as "he" or "she."

4. For a discussion of these concepts see Devor, *Gender Blending*, Garber, *Vested Interests*, 128–164, and Ponse, *Identities in the Lesbian World*.

5. This concept was developed by Rich, "Compulsory Heterosexuality and Lesbian Existence," 631.

6. See Adler, "The Virgin in the Brothel," 32.

7. See Kimelman, "Homosexuality and Family-Centered Judaism," 53–57 and Levado, "Family Values: A Reply to Reuven Kimelman," 57–60.

8. Lamm, "Judaism and the Modern Jewish Attitude to Homosexuality," 194–205. This article achieved wide circulation and has been reprinted in *Contemporary Jewish Ethics*, ed. Kellner, 375–400 and *Jewish Bioethics*, ed. Bleich and Rosner, 197–218.

9. Lamm, "Judaism and the Modern Attitude to Homosexuality," 198.

10. Freehof, "A Responsum," 31.

11. It is also found in later sources, *Genesis Rabbah* 26:6 and *Leviticus Rabbah* 23:9.

12. See Mannich, "Some Aspects of Egyptian Sexual Life," 330.

13. Cantarella, *Bisexuality in the Ancient World*, 166.

14. See Boswell, *Christianity, Social Tolerance, and Homosexuality*, 26 and 84. Boswell explores the issue of male same-sex marriage in antiquity further in *Same-Sex Unions in Premodern Europe*.

15. *Paidagōgos* 2, 3:21. For further information about the early church and female homoeroticism, consult Brooten, *Love Between Women*.

16. *The Sentences of Pseudo-Phocylides*, line 192.

17. Brooten, "Paul's Views On the Nature of Women and Female Homoeroticism," 64, suggests that the context makes it clear that the reference is to female homosexual behavior.

18. See *Babylonian Talmud* (Soncino: London, 1938), *Yebamot* 76a.

19. For a discussion of the relationship between female homoeroticism and penetration in ancient Jewish texts, see Satlow, " 'They Abused Him Like a Woman'," 16–17.

20. The definition of tribadism is found in the commentary of Rashi (1040–1105) who explains the meaning of mesolelot in the *Babylonian Talmud*: "Like in the intercourse of male and female they rub the genitals against one another" *Yebamot* 76a.

21. Moses Maimonides, *Mishneh Torah, Issurei Bi'ah* 21:8.

22. Lamm, "Judaism and the Modern Attitude to Homosexuality," 203.

23. Kaufman, *The Woman in Jewish Law and Tradition*, 127–128. Earlier works about Jewish women from an Orthodox perspective never mention lesbianism at all.

24. There has been ample discussion on this topic. See for example, Rachel Biale, *Women and Jewish Law*; Plaskow, *Standing Again at Sinai*; Wegner, *Chattel or Person?*.

3. JEWISH LESBIAN INTERPRETATION OF TORAH

1. Arthur Waskow, personal communication.

2. I am indebted to the writings of Rabbi Hershel Matt (of blessed memory) for this interpretation.

3. ben Ari, *Menorah*, 1.

4. Levado, "Gayness and God," 60.

5. Trible, *God and the Rhetoric of Sexuality*, 77.

6. This phrase is often translated as helpmeet, which suggests a relationship of dependency between man and woman at the very start. But the Hebrew phrase may also be understood as meaning counterpart or companion, emphasizing the contradictory ezer (helper) c'negdo (opposite).

7. See Patai, *The Hebrew Goddess*, 180–225 and Koltuv, *The Book of Lilith* for extended discussions of the legends surrounding the figure of Lilith.

8. Plaskow, "The Coming of Lilith," 206.

9. Eilberg-Schwartz, *God's Phallus*, 137–162 and Wolfson, *Through A Speculum*.

10. Contemporary biblical critic Saul Olyan has argued that the only forbidden act was anal penetration. He bases his assumption on a philological analysis of the term "mishkavei ishah," which he translates as "the lying down of a woman." Olyan, " 'And With a Male You Shall Not Lie the Lying Down of a Woman'," 184–186.

11. For this interpretation, see Boswell, *Christianity, Social Tolerance, and Homosexuality*, 100–101. Olyan disagrees with Boswell's interpretation of to'evah. Olyan translates to'evah as "the violation of a socially constructed boundary, the undermining or reversal of what is conventional, the order of things as the ancient might see it." " 'And With a Male'," 180, n. 3.

12. There are many different explanantions for the purity concerns of the biblical text. See Mary Douglas, *Purity and Danger*, and Howard Eilberg-Schwartz, *The Savage in Judaism*, 177–216. Olyan summarizes theirs and other arguments on the relationship between the prohibition in Leviticus and other purity laws. He concludes that the prohibition against anal intercourse between two men should be looked at in the context of impure mixing, presumably between feces and semen, "the mixing of two otherwise polluting substances in the body of the receptive partner," 206.

13. Olyan argues that these two texts not only reflect different punishments but also different sensibilities about homosexual behavior. In Leviticus 18 only the penetrator is held responsible. In Leviticus 20 both men involved in the act are guilty and subject to the death penalty. " 'And With a Male'," 188.

14. See for example, Trible, *God and the Rhetoric of Sexuality*; Schüssler Fiorenza, *In Memory of Her*; Plaskow, *Standing Again at Sinai*; Teubal, *Sarah the Priestess*; and *Reading Ruth*, ed. Kates and Reimer.

15. *Ceremonies of the Heart*, ed. Butler, 13.

16. The story is based on an incident in a novel by Flagg, *Fried Green Tomatoes*, 191.

17. Hirsch, "In Search of Role Models," 84–85.

18. David Biale, *Eros and the Jews*, 15. Biale is not himself suggesting any lesbian connotations when he draws this comparison, though to me they seem unmistakable.

19. See Hirsch, "In Search of Role Models," 84–85.

20. See *Ruth: A New Translation [Anchor Bible]*, ed. Campbell, 22–23.

21. In her feminist commentary on Ruth in *Countertraditions in the Bible*, Pardes does suggest that the defining relationship in the story is

female bonding between Ruth and Naomi, although she does not consider the possibility of a lesbian dimension to this bonding.

22. I am grateful to Lori Lefkovitz for imagining these questions.

4. HAẒNEA LEKHET IM ELOHEKHA: JEWISH LESBIAN VISIBILITY

1. The concept of ahavat ḥesed is difficult to translate. The standard translation is love of mercy, but this is inadequate. Ahavat ḥesed is love that is based on kindness. Perhaps it is the love of which Martin Buber speaks when he defines the "I-Thou" relationship, love that is focused on the well-being of the "thou." I have decided to translate this concept as loving well.

2. As to the origins of lesbianism, evidence comes from people's lives. Some women claim that they have had erotic same-sex attractions from the time they were three; others claim to experience these feelings for the first time late in life. Both groups tell the truth. Women come to terms with lesbianism at different speeds and in different ways. See Plaskow, "Lesbian and Gay Rights," 31–32 for a fuller discussion of the issue of choice and biology.

3. This argument is based on Lorde, "The Uses of the Erotic."

4. Johansson and Percy, *Outing*, 297–298.

5. See interview with Yoel Kahn, *Advocate* (February 12, 1991).

6. Johannson and Percy, *Outing*, 290.

7. The blessing formula "let us bless the source of life" is the work of Marcia Falk. See her "Notes on Composing New Blessings," 39–53. My thanks to Leila Gal Berner for her help with constructing the rest of the blessing.

8. I am grateful to Sarra Levine for reminding me about this connection.

9. Abramowitz, "Growing up in Yeshiva," 26–27.

10. Until a few years ago it was commonly accepted practice in the lesbian community that one does not reveal information about another's sexual orientation. This behavior is crucial to a closeted lesbian who fears being hurt by others who find out about her identity. Recently the gay community has been engaged in debates about the practice of "outing." I have discussed the merits of the practice earlier in this chapter. Observing public ceremonies should not be construed as a license to discuss someone's sexual orientation without their permission. When someone comes out, it makes sense to ask them how many people know and with whom they wish the matter discussed.

11. Cooper, "No Longer Invisible," 84–86, gives a detailed history of the gay synagogue movement.

12. The early history of Beth Simchat Torah (CBST) is detailed in an ethnography of the synagogue by Shokeid, *A Gay Synagogue in New York*, 32–62.

13. Brick, "Judaism in the Gay Community," 83.

14. See Shokeid, *A Gay Synagogue*, 174–182, on how these processes developed at CBST. It is important to note that many of the men who were involved in the gay synagogue movement considered themselves feminists and fought for egalitarian language and feminist innovations along with their lesbian sisters.

15. Maggid, "Joining Together: Building a Worldwide Movement," 165.

16. See Marder, "Getting to Know the Gay and Lesbian Shul," 209–217.

17. Cooper, "No Longer Invisible," 85.

18. The *New York Times* covered the story on four occasions in 1993: March 31, when CBST refused the organizers' suggestion that they could march, but without their banner (B2); April 21, when a compromise was reached that CBST could march with the Reform movement's Zionist group (B12); May 5, when the *Times* profiled Sharon Kleinbaum, "'Luckiest Rabbi in America' Holds Faith Amidst the Hate," [Alex Witchell, C1]; and finally on May 8, when the synagogue was barred from marching, and decided to hold a separate event (A16).

5. AHAVAT ḤESED: TRANSFORMING RELATIONSHIPS

1. Beck, "Why is This Book Different?," xiii.

2. Katz, *Running Fiercely*, 171–183. See the discussion of this work in chapter 9.

3. See Weston, *The Families We Choose*, 40–41.

4. This argument is presented in detail by Ettelbrick, "Since When Was Marriage the Path to Liberation?," 14–17.

5. Examples of Jewish lesbian commitment ceremonies are Silverberg-Willis and Silverberg-Willis, "Gospel Under the Chuppah," 55–70; Leipzig and Mable, "Tikkun Olam," 289–305; and Gal Berner and Gal Primack, "Uncharted Territories," 173–177.

6. The Reform rabbinical association (CCAR) affirmed its commitment to gay and lesbian civil marriage at the 1996 convention. They will take up the issue of religious marriage at a later date. The Reconstructionist rabbinical association (RRA) affirmed its commitment to civil and religious marriage for gay men and lesbians in 1993.

7. See for example Gal Berner and Gal Primack, "Uncharted Territory," 175–178.

8. I am indebted to Rebecca Lillian for the last interpretation.

9. Silverberg-Willis and Silverberg-Willis, "Gospel Under the Chuppah," 55–70.

10. A documentary about a lesbian commitment ceremony conducted by Rabbi Sue Levi Elwell, *Chicks in White Satin*, was nominated for an Academy Award in 1994. It deals with many of the dilemmas involved in lesbian weddings and can be used to trigger conversations about the subject.

11. See Eisenbach-Budner, "Spilling Out Wine," 44.

12. Balka, "Thoughts on Lesbian Parenting," 57–65.

6. Asot Mishpat: The Commitment to Justice

1. This idea was first developed by Gilligan, *In A Different Voice*. It has been debated in feminist scholarship for many years.

2. Heyward, "Sexuality, Love, and Justice," 92.

3. It is my hope that some groups will want to call this event Queer Awareness Week, to signal the inclusion of bisexual and transgendered people in the celebration and learning.

4. It is important to note that the United States is not the only place where a change in the status of gay and lesbian Jews has taken place in recent years. Israel has begun to make changes in its legal system toward the acceptance of lesbian and gay Jews. Israel's decriminalization of homosexuality in 1988 was a very significant change. Prior to that time gay and lesbian Jews were not welcome in Israel under the law of return, which grants any Jew citizenship. Legal and social discrimination kept Israeli lesbians silent for many years. A homophile organization, the Society for the Protection of Personal Rights, has existed in Israel since 1975. Its primary focus has been the protection of the civil rights of gay men and lesbians. Among the leaders of the Israeli feminist movement were many closeted lesbians, some of whom in the past few years have been courageous enough to come out. Kol Isha, the Israeli feminist organization, was known to be a meeting place for lesbians from its inception in the 1970s. One of its leaders, Knesset member Marcia Freedman, came out in 1977 and experienced extreme marginalization in Israeli society. Freedman faced terrible pressure on her family, which ultimately resulted in her leaving Israel, as she describes in her memoirs, *Exile in the Promised Land*. Another Israeli feminist involved in Kol Isha, Chaya Shalom, founded CLAF, the Israeli Lesbian Feminist Organization. In 1993 a lesbian conference sponsored by CLAF was hosted by the Knesset. Knesset Member Yael Dayan has also been a leading supporter of gay and lesbian rights. *Lesbiōt: Israeli Lesbians Talk About Sexuality, Feminism, Judaism and Their Lives*, edited by Tracy Moore, tells the stories of the lives of Israeli lesbians over the last two decades through oral histories.

Clearly, the environment in Israel has become more open, if not yet accepting of lesbianism. Other lesbian support groups, including one known as Orthodykes, meet to deal with the connections between religious observance and lesbianism. (See "On Being Orthodox and Lesbian.") There is even a small gay and lesbian congregation that meets in Tel Aviv. The Israeli Supreme Court has required El Al Airlines to give partnership benefits to one of its employees, opening the door for similar legislation. Things are also improving for lesbians in England (see Elizabeth Sarah's article), France (see Marthe Rosenfeld's article), and in Australia where many Jewish lesbian groups have formed. (Workshop, International Conference of Gay and Lesbian Jews, New York, 1995.)

5. Such films include *Out in Suburbia: The Stories of Eleven Lesbians, Gay Youth, Forbidden Love: The Unashamed Stories of Lesbian Lives, Johanna d'Arc of Mongolia, Oy Gay, Queer Son, Treif, Emily and Gitta* (Jewish themes), *Came Out, It Rained, Went Back In Again, War on Lesbians, First Comes Love* (on marriage), *Damned if You Don't* (Catholic themes), *The Ties That Bind* (Holocaust, mother/daughter themes), *Women Like Us* (lesbian history), *Lifetime Commitment* (legal issues), *No Need to Repent: The Ballad of Rev. Jan Griesinger* (story of a lesbian minister), *Exposure* (intersection of sexual and racial identities).

6. I am grateful to Rebecca Lillian for this suggestion.

7. The New Jewish Agenda National Platform demands that Jewish communal institutions pay attention to the needs of lesbians and gay men, among others, who have been "consistently disregarded."

8. Armstrong describes this event in "New Jewish Agenda Havdallah Service." This tradition was continued by the editors of *Bridges* who sponsored a similar event at the April 1993 march. See "At the March on Washington with *Bridges*." By 1993 there were several non-gay Jewish organizations that illustrated their commitment to gay and lesbian Jewish issues by marching in the parade.

9. See "From the Editors," 4.

10. David Biale comments that "for a Jewish woman to adopt a sexual identity, and even more to adopt a lesbian identity, is to challenge the myths of the asexual Jewish woman." *Eros and the Jews*, 225.

11. Iris Marion Young has begun this work in *Justice and the Politics of Difference*.

12. Many lesbians resent the claims of bisexuals that they are the most stigmatized group, accepted neither by heterosexuals or lesbians. Lesbians point out the danger of living openly as lesbian as compared to the relative protection of heterosexual privilege for bisexuals who live with men but want access to the culture and companionship—sexual and otherwise—of lesbians.

13. See essays by Rich, "Split at the Root," Kaye/Kantrowitz, "Some Notes on Jewish Lesbian Identity," Miriam, "Anti-Semitism in the Lesbian Community," Liza and Penny, "Anti-Semitism in the Lesbian Movement," and Mushroom, "Merrill Mushroom is a Jew."

14. Beck, *Nice Jewish Girls*, xxxi and Klepfisz, *Dreams of an Insomniac*, 80.

15. Rich, "If Not With Others, How?," 209.

16. Bulkin, Pratt, and Smith, *Yours in Struggle*, 95.

17. Beverly Smith with Stein and Golding, "The Possibility of Life Between Us," 25–46.

18. Klepfisz, *Dreams of an Insomniac*, 118.

7. MODERN TEXTS: JEWISH LESBIAN SEXUALITY

1. See for example Vicinus, "They Wonder to Which Sex I Belong," 171–198; *Hidden From History*, ed. Duberman, et al.; Faderman, *Surpassing the Love of Women* and *Odd Girls and Twilight Lovers*, 215–308; Kennedy and Davis, *Boots of Leather, Slippers of Gold* and Smith-Rosenberg, "The Female World of Love and Ritual," 53–76.

2. See Bullough and Bullough, *Cross Dressing, Sex, and Gender*; Garber, *Vested Interests: Cross-Dressing and Cultural Anxiety*; and Newton, "The Mythic Mannish Lesbian," 557–575. See also Devor, *Gender Blending*. Devor looks at women who have been mistaken for men, and the relationship between appearance and desire.

3. Foucault, *The History of Sexuality: An Introduction*; Laqueur, *Making Sex*; and Weeks, *Sexuality and its Discontents*.

4. Gay history in Western antiquity and in early cultures worldwide has received the attention of serious scholars in the last decade. Most of these authors note the paucity of information about female homoeroticism. See, for example, Boswell, *Christianity, Social Tolerance and Homosexuality* and Greenberg, *The Construction of Homo-sexuality*.

5. See Grahn, *Another Mother Tongue*. Lillian Faderman has collected literary texts that illustrate the possibilities of finding such a history in *Chloe Plus Olivia*.

6. The best known example of female homoeroticism in antiquity is the Greek poet Sappho (612–560 BCE). The term "lesbian," which did not come into common use to refer to female homoeroticism until the nineteenth century, derives from the island of Lesbos on which Sappho lived. There is scholarly dispute over whether or not Sappho herself was a lover of women. There is general agreement that at least between the sixth and fourth centuries BCE erotic love between women was part of the fabric of ancient Greek civilization. See Hallett, "Sappho and Her Social Context,"; Stigers, "Romantic Sensuality, Poetic Sense"; and Eva Cantarella,

Bisexuality in the Ancient World. Bernadette Brooten argues that marriages between women existed in antiquity in her work on female homoeroticism in the Ancient World (quoted in an interview with Eduoard Fontenot, "Of Spells and Lesbians in Ancient Rome," 12.)

7. Wiesen Cook, "Review Essay: *The Life of Lorena Hickok,*" 511.

8. The lesbians I have chosen to include all had meaningful relationships to their Jewish identity as well. For the purposes of this book, I have omitted discussing the lives of lesbians such as the painter Gluck, writer Jane Bowles, or members of Natalie Barney's circle, all of whom identified as Jews but for whom that identification had little or no meaning in their lives. Gertrude Stein and Alice B. Toklas, although also both Jewish, are also omitted from this account. Stein and Toklas both had problematic relationships to their Jewish heritage—Stein was often negative or ambivalent about her Jewishness; Toklas ultimately converted to Christianity. For further information about their connections to Judaism, see Watts, " 'Can Women Have Wishes' " and Orenstein, *The Reflowering of the Goddess,* 50–56.

9. See Diller, *Freud's Jewish Identity,* 209–218.

10. Freud, "Hysterical Fantasies," 151. Freud's emphasis on the innate nature of bisexuality and his insistence that lesbianism was neither an illness nor easily changed through psychoanalysis is evident both in this work and his later "The Psychogenesis of a Case of Homosexuality in a Woman."

11. See Deutsch, "A Footnote to Freud's 'Fragment of an Analysis of a Case of Hysteria'," 42.

12. Freud, "Hysterical Fantasies," 142. Only one interpreter, Lewin, "Dora Revisted," 520–532, suggests that Dora's lesbianism was central to her life and that Freud's inability to see it marred his work in this case. Others suggest that Freud miscalculated the nature of the transference and that Dora saw Freud as representing the women in Dora's life. See Jerre Collins, "Questioning the Unconscious," 243–253.

13. Rich, "Compulsory Heterosexuality and Lesbian Existence," 635–637.

14. Jacobus, "Dora and the Pregnant Madonna," 137–196.

15. Ramas, "Freud's Dora, Dora's Hysteria," 472–510.

16. Ibid., 478.

17. Daniels, *Always a Sister,* 5–12.

18. Wiesen Cook, "Female Support Networks," 51.

19. Ibid., 52.

20. Ibid., 53.

21. Daniels, *Always a Sister,* 72.

22. Ibid.

23. Wiesen Cook argues that "women who love women, who choose women to nurture and support and to create a living environment in which to work creatively and independently, are lesbians." "Female Support Networks," 48.

24. Daniels, *Always a Sister*, 74.

25. The history of this play's production provides important data with which to reconstruct Jewish attitiudes toward lesbianism. Asch wrote the play in Yiddish in 1907. It was performed without incident in Germany, Austria, Poland, Holland, Norway, Sweden, Italy, and in the Yiddish theater of the Lower East Side of New York. The play was produced for seventeen years before any problems arose with its presentation. The first difficulties occurred in 1923 when an English language version, starring well-known Yiddish theatre actor Rudolph Schildkraut, appeared on Broadway. As part of the antivice attitudes of the post World War I era, a citizens group, the Society for the Suppression of Vice, brought charges of obscenity, demanding that the play be shut down. Although the cast was arrested and fined, the play continued to be performed.

In Kaier Curtin's study of this play, he notes that class and cultural differences between Russian and German Jews in the United States played an important role in this episode. German Jews were actively involved in the antivice movement. The Society for the Suppression of Vice was headed by the rabbi of Reform Temple Emanuel, Joseph Silverman. The actors and producers were, of course, part of the Yiddish theater dear to the Russian immigrants.

For further information, see Curtin, *We Can Always Call Them Bulgarians*. Curtin writes extensively about the play, its background, and the reviews it received and should be consulted about the role of this play in the context of the portrayal of gays and lesbians in the American theater.

26. Asch, *The God of Vengeance*, 17.

27. Ibid., 40.

28. Ibid., 59.

29. Ibid., 59–60.

30. Curtin, *We Can Always Call Them Bulgarians*, 29.

31. Singer, "Zeitl and Rickel," 117.

32. Ibid., 199.

33. Unless otherwise indicated, I am indebted for this discussion of Pauline Newman's life to Orleck, *Common Sense and a Little Fire*, which she graciously discussed with me and permitted me to read in manuscript form.

34. Ibid., 71.

35. Chauncey, *Gay New York*, 227–244.

36. See Kessler-Harris, "Organizing the Unorganizable," 14.

8. MODERN TEXTS: LESBIANS AS
GENDER NONCONFORMISTS

1. Ellis, *Studies in the Psychology of Sex*, 195–264 and Krafft-Ebing, *Psychopathia Sexualis*. For a comprehensive discussion, see Faderman, *Odd Girls*, chapter 2 and D'Emilio and Freedman, *Intimate Matters*, 222–235.

2. Horodetzky's main interest was to prove that Hasidic tradition had an important role for women. See his *Leaders in Hasidism*. His efforts have been adequately disproven by Ada Rapoport-Albert, "On Women in Hasidism." They are nonetheless perpetuated in our times in such works as Gershon Winkler's *They Called Her Rebbe*, a book for adolescent girls.

3. Horodetzky, 115.

4. Ibid.

5. Ibid., 116.

6. Rapoport-Albert, "On Women in Hasidism," 495–525.

7. Singer, *Shosha*, 27.

8. Singer, *Yentl the Yeshiva Boy*, 8.

9. Ibid., 20.

10. Ibid., 23.

11. Ibid., 36.

12. Eve Sicular finds a similar cross-dressing motif present in the Yiddish film *Yidl mitn fidl* (1936). Noted Yiddish film star Molly Picon cross-dresses in this film so that she can obtain work as an itinerant klezmer musician. Like Streisand's Yentl, there is no hint of ambiguity in Yidl's sexual desire for the male lead, nor is there any real confusion about Yidl's gender. " 'A yingl mit a yingl hot epes a tam'," 41. See also Sicular, "Gender Rebellion in Yiddish Film," 12–17.

13. In her comments about the film Streisand has vehemently rejected any homoeroticism in the text, even the more obvious male homosexuality in the double entendres between Anshel/Yentl and Avigdor. Garber has a lengthy discussion of Streisand's reading of the text, and of Singer's reaction to it, *Vested Interests*, 63–76. See also Schanfield, "Singer's 'Yentl'," 185–192.

14. Just before her death in 1994 Ruth Seid published a memoir, *The Seasons: Death and Transfiguration*. The memoir does not yield any information about the character of Deborah Brown, but certain details of Ruth Seid's life bear a strong resemblance to the fictional character. Like Deborah, Ruth was the youngest of five in a working class Jewish family in the midwest. She was a writer who loved books and music and did not conform to the expectations of her family. Also like Deborah, Ruth took a job with the WPA, which enabled her family to get off relief, and had her first article published by *New Masses*. Unlike Deborah, Ruth did not

believe in traditional psychotherapy. Much of the memoir focuses on her relationship with Helen, her mentor and patron. As Ruth explains in the memoir, Helen was her therapist who helped her develop as a writer and a human being. Although several reviews refer to Seid herself as a lesbian based on her relationship with Helen, and her obituary mentions her "dear friend, Joan Soffer, with whom she lived for more than 20 years" (*Philadelphia Inquirer*, April 7, 1995, B6), Seid did not define herself as a lesbian and was not interested in discussing her works or her life with the current generation of Jewish lesbians who sought her out. Because of the intensity of oppression in the 1950s, Sinclair never again created a Jewish lesbian character. When her novel *The Changelings* was originally published in 1956, the main character was a young Jewish woman. Judy Vincent was in fact a lesbian in the first draft of the novel, but all references to her lesbianism were omitted when the book was published. Ruth Seid's manuscript drafts and papers are in the Twentieth Century Archives at Mugar Memorial Library, Boston University. I am indebted to Elly Bulkin for pointing this information about *The Changelings* out to me.

15. Sinclair, *Wasteland*, 26.

16. Ibid., 122.

17. Ibid.

18. Ibid., 189.

19. Ibid., 191.

20. Ibid., 273.

21. Decker, *Freud, Dora, and Vienna, 1900*, 2.

22. Gilman, "The Jewish Psyche," 60–103.

23. In photographs of Wolff, she has a strongly masculine appearance. This impression was corroborated by James Steakley, who came to know her at the end of her life. (Personal communication, November, 1994). See Steakley's interview with Wolff, "Love Between Women and Love Between Men."

24. Wolff, *Hindsight*, 2.

25. Ibid., 3.

26. Ibid., 6.

27. Ibid., 26.

28. Ibid., 21.

29. Ibid., 48.

30. Ibid., 7.

31. Ibid., 26.

32. For information about lesbian culture in Weimar Germany, see "Germany: Not Just Memories," 28–29, and "Sixty places to talk, dance and play," 16–18, and about the fate of lesbians under Nazi rule see Fisher, *Aimée and Jaguar* and Schoppmann, *Days of Masquerade*.

33. Wolff, *Hindsight*, 74.

34. Ibid.

35. Wolff, *Magnus Hirschfield*, 377.

36. Wolff, *Hindsight*, 110.

37. Wolff, *A Psychology of Gesture*, 199.

38. Ibid., 200. See also Wolff, *The Hand in Psychological Diagnosis*, 26–29, 112, 193–197.

39. Ibid., 60.

40. Ibid., 215.

41. Ibid., 218.

42. Ibid., 218.

43. Wolff, *Love Between Women*, 41.

44. Ibid., 21.

45. Ibid., 46.

46. Wolff, *Hindsight*, 220.

47. Wolff, *Bisexuality: A Study*, 106.

48. Ibid., 109.

49. Wolff, *Hindsight*, 296.

50. Ibid., 219.

51. Wolff, *Hirschfeld*, 98.

52. Ibid., 402.

53. Wolff, *Hindsight*, 262.

54. Ibid., 266.

55. Ibid., 295.

56. Ibid., 237.

57. Ibid., 155.

58. Wolff, *Hirschfeld*, 103, 285.

9. CONTEMPORARY JEWISH LESBIAN FICTION

1. Bloch, *The Law of Return*, 75.

2. Ibid., 85.

3. Ibid., 93.

4. Bonnie Zimmerman suggests a connection between food and sex in lesbian literature in general, *Safe Sea of Women*, 104–105. This connection is prevalent in Jewish lesbian writing. One of Lesléa Newman's characters writes a series of Yiddish couplets. Many of them are sexual, and several are about the sexual delights of Jewish food and women's bodies (*Harvey Milk*, 70). Jano's story of lovemaking between Yetta and Hannah is a fantasy in which Yetta's hands and mouth on Hannah's nipples turn them into bagels and then challah for their Shabbat meal. "The Woman Who Lied," 116–118.

Judith Stein writes an erotic ode to sour cream, to her the quintessential "Eastern European Jewish food." She describes a scene where she and her girlfriend, "two gorgeous fat dumpling Jewish girls" decide to smear sour cream on each other's breasts and lick it off. As Stein concludes, "See, she really loves sour cream too, nice Yiddish maidl that she is! And me, I'm more and more thrilled about sour cream all the time." "Jewish Food."

Jyl Lynn Felman's protagonist, Esther, goes through a transformation from Jewish to lesbian in "Hot Chicken Wings." In this case, eating treif food is the beginning of Esther's feeling comfortable with her "treif" lesbian desire. She must leave being Jewish in order to be at home in a lesbian identity, as symbolized by the food she eats.

5. Schulman, 59–61.

6. Katz, 115.

7. Ibid., 81.

8. Ibid., 151–152.

9. Rejection by the Jewish family is a common theme in the works of Jewish lesbian writers. It is the focus of the three earliest lesbian novels: Sinclair's *Wasteland* (1946), Ruth Geller's *Triangles* (1984), and Nancy Toder's *Choices* (1980). Family also figures significantly in the more recent works of Jyl Felman and Lesléa Newman. In some stories the Jewish symbolism of family rejection is vivid. In Sara Levi Calderon's *The Two Mujeres*, Valeria's adult son hits her over the head with a family menorah upon finding her with her female lover. Often lesbian relationships cannot survive family pressures. In Ellen Gruber Garvey's "Soup Story," Nan and Michelle separate after Michelle's visit home to her family who ignore her lesbian relationship and pressure her to marry. Nikki and Ilana's relationship ends after a long visit from Ilana's Israeli Holocaust survivor mother, who describes Ilana's lesbianism as a stab in the heart. In Shelley, "The Car O'Tea Belove."

10. Schulman, 59.

11. Katz, 171–183.

12. Galford, 247.

13. Naomi Schemen writes poignantly of a Jewish lesbian seder where the father of one of the women participated with joy. "Accepting his daughter's lesbianism was the improbable route back to his own Jewishness." ("Jewish Lesbian Writing: A Review Essay," 193.)

14. Bloch, 204.

15. Ibid., 216.

16. Ibid., 231.

17. Ibid.

18. Ibid., 248.

19. Galford, 1.

20. Changing names is expressive of identity formation in several Jewish lesbian short stories. Thyme Seagull's protagonist changes her Yiddish sounding name, Cheikie. "It's a tribal name. I belong to a different tribe now." "My Mother Was a Light Housekeeper," 186. Elisheva

Rogin changed her name from Ellen when she immigrated to Israel. In Lesléa Newman's *In Every Laugh a Tear*, the protagonist changes her name from Linda to Shayna when she comes out as a lesbian (1), an interesting reversal of the pattern set by Thyme Seagull and indicative of a change over time in Jewish lesbians' attitudes about claiming their Jewishness.

21. Much lesbian Jewish fiction incorporates fantasies of Jewish lesbians living in the past. In *The Sophie Horowitz Story*, Sophie admires Muffin's dexterity and dark complexion and muses that Muffin was "the kind of woman my grandmother probably made out with in the potato fields of Lithuania." (60) Several Jewish lesbian short stories also fantasize about Jewish lesbians in the past. Teya Schaffer's "With Love, Lena," 157–158, is a story of repressed love between Jewish women immigrants on New York's lower east side. Marcy Alancraig wrote about two Jewish women chicken farmers in Petaluma, California in the 1930s and their mutual attraction. Rheabie and Mae are neighbors who explore their sexual passion despite Rheabie's fears. "Such a Business," 71–76. Susan Ruth Goldberg explores the possibility that Teibl and Chana might have become lovers had the destruction of the Warsaw Ghetto not prevented them. In her letter to Chana in April, 1943 Teibl describes the depth of her love and the intensity of her passion which "I have not had . . . for any young man, ever." "Letter from the Warsaw Ghetto," 31–33.

22. Galford, 235.

23. Ibid.

24. Katz, 159.

25. Ibid., 186.

10. VISIONS FOR THE FUTURE

1. Cleaver, *Know My Name*, provides interpretations of Christian scripture that are helpful in this effort.

Glossary

(Words are from the Hebrew unless otherwise indicated.)

adamah: The earth.

Aḥare Mot: Portion of the Torah that includes the interdiction of male homosexual behavior.

aliyah: The honor of reciting a blessing over the Torah during a public reading.

apikoros (Greek): Skeptic, one who refuses to observe Jewish law and custom.

aufruf (Yiddish): Special aliyah for a bridegroom the Sabbath before his wedding.

bar/bat mitzvah: Literally, son/daughter of the commandments; ritual upon reaching the age of majority.

bet din (pl. **batei din**): Religious court.

bet midrash: House of study.

betulah: Virgin.

bimah: Pulpit.

brit: Literally, covenant. Term used to describe baby-naming ceremonies for girls, which have become popular in recent times. Throughout most of its history, Judaism did not initiate women into the covenant of Israel and had no special ceremonies for the birth of a girl child.

d'var torah: Commentary on a Jewish text during a religious service.

dybbuk: The spirit of a dead person that enters a living person.

ezer c'negdo: Helpmeet, counterpart, companion.

enosh: Man.

farbrente (Yiddish): ardent, zealous.

Ḥabad (Chabad): Sect of Hasidic Jews.

haftarah: Prophetic portion of the Hebrew Bible read every Sabbath.

haggadah (pl. haggadot): Text used at Passover seder.

halakhah: Jewish legal writings.

ḥamez (chametz): Leavened bread, not to be eaten during Passover.

Ḥanukkah (Chanukah): Holiday commemorating the rededication of the temple in the second century B.C.E.

havdallah: Ritual for the closing of the Sabbath.

ḥevruta (chevruta): Learning partners.

ḥuppah (chuppah): Marriage canopy, marriage ceremony.

ketubbah (pl. ketubbot): Marriage contract.

kikombe (African): Cup used during Kwanzaa celebration that represents unity.

Kwanzaa: African-American celebration at the winter solstice.

lashon hara: Gossip, spreading rumors.

lazet min hamezarim (latzet min hametzarim): Neologism for coming out.

mazzah (matzah): Unleavened bread eaten on Passover.

mazzal tov (mazel tov): Greeting of congratulations.

meḥizah (mechitzah): Physical barrier separating the women's section in a traditional synagogue.

mesolelot: Lesbian behavior.

midrash: The process of making commentary to interpret the text.

mikveh: Ritual bath.

mishkavei ishah: Sexual intercourse, penetration.

Mishnah: Ancient compilation of Jewish law.

Mizrayim (Mitzrayim): Egypt; literally, narrow place.

mohel: Ritual circumciser.

nashim: Women.

niddah: A menstruant woman.

nosin: Technical term for Jewish marriage.

payis (Yiddish): Hairlocks worn by Hasidic men in observation of the biblical commandment that prohibits shaving the corners of the head.

Pesaḥ (Pesach): Passover, the spring festival that marks Jewish liberation from Egypt.

priẓut (pritzut): Minor infraction.

rebbitzin (Yiddish): Rabbi's wife.

reyut: Passionate friendship.

Shabbat Shirah: Sabbath during which the portion about crossing the sea to freedom is read.

shammes (Yiddish): Caretaker of the synagogue.

shamor: To keep.

sheva berakhot: The seven wedding blessings.

shiva: Jewish mourning observance.

shul (Yiddish): Synagogue.

tallit: Prayer shawl.

Talmud: Fifth-century compilation of Jewish law, which encompasses the Mishnah and the commentaries on the Mishnah known as gemara. There are two versions of the Talmud, one compiled in Babylonia and the other in Jerusalem. The Babylonian Talmud is the more complete and more commonly referenced work.

tashlikh: Ceremony conducted on the New Year for casting out sins.

tefillin: Leather amulets placed on the head and arms during weekday morning prayers, in fulfillment of the biblical commandment: "You shall bind them for a sign on your hand and they shall be frontlets between your eyes" (Deuteronomy, 6:4). Only adult males are commanded to wear them; recently, however, women have begun to adopt this practice.

to'evah: Forbidden act, abomination.

Torah: The five books of Moses; also refers to Jewish teaching in general.

treif: Not kosher, forbidden.

yiḥud: Private time spent by couples after the wedding ceremony.

ẓaddik (tzaddik): Righteous person.

zakhor: Remember.

ẓedakah (tzedakah): Literally, righteousness; acts of giving, considered obligatory under Jewish law.

Works Cited

"A Woman's Haggadah." Oberlin, Ohio: Miriam's Timbrel, 1984.

"At the March with *Bridges.*" *Bridges: A Journal For Jewish Feminists and Our Friends* 4 (Winter/Spring 1994): 50–58.

"Coming Out, Coming Home: Lesbian and Gay Jews and the Jewish Community." New York: New Jewish Agenda, n.d.

"From the Editors." *Bridges: A Journal For Jewish Feminists and Our Friends* 1 (Spring 1990): 5.

"Germany: Not Just Memories." *Connexions: An International Women's Quarterly* 29 (1989): 28–29.

"Negotiating Boundaries." *The Reconstructionist: A Journal of Contemporary Jewish Thought and Practice* 59 (Fall 1994).

"On Being Orthodox and Lesbian." *Neshama* 5 (Spring 1993): 4–5, 8.

"Report of the Ad-Hoc Committee on Homosexuality and the Rabbinate." *Central Conference of American Rabbis Yearbook.* 100 (1990): 98–112.

"Sixty Places to Talk, Dance, and Sing." *Connexions: An International Women's Quarterly* 3 (January 1982): 16–18.

Abramowitz, Adina. "Growing up in Yeshiva." In *Twice Blessed: On Being Lesbian or Gay and Jewish.* Edited by Christie Balka and Andy Rose. Boston: Beacon, 1989.

Adler, Rachel. "The Virgin in the Brothel: The Legend of Beruriah."
Tikkun 3 (November/December 1988): 28–35, 102–105.

Alancraig, Marcy. "Such a Business." In *Speaking For Ourselves: Short
Stories by Jewish Lesbians*. Edited by Irene Zahava. Freedom, California:
Crossing, 1990.

Armstrong, Toni L. "New Jewish Agenda Havdallah Service and Concert."
Hotwire (March 1988): 20–21, 60–61.

Asch, Sholom. *The God of Vengeance*. Translated by Isaac Goldberg.
Boston: Stratford, 1918.

Balka, Christie. "Thoughts on Lesbian Parenting and the Challenge to
Jewish Communities." *Bridges* 3 (1993): 57–65.

Balka, Christie and Andy Rose, eds. *Twice Blessed: On Being Lesbian or
Gay and Jewish*. Boston: Beacon, 1989.

Bauman, Batya. "Women-Identified Women in Male-Identified Judaism."
In *On Being A Jewish Feminist: A Reader*. Edited by Susannah Heschel.
New York: Schocken, 1983.

Beck, Evelyn Torton. "Why is This Book Different from All Other
Books?" and "Still Different (1989)." In *Nice Jewish Girls: A Lesbian
Anthology*, rev. and updated. Edited by Evelyn Torton Beck. Boston:
Beacon, 1989.

ben Ari, Yehudah. *Menorah* (July/August 1983): 1.

Berman, Phyllis and Arthur Waskow. "The Seder of Rebirth." In *Tikkun*
9 (March/April 1994): 72–75.

Biale, David. *Eros and the Jews: From Biblical Israel to Contemporary
America*. New York: Basic Books, 1992.

———. "Who Was a Jew—Who is a Jew?" In *Disciplinary Boundaries*.
Edited by Wofgang Nutter. New York: Guilford, 1997.

Biale, Rachel. *Women and Jewish Law: An Exploration of Women's Issues
in Halakhic Sources*. New York: Schocken, 1984.

Bleich, David and Fred Rosner, eds. *Jewish Bioethics*. New York:
Sanhedrin, 1980.

Bloch, Alice. *The Law of Return*. Boston: Alyson, 1983.

———. "Scenes from the Life of a Jewish Lesbian." In *On Being A Jewish
Feminist: A Reader*. Edited by Susannah Heschel. New York: Schocken,
1983.

Bornstein, Kate. *Gender Outlaw: On Men, Women, and the Rest of Us*.
New York: Routledge, 1994.

Boswell, John. *Christianity, Social Tolerance, and Homosexuality: Gay
People in Western Europe from the Beginnings of Christianity to the
14th Century*. Chicago: University of Chicago Press, 1981.

———. *Same-Sex Unions in Premodern Europe*. New York: Villard,
1994.

Brick, Barrett L. "Judaism in the Gay Community." In *Positively Gay*. Edited by Betty Berzon and Robert Leighton. Millbrae, Calif.: Celestial Arts, 1979.

Brooten, Bernadette. "Paul's Views On the Nature of Women and Female Homoeroticism." In *Homosexuality and Religion and Philosophy*. Vol. 12, *Studies in Homosexuality*. Edited by Wayne R. Dynes and Stephen Donaldson. New York: Garland, 1992.

————. *Love Between Women: Early Christian Responses to Female Homoeroticism*. Chicago: University of Chicago Press, 1996.

Bulkin, Elly, Minnie Bruce Pratt, and Barbara Smith. *Yours in Struggle: Three Feminist Perspectives on Anti-Semitism and Racism*. Brooklyn, N.Y.: Long Haul, 1984.

Bullough, Vern and Bonnie Bullough. *Cross Dressing, Sex, and Gender*. Philadelphia: University of Pennsylvania Press, 1993.

Butler, Becky, ed. *Ceremonies of the Heart: Celebrating Lesbian Unions*. Seattle, Wash.: Seal, 1990.

Calderon, Sara Levi. *The Two Mujeres*. Translated by Gina Kaufer. San Francisco: Aunt Lute, 1991.

Calhoun, Cheshire. "Separating Lesbian Theory from Feminist Theory." *Ethics* 104 (April 1994): 558–581.

Califia, Pat. *Sapphistry: The Book of Lesbian Sexuality*. Tallahassee, Fla: Naiad, 1980.

Cantarella, Eva. *Bisexuality in the Ancient World*. Translated by Cormac ó Cuilleanáin. New Haven and London: Yale University Press, 1992.

Chauncey, George. *Gay New York: Gender, Urban Culture, and the Making of the Gay World, 1890–1940*. New York: Basic Books, 1994.

Cleaver, Richard. *Know My Name: A Gay Liberation Theology*. Louisville, Ky: Westminster John Knox, 1995.

Clement of Alexandria. *Paidagōgos*. Translated by Simon P. Wood. New York: Fathers of the Church, 1954.

Collins, Jerre et. al. "Questioning the Unconscious: The Dora Archive." In *In Dora's Case: Freud, Feminism, Hysteria*. Edited by Charles Bernheimer and Claire Kahane. New York: Columbia University Press, 1985.

Collins, Patricia Hill. *Black Feminist Thought: Knowledge, Consciousness, and the Politics of Empowerment*. New York: Routledge, 1990.

Cooper, Aaron. "No Longer Invisible: Gay and Lesbian Jews Build a Movement." *Journal of Homosexuality* 18 (1989–90): 83–94.

Curtin, Kaier. *We Can Always Call Them Bulgarians: The Emergence of Lesbians and Gay Men on the American Stage*. Boston: Alyson, 1987.

D'Emilio, John and Estelle Freedman. *Intimate Matters: A History of Sexuality in America*. New York: Harper and Row, 1988.

Daniels, Doris. *Always a Sister: The Feminism of Lillian D. Wald.* New York: Feminist Press, 1989.

Decker, Hannah. *Freud, Dora, and Vienna 1900.* New York: Free Press 1991.

Deutsch, Felix. "A Footnote to Freud's 'Fragment of an Analysis of a Case of Hysteria'." In *In Dora's Case: Freud, Feminism, Hysteria.* Edited by Charles Bernheimer and Claire Kahane. New York: Columbia University Press, 1985.

Devor, Holly. *Gender Blending: Confronting the Limits of Duality.* Bloomington: Indiana University Press, 1989.

Diller, Victor Jerry. *Freud's Jewish Identity: A Case Study in the Impact of Ethnicity.* Cranbury, N.J.: Associated University Presses, 1991.

Douglas, Mary. *Purity and Danger.* London: Routledge, 1966.

Duberman, Martin Bauml, Martha Vicinus, and George Chauncey, Jr., eds. *Hidden From History: Reclaiming the Gay and Lesbian Past.* New York: New American Library, 1989.

Eilberg-Schwartz, Howard. *God's Phallus and Other Problems for Men and Monotheism.* Boston: Beacon, 1994.

———. *The Savage in Judaism.* Bloomington: University of Indiana Press, 1990.

Eisenbach-Budner, Deborah. "Spilling Out Wine: A New Wedding Blessing." *Lilith* 20 (Winter 1995–96): 44.

Ellis, Havelock. *Studies in the Psychology of Sex.* Philadelphia: F. A. Davis, 1928–30.

Ettelbrick, Paula L. "Since When Was Marriage the Path to Liberation?" *Out/look* 6 (Fall 1989): 9, 14–17.

Faderman, Lillian, ed. *Chloe Plus Olivia: An Anthology of Lesbian Literature from the Seventeenth Century to the Present.* New York: Viking, 1994.

Faderman, Lillian. *Odd Girls and Twilight Lovers: A History of Lesbian Life in Twentieth-Century America.* New York: Columbia University Press, 1992.

———. *Surpassing the Love of Women: Romantic Friendship and Love between Women from the Renaissance to the Present.* New York: William Morrow, 1981.

Falk, Marcia. "Notes on Composing New Blessings: Toward a Feminist-Jewish Reconstruction of Prayer." *Journal of Feminist Studies in Religion* 3 (Spring 1987): 39–53.

Feinberg, Leslie. *Stone Butch Blues.* Ithaca, N.Y.: Firebrand, 1993.

Felman, Jyl L. *Hot Chicken Wings.* San Francisco: Aunt Lute, 1992.

Ferris, Helene. "Statement of Purpose and Goals: Conference on

'Lesbian and Gay Jews in the Jewish Community'." April 20, 1986. Photocopy.

Fischer, Erica. *Aimée and Jaguar: A Love Story, Berlin 1943*. Translated by Edna McCown. New York: HarperCollins, 1995.

Flagg, Fannie. *Fried Green Tomatoes at the Whistle Stop Cafe*. New York: McGraw-Hill, 1988.

Fontenot, Eduoard. "Of Spells and Lesbians in Ancient Rome." *Harvard Gay and Lesbian Review* 1 (Spring 1994): 11–14 .

Foucault, Michel. *The History of Sexuality: An Introduction*, Vol. 1. Translated by Robert Hurley. New York: Vintage, 1990.

Freedman, Marcia. *Exile in the Promised Land: A Memoir*. Ithaca, N.Y.: Firebrand, 1990.

Freehof, Solomon R. "A Responsum." *CCAR Journal* 20 (Summer 1973): 31–32.

Freud, Sigmund. "Hysterical Fantasies." In *Dora: An Analysis of a Case of Hysteria*. Edited by Philip Rieff. New York: Collier, 1963.

–––––. "The Psychogenesis of a Case of Homosexuality in a Woman (1920)." In *The Standard Edition of the Complete Psychological Works of Sigmund Freud*. Vol. 18. Translated and edited by James Strachey. London: The Hogarth Press, 1955.

Gal Berner, Leila and Renee Gal Primack. "Uncharted Territory: Lesbian Commitment Ceremonies." In *Lifecycles: Jewish Women on Life Passages and Personal Milestones*. Vol. 1. Edited by Debra Orenstein. Woodstock, Vt.: Jewish Lights, 1994.

Galford, Ellen. *The Dyke and The Dybbuk*. London: Virago, 1993.

Garber, Marjorie. *Vested Interests: Cross-Dressing and Cultural Anxiety*. New York: Routledge, 1992.

Garvey, Ellen Gruber. "Soup Story." In *Speaking For Ourselves: Short Stories by Jewish Lesbians*. Edited by Irene Zahava. Freedom, Calif.: Crossing, 1990.

Geller, Ruth. *Triangles*. Freedom, Calif.: Crossing, 1984.

Gilligan, Carol. *In A Different Voice: Psychological Theory and Women's Development*. Cambridge: Harvard University Press, 1992.

Gilman, Sander. "The Jewish Psyche: Freud, Dora, and the Idea of Hysteria." In *The Jew's Body*. New York: Routledge, 1991.

Goldberg, David Theo and Michael Krausz, eds. *Jewish Identity*. Philadelphia: Temple University Press, 1993.

Goldberg, Susan Ruth. "Letter from the Warsaw Ghetto." In *Speaking For Ourselves: Short Stories by Jewish Lesbians*. Edited by Irene Zahava. Freedom, Calif.: Crossing, 1990.

Goldstein, Elsie. "Letter." *Lilith* 17 (Spring 1992): 2.

Grahn, Judy. *Another Mother Tongue: Gay Words, Gay Worlds.* Boston: Beacon, 1990.

Greenberg, David F. *The Construction of Homosexuality.* Chicago: University of Chicago Press, 1988.

[Grossman, Marlyn]. "Dilemma of a Jewish Lesbian." In *Chutzpah: A Jewish Liberation Anthology.* Edited by Steven Lubet et. al. San Francisco: New Glide, 1977.

Hallett, Judith P. "Sappho and Her Social Context: Sense and Sensuality." *Signs* 4 (Spring 1979): 447–464.

Heyward, Carter. "Sexuality, Love, and Justice." In *Our Passion for Justice: Images of Power, Sexuality, and Liberation.* New York: Pilgrim, 1984.

Hirsch, Jody. "In Search of Role Models." In *Twice Blessed: On Being Lesbian or Gay and Jewish.* Edited by Christie Balka and Andy Rose. Boston: Beacon, 1989.

Hirschfeld, Magnus. *Racism.* Translated and edited by Eden and Cedar Paul. Port Washington, N.Y.: Kennikat, 1973.

Hoagland, Sarah Lucia and Julia Penelope, eds. *For Lesbians Only: A Separatist Anthology.* London: Onlywomen, 1988.

Hollibaugh, Amber and Cherrie Moraga. "What We're Rollin Around in Bed With: Sexual Silences in Feminism." In *Powers of Desire: The Politics of Sexuality.* Edited by Ann Snitow, C. Stansell, and S. Thompson. New York: Monthly Review Press, 1983.

Homosexuality and Judaism: The Reconstructionist Position. Wyncote, Pa.: Federation of Reconstructionist Congregations and Havurot and The Reconstructionist Rabbinical Association, 1992.

Horodetzky, Samuel A. *Leaders of Hasidism.* Translated by Maria Horodetzky-Magasanik. London: Hasefer Agency for Literature, 1928.

Horst, P. W. van der, trans. *The Sentences of Pseudo-Phocylides.* Vol. 4, *Studia Veteris Testamenti Pseudepigrapha.* Leiden: Brill, 1978.

Jacobus, Mary. "Dora and the Pregnant Madonna." In *Reading Woman: Essays in Feminist Criticism.* New York: Columbia University Press, 1986.

Jano. "The Woman Who Lied." In *Speaking For Ourselves: Short Stories by Jewish Lesbians.* Edited by Irene Zahava. Freedom, Calif.: Crossing, 1990.

Johansson, Warren and William Percy. *Outing: Shattering the Conspiracy of Silence.* New York: Haworth, 1994.

Kaplan, Marion. *The Jewish Feminist Movement in Germany: The Campaigns of the Judischer Frauenbund 1904–1938.* Westport, Conn.: Greenwood, 1979.

Kaplan, Mordecai. *Judaism as a Civilization*. New York: Schocken, 1967.

Kates, Judith A. and Gail Twersky Reimer, eds. *Reading Ruth: Contemporary Women Reclaim a Sacred Story*. New York: Ballantine, 1994.

Katz, Judith. *Running Fiercely Toward a High Thin Sound*. Ithaca, N.Y.: Firebrand, 1992.

Kaufman, Michael. *The Woman in Jewish Law and Tradition*. Northvale, N.J.: Jason Aaronson, 1993.

Kaye/Kantrowitz, Melanie. "Some Notes on Jewish Lesbian Identity." In *Nice Jewish Girls: A Lesbian Anthology*, rev. and updated. Edited by Evelyn Torton Beck. Boston: Beacon, 1989.

Kaye/Kantrowitz, Melanie and Irena Klepfisz, eds. *Tribe of Dina: A Jewish Women's Anthology*. Montpelier, Vt.: Sinister Wisdom, 1986.

Kellner, Menachem, ed. *Contemporary Jewish Ethics*. New York: Sanhedrin, 1978.

Kennedy, Elizabeth L. and Madelyn Davis. *Boots of Leather, Slippers of Gold: The History of a Lesbian Community*. New York: Routledge, 1993.

Kessler-Harris, Alice. "Organizing the Unorganizable: Three Jewish Women and Their Unions." *Labor History* 17 (Winter 1976): 5–23.

Kimelman, Reuven. "Homosexuality and Family-Centered Judaism." *Tikkun* 9 (July/August 1994): 53–57.

Klepfisz, Irena. *Dreams of an Insomniac: Jewish Feminist Essays, Speeches, and Diatribes*. Portland, Ore.: Eighth Mountain, 1990.

Koltun, Elizabeth, ed. *The Jewish Woman: New Perspectives*. New York: Schocken, 1976.

Koltuv, Barbara Black. *The Book of Lilith*. York Beach, Me.: Nicolas-Hays, 1991.

Krafft-Ebing, Richard von. *Psychopathia Sexualis with Specific Reference to Antipathic Sexual Instinct: A Medio-Forensic Study*. London, 1899.

Lamm, Norman. "Judaism and the Modern Jewish Attitude to Homosexuality." *Encyclopedia Judaica Yearbook* (1974).

Laqueur, Thomas. *Making Sex: Body and Gender from the Greeks to Freud*. Cambridge: Harvard University Press, 1990.

Leipzig, Roseanne and Judy Mable. "Tikkun Olam: Healing of the World." *Ceremonies of the Heart: Celebrating Lesbian Unions*. Edited by Becky Butler. Seattle, Wash.: Seal, 1990.

Levado, Yaakov [pseud.]. "Family Values: A Reply to Reuven Kimelman." *Tikkun* 9 (July/August 1994): 57–60.

——. "Gayness and God, Wrestlings of an Orthodox Rabbi." *Tikkun* 8 (September/October 1993): 54–60.

Lewin, Karl K. "Dora Revisted." *Psychoanalytic Review* 60 (1973–74): 520–532.

Liza and Penny. "Anti-Semitism in the Lesbian Movement." *Dyke* 5 (Fall 1977): 20.

Lorde, Audre. "The Uses of the Erotic: The Erotic as Power." In *Sister/ Outsider*. Trumansburg, N.Y.: Crossing, 1984.

Maggid, Aliza. "Joining Together: Building a Worldwide Movement." In *Twice Blessed: On Being Lesbian or Gay and Jewish*. Edited by Christie Balka and Andy Rose. Boston: Beacon, 1989.

Mannich, Lise. "Some Aspects of Egyptian Sexual Life." In *Homosexuality in the Ancient World*. Vol. 1, *Studies In Homosexuality*. Edited by Wayne R. Dynes and Stephen Donaldson. New York: Garland, 1992.

Marcus, Jacob R., ed. *The American Jewish Woman: A Documentary History*. New York: KTAV, 1981.

Marcus, Steven. "Freud and Dora: Story, History, Case History." In *In Dora's Case: Freud, Feminism, Hysteria*. Edited by Charles Bernheimer and Claire Kahane. New York: Columbia University Press, 1985.

Marder, Janet. "Getting To Know the Gay and Lesbian Shul: A Rabbi Moves from Tolerance to Acceptance." In *Twice Blessed: On Being Lesbian or Gay and Jewish*. Edited by Christie Balka and Andy Rose. Boston: Beacon, 1989.

Matt, Herschel. "Homosexual Rabbis." *Conservative Judaism* 39 (1987): 29–33.

––––––. "Sin, Crime, Sickness, or Alternative Life-Style?: A Jewish Approach to Homosexuality." *Judaism* 27 (1978): 13–24.

Mazow, Julia Wolf, ed. *The Woman Who Lost Her Names: Selected Writings of American Jewish Women*. San Francisco: Harper and Row, 1980.

Merkin, Daphne. "A Closet of One's Own: On Not Becoming A Lesbian." *Tikkun* 10 (November/December 1995): 21–24, 93–94.

Miriam, Selma. "Anti-Semitism in the Lesbian Community: A Collage of Mostly Bad News by One Jewish Dyke." *Sinister Wisdom* 19 (1982): 25.

Moore, Tracy, ed. *Lesbiōt: Israeli Lesbians Talk about Sexuality, Feminism, Judaism, and Their Lives*. London: Cassell, 1995.

Mushroom, Merrill. "Merrill Mushroom is a Jew." *Common Lives, Lesbian Lives* 7 (Spring 1983): 78–85.

Nestle, Joan, ed. *The Persistent Desire: A Femme-Butch Reader*. Boston: Alyson, 1992.

Newman, Lesléa. *In Every Laugh a Tear*. Norwich, Vt.: New Victoria, 1992.

————. *A Letter to Harvey Milk*. Ithaca, N.Y.: Firebrand, 1988.

Newton, Esther. "The Mythic Mannish Lesbian: Radclyffe Hall and the New Woman." *Signs: Journal of Women and Culture in Society* 9 (Summer 1984): 557–575.

Olyan, Saul. "'And With a Male You Shall Not Lie the Lying Down of a Woman': On the Meaning and Significance of Leviticus 18:22 and 20:13." *Journal of the History of Sexuality* 5 (October 1994): 179–206.

Orenstein, Gloria Feman. *The Reflowering of the Goddess*. Elmsford, N.Y.: Pergamon, 1990.

Orleck, Annelise. *Common Sense and a Little Fire: Women and Working Class Politics in the United States, 1900–1965*. Chapel Hill, N.C.: University of North Carolina Press, 1995.

Pardes, Ilana. *Countertraditions in the Bible: A Feminist Approach*. Cambridge: Harvard University Press, 1992.

Patai, Raphael. *The Hebrew Goddess*. New York: Avon, 1978.

Plaskow, Judith. "The Coming of Lilith: Toward a Feminist Theology." In *Womanspirit Rising: A Feminist Reader in Religion*. Edited by Carol Christ and J. Plaskow. San Francisco: Harper and Row, 1979.

————. "Lesbian and Gay Rights: Asking the Right Questions." *Tikkun* 9 (March/April 1994): 31–32.

————. *Standing Again at Sinai: Judaism from a Feminist Perspective*. San Francisco: Harper and Row, 1990.

Ponse, Barbara. *Identities in the Lesbian World: The Social Construction of Self*. Westport, Conn.: Greenwood, 1978.

Ramas, Maria. "Freud's Dora, Dora's Hysteria: The Negation of A Woman's Rebellion." *Feminist Studies* 6 (Fall 1980): 472–510.

Rapoport-Albert, Ada. "On Women in Hasidism: S. A. Horodecky and the Maid of Ludmir Tradition." In *Jewish History: Essays in Honor of Chimen Abramsky*. Edited by Ada Rapoport-Albert and Steven J. Zipperstein. London: Peter Halban, 1988.

Reagon, Bernice Johnson. "Coalition Politics: Turning the Century." In *Home Girls: A Black Feminist Anthology*. Edited by Barbara Smith. New York: Kitchen Table Women of Color, 1983.

Rich, Adrienne. "Compulsory Heterosexuality and Lesbian Existence." In *Signs: Journal of Women in Culture and Society* 5 (Summer 1980): 631–660.

————. "If Not With Others, How?" In *Blood, Bread and Poetry: Selected Prose 1979–1985*. New York: Norton, 1986.

———. "Split at the Root." In *Nice Jewish Girls: A Lesbian Anthology*, rev. and updated. Edited by Evelyn Torton Beck. Boston: Beacon, 1989.

Rogow, Faith. "Why Is This Decade Different From All Other Decades? A Look at the Rise of Jewish Lesbian Feminism." *Bridges* 1 (Spring 1990): 67–79.

Rosenblum, Barbara and Sandra Butler. *Cancer in Two Voices*. San Francisco: Spinster, 1991.

Rosenfeld, Marthe. "Jewish Lesbians in France." In *Lesbian Philosophies and Cultures*. Edited by Jeffner Allen. Albany, N.Y.: State University of New York Press, 1990.

Rubin, Gayle. "Thinking Sex: Notes for a Radical Theory of the Politics of Sexuality." In *Pleasure and Danger: Exploring Female Sexuality*. Edited by Carol Vance. Boston: Routledge and Kegan Paul, 1984.

Ruth: A New Translation [Anchor Bible]. Introduction by Edward F. Campbell. Garden City, N.Y.: Doubleday, 1975.

Sarah, Elizabeth. "Judaism and Lesbianism: A Tale of Life on the Margins of the Text." *Jewish Quarterly* 40 (1993): 20–23.

Satlow, Michael. " 'They Abused Him Like a Woman': Homoeroticism, Gender Blurring, and the Rabbis in Late Antiquity." *Journal of the History of Sexuality* 5 (1994): 1–25.

Schaffer, Teya. "With Love, Lena." In *Tribe of Dina: A Jewish Women's Anthology*. Edited by Melanie Kaye/Kantrowitz and Irena Klepfisz. Montpelier, Vt.: Sinister Wisdom, 1986.

Schanfield, Lillian. "Singer's 'Yentl': The Fantastic Case of a Perplexed Soul." In *Spectrum of the Fantastic: Selected Essays from the Sixth International Conference on the Fantastic in the Arts*. Edited by Donald Palumbo. New York: Greenwood, 1988.

Schemen, Naomi. "Jewish Lesbian Writing: A Review Essay." *Hypatia* 7 (1992): 186–194.

Schneider, Susan Weidman. *Jewish and Female: Choices and Changes in Our Lives Today*. New York: Simon and Schuster, 1984.

Schoppmann, Claudia. *Days of Masquerade: Life Stories of Lesbians During the Third Reich*. Translated by Allison Brown. New York: Columbia University Press, 1996.

Schulman, Sarah. *The Sophie Horowitz Story*. Tallahassee, Fla.: Naiad, 1984.

Schüssler Fiorenza, Elisabeth. *In Memory of Her: A Feminist Theological Reconstruction of Christian Origins*. New York: Crossroad, 1989.

Seagull, Thyme S. "My Mother Was a Light Housekeeper." In *The Woman Who Lost Her Names: Selected Writings by American Jewish*

Women. Edited by Julia W. Mazow. San Francisco: Harper and Row, 1980.

Seid, Ruth. *The Seasons: Death and Transfiguration.* New York: Feminist Press, 1993.

[Sinclair, Jo]. *The Changelings.* New York: Feminist Press, 1985.

————. *Wasteland.* New York: Harper and Brothers, 1946.

Shelley, Martha. "The Car O'Tea Belove." In *Speaking For Ourselves: Short Stories by Jewish Lesbians.* Edited by Irene Zahava. Freedom, Calif.: Crossing, 1990.

Shokeid, Moshe. *A Gay Synagogue in New York.* New York: Columbia University Press, 1995.

Sicular, Eve. " 'A yingl mit a yingl hot epes a tam': The Celluloid Closet of Yiddish Film." *Jewish Folklore and Ethnology Review* 16 (1994): 40–45.

————. "Gender Rebellion in Yiddish Film (It's Not Victor/Victoria!)" *Lilith* 20 (Winter 1995–96): 12–17.

Silberstein, Laurence. "Others Within and Others Without: Rethinking Jewish Identity and Culture." In *The Other in Jewish Thought and History: Constructions of Jewish Culture and Identity.* Edited by Laurence Silberstein and Robert Cohn. New York: New York University Press, 1994.

Silverberg-Willis, Luana and Yael Silverberg-Willis. "Gospel Under the Chuppah." *Ceremonies of the Heart: Celebrating Lesbian Unions.* Edited by Becky Butler. Seattle, Wash.: Seal, 1990.

Singer, Isaac Bashevis. *Shosha.* New York: Farrar, Straus and Giroux, 1978.

————. *Yentl the Yeshiva Boy.* Translated by Marion Magid and Elizabeth Pollet. New York: Farrar, Straus and Giroux, 1983.

————. "Zeitl and Rickel." In *The Seance and Other Stories.* New York: Farrar, Straus and Giroux, 1964.

Smith-Rosenberg, Carroll. "The Female World of Love and Ritual: Relations Between Women in Nineteenth-Century America." In *Disorderly Conduct: Visions of Gender in Victorian America.* New York: Knopf, 1985.

Smith, Beverly with Judith Stein and Priscilla Golding. "The Possibility of Life Between Us: A Dialogue Between Black and Jewish Women." *Conditions* 7 (1981): 25–46.

Steakley, James D. "Love Between Women and Love Between Men: Interview with Charlotte Wolff." *New German Critique* 23 (Spring/Summer 1981): 73–81.

Stein, Judith. "Jewish Food: A Short Thought." Photocopy.

———. *A New Haggadah: A Jewish Lesbian Seder*. Cambridge, Mass.: Bobbeh Meiseh, 1984.

Stigers, Eva Stehle. "Romantic Sensuality, Poetic Sense: A Response to Hallett on Sappho." *Signs* 4 (Spring 1979): 465–471.

Taylor, Verta and Leila J. Rupp. "Women's Culture and Lesbian Feminist Activism: A Reconsideration of Cultural Feminism." *Signs* 19 (Autumn 1993): 32–61.

Teubal, Savina. *Sarah the Priestess: The First Matriarch of Genesis*. Athens, Ohio: Swallow, 1984.

Toder, Nancy. *Choices*. Boston: Alyson, 1980.

Towarnicky, Carol. "Accepting or Embracing." *The New Menorah: The P'nai Or Journal of Jewish Renewal* 23, 2d series (Spring 1991): 13, 18.

Trible, Phyllis. *God and the Rhetoric of Sexuality*. Philadelphia: Fortress, 1978.

Vicinus, Martha. " 'They Wonder to Which Sex I Belong': The Historical Roots of Modern Lesbian Identity." In *Homosexuality, Which Homosexuality?* Edited by Dennis Altman, et. al. Amsterdam: Schorer, 1989.

Warner, Michael. "Introduction." In *Fear of a Queer Planet: Queer Politics and Social Theory*. Minneapolis: University of Minnesota Press, 1993.

Watts, Linda. " 'Can Women have Wishes': Gender and Spiritual Narrative in Gertrude Stein's *Lend a Hand or Four Religions*." *Journal of Feminist Studies in Religion* 10 (1994): 49–72.

Weeks, Jeffrey. *Sexuality and Its Discontents: Meanings, Myths and Modern Sexualities*. London: Routledge and Kegan Paul, 1985.

Wegner, Judith. *Chattel or Person? The Status of Women in the Mishnah*. New York: Oxford University Press, 1988.

Weston, Kath. *The Families We Choose: Lesbians, Gays, Kinship*. New York: Columbia University Press, 1991.

Wiesen Cook, Blanche. "Female Support Networks and Political Activism: Lillian Wald, Crystal Eastman, Emma Goldman." *Chrysalis* 3 (1977): 43–61.

———. "Review Essay: *The Life of Lorena Hickok: ER's Friend* by Doris Faber." *Feminist Studies* 6 (Fall 1980): 511–516.

Winkler, Gershon. *They Called Her Rebbe: The Maid of Ludomir*. New York: Judaica, 1991.

Wolff, Charlotte. *Bisexuality: A Study*. London: Quartet, 1977.

———. *The Hand in Psychological Diagnosis*. New York: Philosophical Library, 1952.

———. *Hindsight*. London: Quartet, 1980.

———. *Love Between Women*. London: Duckworth, 1971.

————. *Magnus Hirschfield: A Portrait of a Pioneer in Sexology*. London: Quartet, 1986.

————. *On the Way to Myself: Communications to a Friend*. London: Methuen, 1969.

————. *A Psychology of Gesture*. London: Methuen, 1945.

Wolff, Elliot R. *Through A Speculum That Shines: Vision and Imagination in Medieval Jewish Mysticism*. Princeton: Princeton University Press, 1994.

Young, Iris Marion. *Justice and the Politics of Difference*. Princeton: Princeton University Press, 1990.

Zahava, Irene, ed. *Speaking for Ourselves: Short Stories by Jewish Lesbians*. Freedom, Calif.: Crossing, 1990.

Zimmerman, Bonnie. *The Safe Sea of Women: Lesbian Fiction 1969–1989*. Boston: Beacon, 1993.

Index

Thomas Waugh, *Hard to Imagine: Gay Male Eroticism in Photography and Film from Their Beginnings to Stonewall*

Kath Weston, *Families We Choose: Lesbians, Gays, Kinship*

Kath Weston, *Render Me, Gender Me: Lesbians Talk Sex, Class, Color, Nation, Studmuffins . . .*

Carter Wilson, *Hidden in the Blood: A Personal Investigation of AIDS in the Yucatán*

Jacquelyn Zita, *Body Talk: Philosophical Reflections on Sex and Gender*

Bk Micah
Do Justice   asot mishpat
Love well   ahavet hesed
Walk modestly w/God   haznea lekhet im elo heka

✓ Rites of Passage

✓ Miriam   Old Test   ✓ Lilith Old T.

✓ Canceling 2 Voices   ✓ Dyke & Dybbuk
                              - Galford
✓ Sifra

✓ God of Vengeance Sholom Asch

Zeitel & Rickel - Issac Bashevis Singer Sht Story

Yentl   Running Fiercely
                         Toward a High
Jo Sinclair W's the love   Pitched Sound
                              Katz
Wolff Laws Between OT
        On the Way to Myself

                         Kol Isha ot
Lesbrōt   community
                         in Israel
Law of Return: Alice Bloch

CPSIA information can be obtained at www.ICGtesting.com
Printed in the USA
LVOW11s0129280815

451766LV00002B/25/P